Historic Churches *of the* World

CHRIST CHURCH, PHILADELPHIA. *(See page 249)*

Historic Churches
of the World

BY

ROBERT B. LUDY, M. D.

Acting-Assistant Surgeon, U. S. A., Spanish-American War;
Former Lecturer on Practice of Medicine in Temple University
of Philadelphia; Member of Historical Society of Pennsylvania

Author of

*Answers to Questions Prescribed by Medical, Dental and
Pharmaceutical State Boards, Etc.*

1926
THE STRATFORD COMPANY
Publishers
BOSTON, MASSACHUSETTS

THE CHURCH UNIVERSAL

One Holy Church of God appears
    Through every age and race,
Unwasted by the lapse of years,
    Unchanged by changing place.

From oldest time, on farthest shores,
    Beneath the pine or palm,
One unseen Presence she adores,
    With silence or with psalm.

Her priests are all God's faithful sons,
    To serve the world raised up;
The pure in heart her baptized ones;
    Love her communion cup.

The Truth is her prophetic gift,
    The soul her sacred page;
And feet on mercy's errands swift
    Do make her pilgrimage.

O Living Church, thine errand speed;
    Fulfill thy task sublime;
With bread of life earth's hunger feed;
    Redeem the present time!

—Samuel Longfellow

INTRODUCTION

The future safety of the world will depend in a large measure upon the religious training of the people who inhabit every quarter of the globe. If we ever attain everlasting peace—and this is not the most difficult problem which confronts all of us,—the greatest credit will belong to religion in some form.

The outward landmarks of all the religions of the world today are the Cathedrals, Churches, Missions, Meeting Houses, Synagogues, Tabernacles and other places of worship which one has in his own locality and which the world-tourist finds in his travels.

Wherever one goes, he will find a place of worship. True, one will also find public buildings, libraries, art galleries with priceless treasures; museums with wonderful collections, and thousands of structures of every description, all worthy of visit and study. Yet in and around these notable structures, one will find the Cathedral, or the Church, or the little Mission—many of them possibly empty for the moment, but all holding a mighty influence over the people in their own localities. To this date, with science and invention making their greatest strides and accomplishing the most wonderful and almost impossible achievements, no one has ever been able to measure the vast amount of good which has been accomplished through religion.

We hear almost daily in our contacts with business and professional men that religion does not seem to have the same grip upon mankind that it had one, two, or more generations ago. The writer has heard this expression of thought many times and in many countries. He does not believe the statement. As a close student of human nature, and from his observations made in every part of the world, he is fully convinced that religion is stronger today than ever.

This book is not a treatise on religion. Neither is it offered at this time, when the United States of America is observing its one hundred and fiftieth anniversary of independence, as an effort to strengthen religion in any way.

It is presented, however, in response to a growing demand from all sections which is conclusively demonstrating that the people of every class are becoming more religious day by day. In consequence, there has been a decided reawakening of interest in the history of the many places of worship throughout the world. The short-distance motor tourist has shown an increasing tendency to visit the Cathedrals, Churches and Missions which he passes in his journeyings. The traveler to distant points, whether in this country or abroad, has generally been interested in visiting notable places of worship. In fact, no traveler felt that he had seen everything of value unless he had visited the famous Cathedrals and Churches.

This interest exists today in a greater degree, for the reason that methods of travel and transportation are vastly superior to the traveling conveniences of yesterday. While the number of travelers is many times increased, there has been felt among all classes a keen desire for handy works of reference briefly describing the important and notable places of worship, not only in the United States, but throughout the world.

In a great measure, it was this growing demand which prompted the writer to compile the numerous interesting facts contained in this volume. As a result of many years of travel in all the countries mentioned, he was asked by many of his acquaintances to bring together in one handy volume some of the noteworthy facts relating to the old and modern places of worship which he has visited.

This work is not designed as a history. If it satisfies some of your demands for information regarding many places of worship, the writer will feel much rewarded for his efforts. If it should create in anyone's mind a greater desire to help carry on the work for which the Cathedral, the Church, or any other place of worship is the outward symbol, then he will feel doubly gratified and repaid for the hours spent in preparing this work.

To many of my friends and acquaintances, I am deeply indebted for their valued help in compiling this work. Many of the historical facts have been taken from standard works of reference. The writer desires to take this opportunity to convey his sincerest thanks for the valued and much appreciated assistance most generously given him by Miss Helen M. Lehman, of Belleville, New Jersey; Mr. William W. Matos, the Rev. Geo. W. Swope, D. D., and Mr. John Curtis, of Philadelphia, and also to the officials of the Historical Society of Pennsylvania, whose many courtesies will never be forgotten.

ROBERT B. LUDY, M. D.

Atlantic City
March 1, 1926

FOREWORD

The altar, a sacred place of worship, was the primitive form of church. Out in the open, and usually on the tops of hills or elevated spots, these places of worship were fittingly known as "High Places." It was customary to erect an altar where some new revelation from Heaven had been received and to set up memorial stones marking it as the site of an event of peculiar interest.

With God's fuller revelation of Himself, came, first the tabernacle, a "Tent of Meeting," set up in the midst of the camp at every resting place; and later the temple, constructed on the same plan as the tabernacle, but of more durable and costly materials, more ornate and elaborate in appearance. Accessories were grander and the effect much more imposing. Extensive ceremonial worship in magnificent structures took the place of simple votive offerings at primitive shrines.

Not different is the story of the chapel and the cathedral, the more modern form of church. With the magnificent temple in ruins, persecuted worshippers knelt in worship, not at rustic altars in the open, but at candlelit shrines of underground chapels within the catacombs, with guards at their secret entrances. On the sites of these chapels and on others sacred to the martyrdom of early Christians, sprang up medieval cathedrals. Altar, tabernacle, temple, chapel, cathedral, synagogue, church, were each a vitally significant episode in the story of the living church, and her worship of

> The Unseen Presence she adores
> With silence or with psalm.

As the primitive chapels were the forerunners of the church and its attendant civilization in the Old World, so were humble missions the forerunners of the church and its beneficent influences in the New. Adventurers sought to win new dominions for their sovereigns, and to extend their religion. The accomplishment of the latter made possible the former. Ahead of the armed soldier went the cowled monk, and the pious, praying, self-renunciating priest. About his humble mission grew up the cathedral, in the New World as in the Old. Later came the Colonial "Church-in-the-Fort" and meeting house, about which grew up big cities. Again, in the newness of the New World, the primitive altar was erected, this time the cell and cloister of the Franciscan Padre, whose "feet on mercy's errands swift" made tireless pilgrimage; and Plymouth Rock still stands sacred to the Pilgrim Fathers— their "faith's pure shrine."

And so it is that, whether in the Old World or in the New—Old Mexico, New Mexico, New England, or elsewhere; in countries old enough to claim the romance of a past — everywhere there are historic churches, cherished monuments of the past, final evidence of the abiding presence and ultimate triumph of the Church Universal, which ever constant appears

> Through every age and race,
> Unwasted by the lapse of years,
> Unchanged by changing place.

CONTENTS

(Part I)

PAGE

INTRODUCTION v

FOREWORD ix

OLD WORLD CHURCHES

Pre-Christian Temples and Shrines . . 3

Early Christian or Basilican Churches . . 21

Mosques, Temples of Mahomet . . . 35

Medieval Cathedrals 49

(Part II)

NEW WORLD CHURCHES

Early Missions, Cathedrals, and Churches . 159

Colonial Churches:

New England 187

Middle States 216

Southern States 287

Modern Cathedrals, Chapels, and Churches . 299

BIBLIOGRAPHY 317

INDEX 321

Illustrations

Opposite Page

Alamo, Texas 166
Amiens Cathedral, France 110
Augustus Lutheran Church, Trappe, Pa. 258
Brick Reformed Church, North Carolina . . . 294
Bruton Parish Church, Williamsburg, Va. . . . 286
Canterbury Cathedral, Kent, England, Exterior and
    Interior Views 54
Cathedral of the Assumption, Moscow 142
Cathedral, Holy Trinity, Quebec 164
Cathedral, Mexico City 158
Cathedral, Mexico City, Interior 160
Cathedral of Monreale, Sicily 30
Cathedral of Monreale, Sicily, Interior 32
Cathedral of Our Lady of Guadalupe, Mexico . . . 178
Cathedral of Rouen, France 142
Cathedral of St. Andrew, Wells, England . . . 122
Cathedral of St. John Lateran, Rome 28
Chartres Cathedral, France 106
Christ Church, Alexandria, Va. 288
Christ Church, Philadelphia . . . . *Frontispiece,* 248
Christ Church, Philadelphia, Interior 250
Church of the Holy Sepulchre, Jerusalem . . . 26
Church of the Nativity, Bethlehem 24
Clock in Strassburg Cathedral 112
Collegiate Church (Dutch Reformed) New York City . 216
Cologne Cathedral 84
Columbus Cathedral, Havana, Cuba 162
Donegal Reformed Church, Milton Grove, Pa. . . . 282
Durham Cathedral, England 96

xiii

ILLUSTRATIONS

Opposite Page

Ely Cathedral, England 118
Exeter Cathedral, England 128
First Baptist Church, Providence, R. I. 206
First Church, Boston 200
First Church of Christ, Scientist, Boston 304
First Huguenot Church, New York City 270
First (Tabor) Reformed Church of Lebanon, Pa. . . 282
Friends' Meeting House, Merion, Pa. 246
Friends' Meeting House, Philadelphia 274
Gloria Dei (Old Swedes') Church, Philadelphia . . 242
Gloria Dei (Old Swedes') Church, Philadelphia, Interior . 244
Gloucester Cathedral, England 90
Golden Pagoda, Rangoon 10
Grand Mosque of Damascus, Egypt 44
John Street Methodist Church, New York City . . . 230
King's Chapel, Boston 202
Leaning Tower and Cathedral of Pisa 102
Lincoln Cathedral, England 92
Lincoln Cathedral, England, Interior 94
"Little Church Around the Corner," New York City . 226
Martin Luther's Church, Wittenberg 86
Meeting House-on-the-Green, Lexington, Mass. . . 208
Milan Cathedral, Italy 98
Mission of Concepcion, San Antonio, Texas . . . 164
Moravian Church, Bethlehem, Pa. 266
Mormon Temple, Salt Lake City, Utah 300
Mosque of Cordova, Spain 40
Mosque of Omar, Jerusalem 38
Mosque of the Sultan Hassan, Cairo 42
Notre Dame, Antwerp 144
Notre Dame, Paris 72
Notre Dame, Paris Interior 74
Old Dutch Church, Tarrytown, N. Y. 236

ILLUSTRATIONS

Opposite Page

Old North Church, Boston 192

"Old Ship" Church, Hingham, Mass. 198

Old South Church, Boston 196

Old South Church, Newburyport, Mass. . . . 212

Old Swedes' Church, Wilmington, Del. . . . 238

Old Tennent Church, Monmouth Battlefield, N. J. . 234

Peterborough Cathedral, England 120

Pantheon, Rome 18

Parthenon, Athens 14

Rheims Cathedral, France 108

Ruins, First Protestant Church in America, Jamestown, Va. 186

Russian Orthodox Church, Sitka, Alaska . . . 176

Salisbury Cathedral, England 70

San Domingo Cathedral, San Domingo . . . 162

San Gabriel Campanile, or Bell Tower, California . 170

San Gabriel Mission, California 170

San Juan Capistrano Mission, California . . . 172

Santa Barbara Mission, California 172

Santa Croce, Florence, Italy 138

Santa Maria Della Salute, Venice 88

Santa Maria Maggiore, Rome 20

Santa Maria Maggiore, Rome, Interior 22

Santa Maria Novello, Florence 56

St. Albans, England 114

St. Albans, England, Interior 116

St. Anne de Beaupre, Quebec 174

St. David's Church, Radnor, Pa. 286

St. David's Church, Radnor, Pa., Interior . . . 284

St. George's Chapel, Windsor, England . . . 130

St. George's Methodist Episcopal Church, Philadelphia . 252

St. Gervais, Geneva, Switzerland 100

St. Isaac's Cathedral, Leningrad 140

St. John's Church, Portsmouth, N. H. . . . 208

ILLUSTRATIONS

Opposite Page

St. Joseph's, St. Augustine, Florida 180
St. Louis Cathedral, New Orleans, La. 300
St. Luke's, Smithfield, Va. 290
St. Mark's, Venice 50
St. Mark's, Venice, Interior 52
St. Michael's Church, Charleston, S. C. 292
St. Michael's Evangelical Lutheran Church, Philadelphia . 272
St. Patrick's Cathedral, New York City 302
St. Paul's Church, New York City 224
St. Paul's Church, Norfolk, Va. 292
St. Paul's, London 66
St. Peter's Church, Albany, N. Y. 224
St. Peter's Church, Philadelphia 276
St. Peter's, Rome 80
St. Peter's, Rome, Interior 82
St. Pierre, Geneva, Switzerland, Interior 100
St. Sophia, Constantinople 46
Swamp Church, New Hanover, Pa. 246
Tell's Chapel, Lake Lucerne, Switzerland 126
Temple of Diana, Ephesus 16
Temple of Edfu, Egypt 6
Temple of Nikko, Japan 12
Toledo Cathedral, Spain 104
Trinity Church, Boston 210
Trinity Church, New York City 220
Westminster Abbey, London, West Front 58
Westminster Abbey, London, Nave 60
Winchester Cathedral, Hampshire, England . . . 114
Winchester Cathedral, Hampshire, England, Interior . 116
World's Smallest Church, Kentucky 296
York Minster, England 124
York Minster, England, Interior 126
Zion Evangelical Lutheran Church, Philadelphia . . 280

Part I

OLD WORLD CHURCHES

PRE-CHRISTIAN TEMPLES AND SHRINES

The thoughtful observer of historic churches sees in Oriental temples and shrines, even though of pre-Christian origin, a deep significance and much beauty. To those who knelt in their inner sanctuaries they represented the ideal of human worship and Divine beauty, even as do our churches to us today. For this the world, in its "discovery of God," is deeply indebted. In the triumphant onward march of the Church Universal they, too, have played their part, recognition and appreciation of which Lowell thus fittingly expresses in his familiar lines on "The Church":

> I love the rites of English Church,
> I love to hear and see
> The priest and people reading slow,
> The solemn Litany.
>
> But when I hear the creed that saith,
> This Church alone is His,
> I feel within my soul that He
> Has purer shrines than this.
>
> For His is not the builded Church
> Nor organ-shaken dome,
> In everything that lovely is,
> God lives and has His home.

TEMPLE OF EDFU
EGYPT

In Egypt, land of Time's most ancient monuments, some fifty miles southeast of Thebes, stands Edfu, "perfect Temple of Worship." It is about two thousand years old, but still is one of the best preserved monuments of its day. It was begun two centuries before Christ by Ptolemy III, completed in 57 B.C. and dedicated to Horus, son of Isis and Osiris and symbol of the sun. Entering the doorway guarded by a small sphinx, and proceeding through long vistas of immense pillars, the inner hall, or "Divine House," of the Temple is reached. In this far off sanctuary, entered only by the priests, whose cells surround it, is the inmost chamber with black roof and altar of granite, and a polished granite shrine sacred to the god Horus. The massive Temple was built to house this shrine.

Previous to 1860 the Temple had been in ruins and nomad Arabs had built shabby lean-to sheds against its walls, but Mariette in that year restored it to its former austere beauty and massive grandeur.

Hichens thus gratefully expresses his admiration of this Temple of Worship:

"There is one Temple on the Nile which seems to embrace in its arms all the worship of the past; to be full of prayers and solemn praises; to be the holder, the noble keeper of the sacred longings of the unearthly desires and aspirations of the dead. It is the Temple of Edfu. From the other Temples it stands apart. It is the Temple of the inward flame, of the secret soul of man; of that mystery within us that is exquisitely sensitive and exquisitely alive; that has longings it

[5]

cannot tell and sorrows it dare not whisper. Edfu is the Temple of the 'Hidden One.' Pure and perfect in its design—broad propylon, great open courtyard with pillared galleries, halls, chambers, sanctuary. Its dignity and sobriety are matchless. It is not pagan. It is not Christian. It is a place in which to worship according to the dictates of your heart."

TEMPLE OF EDFU, EGYPT. *(See page 5)*

SOLOMON'S TEMPLE
JERUSALEM

Solomon's Temple, "the Jewish Temple *par excellence*," as planned by King David but built by his son, King Solomon, was in its famed magnificence and its fabulous treasure the pride of the Hebrews and the envy of the surrounding nations.

The Temple proper, or sanctuary, was modeled after the tabernacle, or "Tent of Meeting," which, constructed in the wilderness, accompanied the Jewish nation in its wanderings, and was set up in the midst of the camp at every resting place. The Temple occupied the summit of Mount Moriah, the spot where Abraham is said to have gone to offer up Isaac and where later David raised an altar to Jehovah, after taking Jerusalem from the Jebusites, to whom it originally belonged. On this sacred site the Temple altar ever afterward stood.

The Temple proper, or sanctuary, was sacred to the priesthood. On the north, east and west sides was a terrace, the upper level forming the courts of the Israelites; next below it the courts of the women; the whole rising like a pyramid from a plateau which formed the court of the Gentiles.

The treasurers of the Temple had charge of the sacred vessels of gold and silver, the rich vestments of the priests, flour, wine, oil, and frankincense for the offerings, and large sums of money belonging partly to the Temple, and partly to private individuals who deposited it there for safety. Police saw that the regulations were observed day and night. Prominent among those

[7]

connected with the Temple services were the musicians, whose duty it was to accompany some of these services, such as the daily burnt offerings, with singing and playing on the cymbal, the psaltery and the harp.

Solomon's Temple, built 1012 or 975 B.C., and destroyed by Nebuchadnezzar in 586 B.C., was succeeded by Zerubbabel's Temple, built on its site upon the return of the Israelites from captivity about 516 B.C. This Temple was larger but less sumptuous than Solomon's. It was desecrated by Antiochus Epiphanes (167 B.C.) and was replaced by one built on the ruins by Herod the Great (16 B.C.-29 A.D.). Herod's Temple was in five levels and similar in plan to Solomon's, and surpassed both its predecessors in magnificence. The Royal Porch of Corinthian columns was one of its chief architectural features. Herod's Temple was destroyed by the army of Titus in 70 A.D.

GOLDEN PAGODA

RANGOON

The Golden Pagoda (Sway Dagohn), one of the
most ancient and venerated Oriental shrines in existence, is believed by its worshippers to have been erected
in 588 B.C., on a spot for many previous centuries
sacred to the relics of three succeeding Buddhas, which
were discovered there at the time of its erection. Pilgrims journey to this historic shrine from countries as
far distant as Siam and Korea.

The Golden Pagoda, a marvelously striking structure of exquisite design and form, three hundred seventy feet high and crowned by an umbrella shaped
room (called Htee), raises its glittering head from
among a wondrous company of profusely carved
shrines and smaller Temples, the color and cunning
workmanship of which are fit adornments to this stupendous monument. In nearby quaintly carved and
gilded monasteries dwell yellow robed monks, who
offer prayers and perform other religious rites.

All about are frescoes and brass, wood, stone and
marble images of Buddha (560-480 B.C.) and various saints. Smaller pagodas cluster about. Large
carved elephants and deep urn-shaped vessels beseech
offerings of food for Buddha. Small golden pagodas,
here and there, are entwined with beautiful silks woven
in a single night by devout worshippers.

The Htee is lavishly studded with precious stones
and about it are hung scores of tiny gold and jeweled

[9]

bells, which when lightly swaying in the breeze tinkle a sweet and tender melody. This quaint roof is said to have cost $250,000.

EMERALD BUDDHA
BANGKOK

In Bangkok, the city of Temples, is the famous Wat Phra Kao or Royal Temple for the Emerald Buddha— a magnificent green jade figure discovered in 1436. It is enthroned on the top of a high altar, above a gorgeous array of colored vases, gold, silver, and bronze images of Buddha, lamps, candlesticks, and flickering tapers.

According to the seasons of the year the image is attired in different gold ornaments and robes.

THE GOLDEN PAGODA, RANGOON.   (*See page 9*)

THE TEMPLE OF HEAVEN
PEKING

Peking, the ancient Tartar city of Kublai Khan, until the present century was born, held in its heart another city, "The Imperial City," sacred to the Emperor and the imperial family; a city of mystery around which have been woven legend and story, and which was supposed to hold vast treasures of art, gold, silver and jewels. But there came the uprising among the people which caused the civilized nations of the world to intervene. An allied army marched to the Chinese capital, penetrated to the sacred inner city and found much that was dross, little that was real; but it found quaint relics of a long-distant past. Probably the greatest of these was the Temple of Heaven, sacred to Confucius (551-479 B.C.), and where the Emperors of China paid homage and made sacrifice.

There it rises, a mighty red, circular building, surmounted by two roofs resembling inverted saucers. It is approached from different sides by alabaster stairways of oriental magnificence, bisected by marble panels upon which are chiseled dragons in bold relief. These stairways bring one to the ante-Temple, or porch, with its ancient stone tablets and stone drums antedating more than a score of centuries. Inside all is color and magnificence. There are massive teakwood columns reaching to a paneled ceiling high above in the shadows; thick coir mattings cover the stone floor, and behind the altar is a red wooden shrine holding the tiny

[11]

sacred tablet of Confucius, China's greatest teacher. Upon the dark red walls are hung the votive tablets from the long line of worshipping Emperors who have paid him homage.

TEMPLE OF NIKKO, JAPAN. *(See page 13)*

TEMPLES OF NIKKO

JAPAN

On the Holy Mountain of Nikko, the Mecca of Japan, is the Sanctuary of Shinto, a series of enchanting Temples of bronze and lacquer with roofs of gold, in which guardian priests chant hymns and white robed priestesses perform sacred dances among waving fans. Now and then an enormous bronze gong or a monstrous prayer drum calls to devotions. From a vast Temple entirely blood red covered by an enormous black and gold roof, and entered by granite steps, comes a curious religious music.

Within everything is of black and gold lacquer and there are long curtains of black and gold brocade. Larger golden vases hold bunches of tall golden lotus and branches of full grown cherry blossoms. Bronze and gold replace stone and plaster. The walls are of gold and the ceilings are supported on columns of gold—yellow gold, red gold, green gold—gold that is vital or tarnished, gold that is brilliant or lusterless. And yet, despite so much richness, nothing is overcharged. The effect of the ensemble is simple and restful, and the details are harmonious and exquisite.

"In the Sanctuary of Shinto neither human figures nor idols have a part. Nothing stands upon the altars but large vases of gold filled with natural flowers or gigantic flowers of gold. A solemn hour on the Holy Mountain is at nightfall when the Temple closes. No lamp has ever shone upon these treasures, which have thus slept in darkness in the very heart of Japan for many long centuries."—*Pierre Loti.*

[13]

THE PARTHENON
ATHENS

The Parthenon, Temple of Athena at Athens,
holds a distinctive place among ancient Temples of worship. It was the chief structure of the city and though
boasting no remarkable size, it stood unparalleled in its
time the pride of every Athenian, as it does today, the
world's finest example of Greek architecture. Its unexcelled beauty lay in its extreme simplicity and harmonious proportions. In its sanctuary stood the colossal gold and ivory statue of Athena, patron goddess
of the city, in whose honor the Temple had been erected.

In plan the Parthenon was rectangular, one story
high, and included only two chambers; one storing the
sacred vessels and furniture needed in worship, and the
other, facing the east, enshrining the sacred statue.

Since the Greek Temple was designed primarily to
house the statue of the particular god or goddess worshipped, rather than to serve a congregation of worshippers, there was little interior ornamentation of the
Parthenon. Doric columns, marvels of exquisite
workmanship, surrounded the exterior. The frieze
and pediments were adorned with sculptured reliefs
and statues of life-like colors, which today are treasured
in museums as among the world's choicest specimens of
art. Among the best known are "The Fates" and
"Theseus" in the British Museum, the work of Phidias, under whose superintendence the remarkable decoration of the Temple was executed.

The Parthenon, begun in 447 B.C., was rebuilt under Pericles. After serving as a Temple for some nine

THE PARTHENON, ATHENS.

centuries, it was turned into a Christian church, and later into a Moslem mosque. When the Venetians bombarded Athens (1687) its walls were partially demolished by an explosion caused by a shell hurled into the center of the building, which at that time was being used by the Turks as a powder magazine. Though it has passed through the hands of several nations, the Parthenon is still remarkably well preserved.

The Metropolitan Museum, New York City, treasures a restored model of this classic edifice.

TEMPLE OF DIANA
EPHESUS

Ephesus, famed city of the ancient world, owed much of its repute to its world-renowned Greek Temple of Diana and its widespread worship of the great Nature goddess. There St. Paul, the first Christian missionary, met the defiant challenge, "Great is Diana of the Ephesians." Silversmiths, we are told in the Scriptures (Acts XIX), who had their wealth by their craft of making silver shrines for Diana, "aroused confusion against this Paul, who had persuaded and turned away much people, not alone at Ephesus but almost throughout all Asia, saying that there be no gods which are made with hands." The religious Ephesians feared that the temple of the great goddess Diana would be despised and her magnificence destroyed, whom all Asia and the world worshipped.

In 356 B.C., a former Temple of Diana, erected about 430 B.C., was burned and a second one built by the Ionians. This Temple, the one visited by St. Paul, judged by its ruins to have been one of the largest Temples ever built, takes its place among the Seven Wonders of the ancient world. Its splendor was proverbial. Massive inscribed columns of the peristyle indicate that they were gifts from communities, celebrated individuals and kings. Fragments of sculptured frieze abound with subjects picturing in relief the mythological stories of Diana, Hercules, Theseus, and the Amazons. The altar was decorated with the works of Phidias and Praxiteles. The statue of the goddess was reputed to have fallen from Jupiter.

TEMPLE OF DIANA, EPHESUS.

After the Edict of Theodosius in 381, closing all the pagan Temples, materials of the Temple of Diana as well as those of other Temples, were used in the building of Christian churches. The green jasper columns supporting the dome of St. Sophia are said to have been taken from this historic Ephesian temple.

THE PANTHEON

Unique among Rome's historic buildings stands the Pantheon, "Temple of All Gods" and "Pride of Rome," said to be the only ancient Roman building still standing virtually complete.

This stupendous edifice, boasting the world's largest rotunda and dome, occupies the site of the Temple of Jupiter, erected by Agrippa in the reign of Augustus, 27 B.C., and destroyed by fire in 80 A.D. Some forty years later Hadrian built the present Pantheon, retaining the Greek portico and Corinthian pillar plan almost unchanged, but adding the massive rotunda and the vast dome. The concrete walls of the rotunda are about twenty feet thick. The exterior, veneered with porphyry and marble, was enriched with Corinthian pilasters and sculptured ornament, some of which may yet be seen. Wall niches were filled with statuary, with Jupiter as the central figure, surrounded by his gods and goddesses. The pediment of the portico was adorned with bronze reliefs representing a battle of gods and giants.

The interior of the rotunda, originally faced with valuable Oriental marble and crowned with its vast dome the height of which equals its diameter ($142\frac{1}{2}$ feet), is the principal architectural wonder of the edifice. Through the central opening, twenty-seven feet in diameter, piercing the summit of the dome appears the open vault of the sky. It is the only source of light to the interior. It appears like a gigantic eye looking toward Heaven, and has been pronounced the noblest

THE PANTHEON, ROME.

conception of lighting to be found in any edifice in Europe. The Pantheon was once a pagan temple; to-day it is a Christian church and a burial place for illustrious dead. Here lies Raphael, immortalized by his pictures, so many of which in reverence visualize Christ, the Madonna and scenes sacred to Christian belief; and since Italy became united, the Pantheon has provided sepulchre for her Kings—Victor Emanuel II and Humbert.

Thrilled by the sight of it Byron wrote:

> Simple, erect, serene, austere, sublime,
> Shrine of all saints and temple of all gods,
> From Jove to Jesus—spared and blest by time;
>   Sanctuary and home
> Of Art and Piety—Pantheon
>   Pride of Rome.
>
>   —*"Childe Harold," Canto IV.*

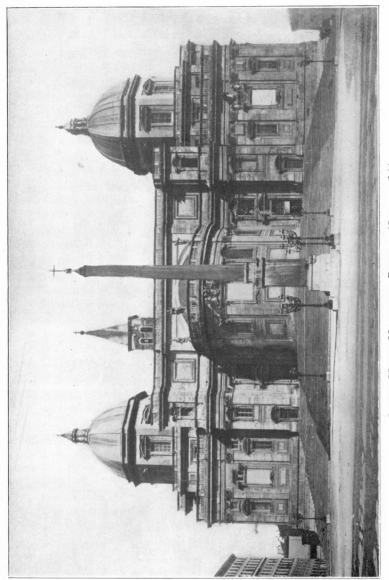

SANTA MARIA MAGGIORE, ROME. *(See page 26)*

EARLY CHRISTIAN OR BASILICAN CHURCHES

When they were come in, they went up into an upper
room . . . and they continued steadfastly in the
apostles' doctrine and fellowship and in breaking of
bread and in prayers.—Acts I, 13; II, 42.

By the close of the first century and for the two succeeding centuries of the Christian Era, Christianity was
under persecution. There were no separate buildings
for worship. Worshippers met in upper rooms of private houses or huddled together in the dark subterra-
nean passages of the catacombs to sing hymns, listen to
the reading of the Scriptures, and partake of the sacrificial meal in memory of the Last Supper of Jesus with
His Disciples. The gatherings at cemeteries to celebrate
the anniversaries of the death of early Christian martyrs probably gave rise to chapels in or connected with
the cemeteries and guarding the entrances to the catacombs.

Early in the fourth century came a more open form
of worship. Under the leadership of Constantine the
age of church building began. This was the day of
Basilican type of church, several of which Constantine
founded in Rome and elsewhere through his empire.
They were modeled after the Roman Basilica, a large
colonnaded building used for the transaction of business and legal affairs, the plain exterior and spacious interior arrangement of which met the demands of the
early Christian ideals both of structure and of ritual
worship. So admirably did the Basilican Church meet

the requirements of the early Christians that its plan was generally adopted later for the magnificent medieval Cathedrals.

In the words of Victor Hugo:

"Whatever may be the carved and nicely wrought exterior of a cathedral, we always find beneath it, if only in rudimentary and dormant state, the Roman Basilica. . . . The trunk of the tree is fixed, the foliage is variable."

The semi-circular end of the Basilica, where the judges sat, became, accordingly, the sanctuary for the presbyters and the bishops. The congregation occupied a central hall or nave. Above the columns surrounding the nave rose another story, called the clerestory, the walls of which were pierced with windows affording extra light. The approach was generally made through a colonnaded atrium, or forecourt, surrounded by a covered arcade. The church, whose apse was dignified by the Cathedra (Greek Kathedra), or chair of the bishop, became the cathedral, or Episcopal Church among parish churches, and the city growing up around it the Cathedral City of the diocese.

Strictly speaking then, while chapels and cathedrals were churches, in that they were houses sacred to divine worship, there was a clearly defined distinction between the two forms even in early Christian church days. In cathedrals, full services were performed and sacraments administered. In chapels or oratories, such as those connected with the catacombs, only prayers were offered. Royal families later had Palatine churches and chapels, and monasteries their abbey churches. The Pontifical Church was supreme over all.

Until the sixth century the Basilican form of church prevailed, at which time the Byzantine influence began

Santa Maria Maggiore, Rome. Interior. *(See page 26)*

to creep in, noticeably modifying the general type of church structure. Later came the medieval cathedral in all its magnificent splendor.

CHURCH OF THE NATIVITY, BETHLEHEM.   Exterior and Interior views.
(See page 25)

CHURCH OF THE NATIVITY

BETHLEHEM

Built over the supposed site of the Khan sheltering the Manger of Bethlehem is the oldest Christian church in the Orient, and to Christians the most sacred in the world, the Church of the Nativity, built by Constantine in 327. Its walls, battered by the storms of seventeen centuries, and pierced by two or three little grated windows, have been likened to a fortification that has stoutly resisted many assaults.

But it is not neglect that gives this revered edifice its worn appearance inside and out. Monarchs have vied with each other in decorating the nave, which is believed to be the oldest specimen of Christian architecture in the world. There are rows of great marble pillars, remnants of once brilliant paintings now dim and tattered by age, and in the clerestory may still be seen some fragments of ancient mosaics. Costly draperies of embroidered silks are hung upon the marble walls.

On each side of the low doorway the rough stone walls are blackened by the hands of millions of devotees who have made the sacred pilgrimage to the shrine of the waxen baby that lies in the manger cradle of marble in the basement chamber, called the "Grotto of the Nativity," a cavern about forty feet long by ten feet wide, reached by two descending stairways and lighted by thirty pendent incense lamps. A silver star in the pavement marks the traditional spot of the Christ Child's birth. Among the many gilt-ornamented altars under the dim swinging lamps is one known as The Altar of the Innocents, marking the reputed burial place of two thousand children slain by Herod.

Underneath the floor to the north of the Grotto is the cell in which St. Jerome lived peacefully for several years while translating the Bible under the direction of Pope Damasus, at intervals from 385 to 404. His version in what became commonly known as the "Vulgate," because of its general use, was the only Bible known to western Christendom for some thousand years.

St. James' Chapel and tomb are here.

SANTA MARIA MAGGIORE
ROME

Among the best preserved and most perfect examples of early Christian Basilicas is Santa Maria Maggiore, built in 432 and but little altered. Its plan is that of the original Roman Basilica, with nave and single aisles. The interior of the nave, dating from the fourth century, is adorned with mosaic decorations of the fifth century. "The square side chapels built out from each side of the single side aisles during the Renaissance and surmounted by domes," says Caffin, "suggest the later Byzantine influence."

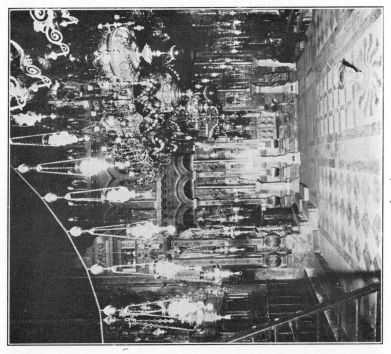

Interior

Exterior

CHURCH OF THE HOLY SEPULCHRE, JERUSALEM. *(See page 27)*

CHURCH OF THE HOLY SEPULCHRE
JERUSALEM

In the heart of Jerusalem is another sacred shrine of the Holy Land, the Church of the Holy Sepulchre, "A Church within a Church," erected on the site of a Temple dedicated about 135 by Hadrian, over the traditional site of Christ's Crucifixion and Burial. The record is that Constantine, after the great Council of Nicea, in 325, wishing to find and to consecrate the spots sacred to the Crucifixion and Resurrection, decided upon this site as correct.

Constantine's Church, completed about 336, suffered some damage at the hands of the Persians in 614, but was spared by Caliph Omar (successor to Mohammed) when he captured Jerusalem in 636.

In 1010, another caliphate virtually destroyed the church, but in the twelfth century it was restored and enlarged by the Crusaders, after their capture of Jerusalem (1099), becoming at that time the center of a group of ecclesiastical buildings.

The present edifice dates from 1810, when the church, which had been nearly destroyed by fire, was restored after the plan of the Crusaders.

There is a high central dome under which is a marble chapel, and before this chapel great numbers of candles are flickering and burning lamps are smoking, while all about are a profusion of crosses and candelabra and much shining brass. More than forty lamps are hung within the tomb, or Holy Sepulchre. They are of blue, red, green and purple, and are constantly tended. In the ante-chamber, framed in brass, is a stone, believed

[27]

to be the rock that was rolled away from the mouth of the tomb by angels on the morning of the Resurrection.

In Golgotha Chapel stands the altar, resplendent with golden crosses, burning tapers and sacred pictures, and under it a hole, bordered with brass in the marble pavement, revered as the spot where the Cross was planted.

The Stone of Unction, a cracked marble slab, traditionally the actual rock on which the Body of Jesus lay and was anointed for burial, is worn with the kisses of countless worshippers.

The Chapel of St. Helena, a subcellar entered by thirty descending steps dimly lighted by candles, is sacred to the Empress Helena, Constantine's mother, who, tradition says, visited the Holy Land at the time of the founding of the church and conducted the excavations which revealed the true Cross and two others, supposedly those of the two thieves, Christ's companions in crucifixion. This True Cross now exists in small pieces in the sacred reliquaries of many of the world's most famous cathedrals and chapels.

CHURCH OF ST. SIMEON STYLITES
KELAT-SEMAN

In Syria is another of the Basilican type, the Church of St. Simeon Stylites, whose court contained the renowned eighty-foot pillar on which this saint, according to tradition, spent thirty years in meditation and prayer.

CATHEDRAL OF ST. JOHN LATERAN, ROME. *(See page 29)*

ST. JOHN LATERAN
ROME

St. John Lateran, the earliest of Rome's three vast five-aisled Basilicas of the fourth century, dedicated to St. John, St. Paul and St. Peter, though completely transformed by its frequent remodelings, still preserves its original basilican form.

This historic church—more than a cathedral, in that it was the mother of Basilican churches and the seat of the Pope until succeeded by St. Peter's in the fifteenth century—is said to occupy the site of a palace confiscated by Nero and later made his imperial residence. Constantine, in 312 gave the palace to the Pope, and in 324 Pope Silvester I erected the first Basilican church of St. John Lateran. The solemn entrance of the Pope into his office is celebrated by his taking possession of this church. At St. Peter's he is Pope, at St. John's, Bishop of Rome.

The Lateran Palace nearby was the habitual home of the Popes from the fourth century until their migration to Avignon. After their return they took up their residence in the Vatican.

———————•◆•———————

CATHEDRAL OF MONREALE
SICILY

The Cathedral of Monreale, near Palermo, also Basilican in plan, is noted for its mosaics of Biblical subjects framed in arabesque borders, again denoting Byzantine influence.

[29]

OLD ST. PETER'S
ROME

Old St. Peter's (the Cathedral Church of St. Peter), the second Basilican church erected near the supposed site of St. Peter's martyrdom in the circus of Nero, though demolished in 1506 to make way for the present St. Peter's is preserved in the record of its plan. This shows that the Basilica building was approached by an atrium, or open court bordered by colonnades or arcades, with a fountain in the centre with the waters of which worshippers sprinkled themselves. This symbol of purification is typified by the vessel of holy water just inside the entrances to Catholic churches. The principal façade is pictured in Raphael's mural painting, "Incendio del Borgo," in the Vatican.

It was in this church that Charlemagne, the warrior-statesman, was crowned head of the Holy Roman Empire on Christmas day, 800.

ST. STEFANO ROTONDO
ROME

St. Stefano Rotondo, built in the fifth century, is said to be the largest circular church in existence. Instead of its one-time rich decorations of marble veneers and mosaics, one now sees "horribly naturalistic scenes of martyrdom executed at the end of the seventeenth century."

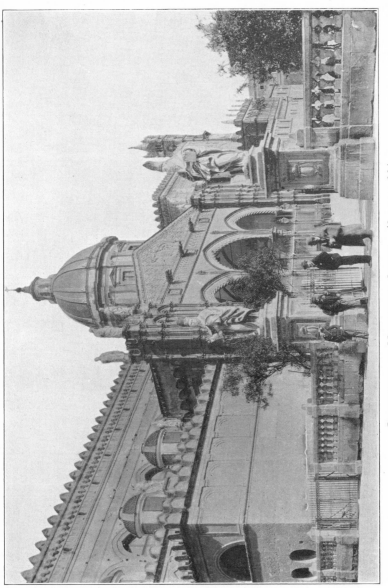

CATHEDRAL OF MONREALE, SICILY. *(See page 29)*

ST. VITALE

St. Vitale, at Ravenna, at one time the chief port by which the trade of Constantinople (or Byzantium) entered Italy, was built by the Emperor Justinian about 536, probably as a Court church after routing the Goths through his general, Belisarius. It is a notable example of Byzantine influence in church building, although its domical arrangement may have been originally derived from that of the Pantheon. This early Christian church later became the model for Charlemagne's Royal Tomb Church at Aix-la-Chappelle (796-814). It preserves among its relics a mosaic of Justinian, dating from 547.

ST. CLEMENT'S
ROME

St. Clement's, another notable example of early Basilican churches still standing in Rome, has aisles terminating in apses. Another suggestion of the Byzantine influence on early church architecture shows also in the adoption of domes to replace the flat wooden roofs of the Basilican church.

ST. APOLLINARE NUOVO
RAVENNA

The Basilican church of St. Apollinare Nuovo remains a monument of Theodoric the Great. Its marble columns imported from Constantinople and rich interior mosaic decorations of martyrs and saints bespeak Byzantine artist and artisan influences, as do also the mosaics which adorn the larger Basilican church of St. Apollinare in Classe.

Ravenna was famous for its mosaics—a kind of picture decoration formed from small pieces of colored glass set in cement against a wall or other surface to be ornamented,—one of the richest forms of decoration. Mosaics were used even in early Christian churches and lavishly in medieval cathedrals.

The manufacture of mosaics was at one time a great industry in Italy. They were used not only for ornamentation but for the reproduction of paintings. It is said that one factory kept no less than 25,000 different shades and tints of colored glass, so that it was possible to imitate any shade or color of a painting, and at a little distance these mosaic copies often could hardly be told from the original paintings. The most noted mosaics were those of Ravenna, which people went from all parts of the world to see and study.

CATHEDRAL OF MONREALE, SICILY. Interior. *(See page 29)*

ST. PAUL-WITHOUT-THE-WALLS

ROME

One of the finest examples of early Christian churches is St. Paul-Without-the-Walls, the original of which was begun in 380 by Theodosius and destroyed by fire in 1823. Under the altar of the original church were the remains of St. Paul. The present building, completed in 1854, preserves the plan of the old church, which is much like that of Old St. Peter's.

Other Emperors and other Popes contributed to its construction and adornment. Commemorating the munificence of the latter are portrait medallions of these emiment heads of the Catholic church, arranged in a band above the arches of the arcade on each side of the nave. Above them the walls are faced with rare marbles encasing panels of paintings representing incidents in the life of St. Paul.

Amid the somewhat extreme sumptuousness of the interior of the modern church a feeling of the older character of a Basilican church is preserved in the mosaics of the fifth century which adorn the Arch of Triumph, and in those of the apse, which date from the early part of the thirteenth century.

MONASTERY OF MAR SABA

On the way "up to Jerusalem," one sees, among other historic structures, the picturesque Monastery of Mar Saba. Here forty monks still inhabit the cells which cluster around the grave of St. Sabias, its founder, who died in 532. In this monastic fortress in the eighth century lived Stephen, the Sabiate, so gifted with the supreme talent of embodying in simple hymns the essence of divine life that one of his hymns still lives and profoundly touches the hearts of Christian worshippers everywhere. Paraphrasing his hymn known as "The Song of Stephen the Sabiate," Dr. Neale has given the Christian world its much beloved

> Art thou weary, art thou languid
> Art thou sore distressed?
> "Come to me," said One, "and coming
> Be at rest."

Thus the eighth century hymn, originally chanted "on the stern ramparts of this outpost of eastern Christendom, already threatened with submersion beneath the flood of Moslem conquest," has become the priceless heritage of twentieth century worship.

MOSQUES, TEMPLES OF MAHOMET

Throughout the Orient, northern Africa and southern Europe one sees everywhere the mosque, sacred to Moslem worship, with its beautiful minarets from the balcony of which "the faithful" are called to prayer. In style of architecture, arrangement and decoration, this house of worship is unique. Many ancient ones were early Christian churches which the Moslems seized and remodeled to suit their own form of worship. Newer mosques, still standing in Egypt and some cathedrals still in Spain are striking examples of the artistic genius and religious zeal of the Moor.

Characteristic of all mosques, besides the ever-present minaret, are the Holy Prayer niches, pulpit, reading desk and Fountain of Ablution. Thrice daily from the minaret sounds the summons to prayer. In the morning the muezzin, or caller, mounts to the first balcony; at noon to the second, and at sunset to the top. And the faithful never miss their prayers.

THE GREAT MOSQUE
MECCA

In Mecca, the metropolis of ancient Arabian commerce and the center of early Moslem religion, situated about fifty miles east of the Red Sea, stands the Mosque of Mecca, the Moslem "House of God, and Prohibited." The present "sacred area" (erected 1566-1574), three hundred yards square, with nineteen gateways, and accommodating as many as 35,000 worshippers, is much more imposing than that of Mohammed's time. The earliest form of mosque was a simple arrangement of open-arcaded court with prayer halls affording protection to worshippers.

The chief sanctuary of the mosque at Mecca is the Kaaba, a cube-shaped building (forty feet long, thirty-three feet wide, and fifty feet high), occupying the center of the mosque. The Kaaba holds embedded in its southeast corner walls a small Black Stone, the object of veneration which gives the Kaaba its sanctity. The Mohammedans connect the building of the first Kaaba with Abraham, and treasure the legend that the Black Stone, once white but now black from the kisses of millions of sinners' lips, came from Heaven. The ancient Stone, now broken in pieces, is held together by silver bands.

Pilgrims to Mecca enter the courtyard, walk seven times around the Kaaba (seven being the holy number in Islam), and kiss the Stone. Every year, history relates, Arab tribes ceased fighting for four months and went up to Mecca to buy and sell and to pay homage to the Kaaba and its Black Stone.

Although this most ancient of mosques has been rebuilt several times since the days of Mohammed, its interior, rich with beautiful mosaic pavements, intricate Arabic mural inscriptions, lamps of massive gold suspended from the ceiling, and the ever-present prayer rug, remains much as it was in the days of Islam's greatest prophet.

The first caliphs kept the sacred building covered with costly Egyptian hangings, three new ones being provided each year. The present covering, a magnificent black brocade, embroidered in all-over design, which extends thirty-three feet from the bottom, is sent new from Cairo each year. The design depicts a golden legend, composed of extracts from the Koran. The Mosque at Mecca is the only one having seven minarets.

THE MOSQUE OF OMAR, JERUSALEM. *(See page 39)*

THE MOSQUE OF OMAR

JERUSALEM

In Jerusalem, "city sacred to Christian and Jew alike, and, after Mecca, the most sacred Mohammedan city," stands the Mosque of Omar, more correctly known among historic churches as "The Dome of the Rock." It marks the traditional site of David's altar of burnt offerings and the Great Altar of Burnt Offerings in Solomon's Temple later erected over this sacred spot. The original Mosque was built about 690 A.D., by the successor of Caliph Omar, who, we are told, piously cleared the débris from the hallowed place as soon as he conquered Palestine. There were many restorations, the walls enclosing the structure having been built in the ninth century. The great dome built over the Sakhrah or Sacred Rock were rebuilt by Saladin in 1189.

It stands in the center of a group of buildings in a courtyard entered through eight gateways—an edifice of beautifully wrought marble. It is a structure of blue, but as one writer says, "a blue so exquisite and rare that it seems to be some old enchanted palace made of turquoise."

The interior shows two concentric rows of pillars, one octagonal, the other circular, supporting the magnificent dome. The columns, composed of red porphyry and different colors of marble, with gilded capitals, stand out resplendent against marble walls, arranged in symmetrical arabesque designs like beautiful inlaid work. The dome and windows are of many-colored glass, giving prismatic loveliness to the light as it shines through. The masonry is covered with mosaics so delicately and expertly fashioned that they resemble rich tapestries and brocades, and antique Persian and Turkish rugs of delicate hues, priceless, magnificent, are spread upon the marble pavement.

Among its relics are the Stone of Abraham and the relics of Mohammed.

With the exception of the dome, which was restored in the twelfth century, the Crusaders found the mosque very much in its present condition. They converted it into a church and placed their altar in the center on David's rock, but after the fall of the Franks, Saladin restored it to its Moslem faith.

Mosque of Cordova. Spain. *(See page 41)*

MOSQUE OF CORDOVA

SPAIN

The Mosque of Cordova, begun in 786, and ranking second in size to the great Mosque of Mecca, still stands, a marvelous memorial of Cordova's supremacy as the most learned, cultured and prosperous caliphate in all Islam. It fulfilled the desire of its builders to construct a mosque which would surpass those of Bagdad, Damascus and Jerusalem.

After the expulsion of the Moors this magnificent mosque was converted into a cathedral. It was repeatedly enlarged until it reached its present dimensions, (570 by 425 feet). The most striking feature of the interior is a great forest of pillars supporting open horse-shoe arches in two tiers. Originally there were about twelve hundred of these pillars, but many of them have been destroyed.

Like most of these ancient mosques the interior is richly colorful in its porphyry, jasper, breccia and many hued marbles. Most of them are ancient, and were carried to Cordova by Arabs from northern Spain, Roman Africa and Gaul. Some belonged to the Temple of Janus which ages ago stood upon this site.

The decorations are of Moorish lavishness and ornate design. There is a dazzling array of crystal, bas-reliefs, gold work and hundreds of lamps filled with perfumed oil bring flash and sparkle from the crystal, making the vast interior seem as if encrusted with brilliants.

A treasured possession of the Mosque of Cordova is the Koran, covered with gold and ornamented with pearls.

THE MOSQUE OF SULTAN HASSAN

CAIRO

Not only is the Mosque of Sultan Hassan the most beautiful in Cairo, but by many it is considered the most beautiful in the Moslem world. It was built in 1336, a century before the fall of Constantinople, and typifies the highest development of Saracenic art in Egypt. While not so large as the great Mosque of Damascus, nor built of such costly materials as the Mosque of St. Sofia, it is given preeminence over these because of the perfect unity of its design, perfect proportions and dignified grace. It is a true mosque and was designed as such, while those of St. Sofia and Damascus were originally Christian churches and show evidences of adaptation.

Within the great, open, quadrangular marble court, more than one hundred feet square, with walls more than one hundred feet high, are vast side recesses framed by a single arch, forming spacious halls for rest and prayer. The eastern recess, wider and deeper than the other three, forms a dais and contains the Holy Prayer niche and the preacher's pulpit.

In an enormous vaulted sepulchral hall (one hundred feet square), stands a railed-off tomb at the foot of which for five hundred years, it is said—ever since the burial of Sultan Hassan—stood an empty iron-bound coffin which contained a fine copy of the Koran, traditionally accepted as written by Sultan Hassan's own hand. A Khedive collecting choice Arabic manuscripts lately ordered its removal.

Interior

THE MOSQUE OF SULTAN HASSAN. CAIRO.

Exterior

Prominent in the court is the Fountain of Ablution, an indispensable feature of every mosque, at which worshippers wash before they pray or rest. The Mohammedan house of worship is ever open to the homeless wanderer of the faith, offering him shelter by night or day.

The Mosque of Sultan Hassan, like St. Sophia, with its attendant buildings, represents the tendency of mosques built after the thirteenth century, to assume the form of the medieval monastery, having in connection a residence for the priests, and other secular buildings closely connected with the sanctuary of worship.

GRAND MOSQUE OF DAMASCUS

The Grand Mosque of Damascus stands on the former site of a Christian Church of St. John the Baptist, dating from the fifth century, which, in turn, marks the site of an earlier pagan temple, "part of whose hoary front still stands, a magnificent fragment of ancient heavy masonry and carving now brown with age."

Other representative mosques are the Mosque of Amru, at Cairo, one of the oldest in Egypt; El-Aksah, on the temple platform at Jerusalem; Sultan Barbouk, in Egypt, famous for its minarets and dome; the Mosque of Kait-Bey, Egypt, noted for its distinctive decoration of arches; and St. Cristo de la Luz and Santa Maria la Bianca, Mosques of Toledo, now converted into Catholic churches.

The Great Mosque of Ispahan, Persia, includes among its notable features, curious bulbous-shaped domes and minarets of peculiar elegance.

The Mosque of Machpelah, at Hebron, marks the traditional site of the tomb of Abraham, Isaac and Jacob.

The Grand Mosque of Damascus.

ST. SOPHIA
CONSTANTINOPLE

When Constantine made Byzantine his capital, naming it Constantinople, he erected a church to the Divine or Holy Wisdom (Greek, Hagia Sophia). This church was rebuilt by his son Constantine, and again in 415 by Theodosius II, and was destroyed by fire in 532. Justinian (527-565), famous builder of early Christian churches, undertook its reconstruction on a new plan, commanding his generals to search through all the old Temples in existence for columns, alabasters, precious relics, and ornaments, and throughout the kingdom for artisans worthy of the magnificent Christian church he would build.

On Christmas Day of 537, five years after the architects of Miletus had begun work on it, Justinian's church in Constantinople, by far the grandest of all the twenty-five churches which he is said to have erected in the city and its suburbs, was dedicated and the glory of it called forth from its builder the words, "Oh, Solomon, I have surpassed thee." Today the world generally concedes St. Sophia, Justinian's great Hall of Worship, a marvel, not only of construction but also of unity and proportion. It was constructed in less than eight years at a total estimated cost of $64,000,000, and is second only to the world's largest and most magnificent church.

Although the exterior of St. Sophia is disappointing, because of its heavy, "squatty" appearance, its interior is unexcelled in richness and splendor, wholly warranting the distinctive title sometimes given it,

"The Jewel Box of Constantinople." Contributions came from all over the world. Columns of infinite variety and sizes represent the ruined temples of the world—Ephesus, Thebes, Athens and Alexandria. Its collection of priceless marbles, gold and silver vessels, and precious stones is unsurpassed.

The main building is roofed over by a central dome —St. Sophia's chief architectural glory—107 feet in diameter and 179 feet high, supported by four arches, each having a span of nearly a hundred feet and resting upon eight porphyry columns arranged in pairs at the four corners of the nave. The base of the dome has forty-six arched windows.

The mammoth dome, the chief marvel of the Mosque, the plan of which tradition says an angel revealed to Justinian, was built, we are told, of "pumice stone that floats on water, and with bricks from the island of Rhodes, five of which weigh less than an ordinary brick." On the top in white letters, some nine yards long, on a black background, one reads, "Allah is the light of heaven and earth," the sentence pronounced by Mahomet II, seated on his white horse in front of the high altar on the day of his entry into the captured city of Constantinople, marking his conquest of the Byzantine Empire (1453). Then the Crescent of the Moor replaced the Christians' Cross.

The "Mihrab," the Holy Place where the spirit of God dwells, is cut in one of the pilasters of the apse, indicating the direction of Mecca, and to the right of it hangs one of Mahomet's prayer carpets. A steep staircase with balustrades of beautifully sculptured marble, leads to the pulpit where the ratib read the Koran, with naked scimeter in his hand to indicate that

ST. SOPHIA, CONSTANTINOPLE.
Upper view shows the mammoth dome, the chief marvel of the Mosque.

the Mosque was acquired by conquest. There are large cartouches of porphyry, which carry inscriptions of Allah, Mahomet and the first four caliphs. Lecterns decorated with mother-of-pearl and copper, are placed here and there, holding manuscript Korans. Faded mosaics decorate the walls, and ancient prayer rugs and mats cover the floor.

When the Ottoman Turks captured Constantinople, this Christian church became a Mohammedan mosque. The story goes that when the triumphant, armor-clad Mahomet rode into St. Sophia, he laid his hand, red with the blood of massacred Christians, on one of the massive pillars, and the impress of it is still there for the inspection of curious visitors. All Christian emblems and decorations were covered with whitewash or stucco, or otherwise obliterated, and great round shield discs, bearing quotations from the Koran in Turkish script, substituted. Four high minarets were erected at each of the exterior angles.

Today, baths, schools, mausoleums and hospitals crowd around the ancient Basilican mosque, by no means heightening its architectural beauty.

MEDIEVAL CATHEDRALS

The medieval conceptions of Christianity are splendidly exemplified in the cathedrals and churches of that period. They show the growth of Christian ideas at a time of which we have all-too-little knowledge. Of the life of the cities they were the hearts. To them the people resorted. They were the refuge of the oppressed and they were the centers of thought and culture of their communities. They were, as one writer aptly says, "mighty Bibles, sources of instruction and inspiration at a time when just this was needed."

In the old days they were ablaze with color, light streaming through windows of many tints to rest upon rich tapestries and hangings, while paintings of masters hung upon ornate walls, and decorations of many kinds were lavishly displayed.

About every gray stone building with its stalwart towers and slender arches pointing skyward, countless age-old legends linger, as thickly as does the ivy that covers their walls. Enshrined in each is not only fascinating historic romance, but stories of their builders and of those who worshipped within them.

"Great buildings," says Victor Hugo, "like great mountains, are the work of centuries." And so it is that cathedral building became a great and honored profession. Cathedral builders not only had to live honorable lives, but each in his line had to be so skilled as to be almost perfect. Powerful guilds controlled styles and ideals, which each generation handed down to the next. In Longfellow's words in "The Golden Legend" immortalizing the Strassburg Cathedral, "The architect built his great heart into these sculptured stones and with him toiled his children."

Religious architecture then, as in all times, became the highest expression of the art of the people, whether classic, Romanesque, Anglo-Norman, Gothic or Renaissance in its outward form. The religious edifice led all others in the progress of building. Churches established the standards of building, as of living. Individual and national life immortalized itself in its churches. "Time was the architect and the nation the mason."

Thus the Gothic Cathedral, says Caffin, "was not only the House of God; it was also the House of Man — the civic center of his religious, social, moral and intellectual life."

ST. MARK'S, VENICE. (*See page 51*)

ST. MARK'S
VENICE

And 'tis a strange and noble pile
Pillared into many an aisle.
Every pillar fair to see—
Marble, jasper, porphyry,
The Church of St. Mark, which stands hard by
With fretted pinnacles on high,
And cupola and minaret,
More like the Mosque of Orient lands
Than the fanes wherein we pray
And Mary's blessed likeness stands.

—"Childe Harold," Canto IV.

St. Mark's, erected by Byzantine builders at the end
of the eleventh century in Venice, City by the Sea, not
only rivals, but stimulates St. Sophia in beauty of construction and decoration. Its model was the Church
of the Holy Apostles in Constantinople, erected by
Constantine and destroyed by the Turks in 1463 to
make room for the Mosque of Sultan Mahomet II.
The church is of Greek Byzantine design, and quite
naturally bears the form of a Greek cross (a cross with
the four arms of equal length), topped with fine, graceful low domes, one in the center and one over each arm
of the cross. Under the high altar of the central dome
rests the remains of St. Mark, Patron Saint of the city,
appropriately guarded by the statues of the twelve
Apostles.

The original St. Mark's was San Marco, a Basilican
chapel attached to the Doge's Palace, and erected in
honor of the acquisition of the bones of St. Mark the
Evangelist, from Alexandria to Venice in 828 A.D., at

which time he was chosen Patron Saint of the city. Tradition makes him the first bishop of the Venetian Isles and people. The chapel was burned in 976, and was wholly reconstructed, substantially on the present plan of St. Mark's. Previous to 1807, St. Mark's was merely a royal chapel, embellished by the successive Doges until the fall of Venice. The city's shrine was increasingly adorned. A law compelled every merchant who journeyed to the Orient to bring back something to beautify it. For five hundred years Venetians have been adorning their church, and the Cathedral of Venice stands today without rival a "marvelous ensemble of embellishment and decoration," one of the most gorgeously beautiful buildings of the world.

The picturesque entrance of fine portals is enriched with shafts of variously colored marbles brought from Jerusalem, Ephesus, Alexandria, Smyrna, Constantinople and other cities of the Orient. "On one," says Stoddard, "the hand of Cleopatra may have rested; another may have cast its shadow on St. Paul; a third may have been looked upon by Jesus."

Four colossal horses of gilded bronze, five feet high and weighing 1,932 pounds, known as the "traveled horses," because they passed through so many lands before arriving at Venice, are set over the central door. They were supposedly brought from Constantinople in 1204. Of these "traveled horses" says Byron:

> Before St. Mark's still glow his steeds of brass,
> Their gilded collars glittering in the sun.

St. Mark's possesses one of the most beautiful of church interiors. Vaults and domes are resplendent in magnificent mosaics of exquisite color schemes set in

ST. MARK'S, VENICE. Interior. *(See page 51)*

gilded backgrounds, picturing the saints and telling the story of their lives. Other mosaics, not attempting to imitate, but reproducing drawings from Titian, adorn the walls. A rich veneer of colored marbles encases the lower part of the walls. The altar screen containing hundreds of precious stones, celebrated as one of the richest and most beautiful pieces of gold and silver work in the world, is displayed at certain seasons.

The famous pigeons, always associated with St. Mark's, are said to have been kept in the square and fed by the city ever since Andrea Dandolo, Doge of Venice and Crusader, received valuable information by carrier pigeons while besieging Candia.

Ruskin, in "The Stones of Venice," suggests that the traveler, when dazzled by the brilliancy of the square of today, try to visualize the scene as it was when St. Mark's was built—a green field divided by a small canal bordered by trees.

CATHEDRAL
NAPLES, ITALY

Naples, the largest city and seaport of Italy, and richer in archeological than architectural interests, has a striking Gothic cathedral, erected 1272-1323, and repeatedly modernized. It is dedicated to St. Januarius and contains among its relics, the celebrated vials in which the liquefication of the Saint's blood is alleged to take place on three annual festivals.

It contains also the tombs of Charles, of Anjou, and Pope Innocent IV, besides numerous fine paintings and statues.

CANTERBURY CATHEDRAL
KENT, ENGLAND

English Cathedrals, says Caffin, are in a very full sense an expression of the nation's growth—a characterization peculiarly fitting to Canterbury Cathedral in Kent, England, the home of the "Mother Church of England." There it was that the monk, St. Augustine, nearly fifteen centuries ago, with forty companions, arrived to carry the gospel to heathen England at the command of Gregory the Great (Gregory II), who viewed the Kingdom of Kent with its Christian Queen, the Frankish Princess Bertha, as a promising mission field. The monks were assigned a residence in Canterbury (sometimes called the first English Christian city), by her husband, Ethelbert, King of Kent. That city to this day remains the religious capital of England and the Archiepiscopal See of the Primate of all England.

Although the close of the sixth century (597) and St. Augustine's arrival in Kent mark the coming of Christianity to England, the new religion had been introduced among the Britons probably as early as the second century by Roman soldiers and merchants. Proof of this was the Christian Queen herself and also her Church of St. Martin's Hill, dating from pre-Saxon times and given her by Ethelbert, as a place of worship, deserted at that time, but formerly used by Roman Christians. This church, as the story goes, St. Augustine reconsecrated under the name of Christ's Church, and made it the scene of his earliest work in Canterbury. In it he baptized King Ethelbert. The present

CANTERBURY CATHEDRAL, KENT, ENGLAND.
Exterior and Interior Views.

St. Martin's at Canterbury, dating from the thirteenth century, and occupying the site of this old church, built before the arrival of St. Augustine, contains some of the Roman bricks used in the original structure, a truly historic church and fittingly called, "The Mother Church of Great Britain," since in it Christian learning and civilization first took root in the Anglo-Saxon race.

The authentic history of Canterbury Cathedral, officially the Cathedral of Christ's Church at Canterbury, began with the Norman Conquest (1067), when Lanfranc, the first Norman Archbishop, erected a splendid church upon a site a mile or so westward from the Old St. Martin's Church (upon which had been erected another more ancient church), the first germ of the present edifice. In 1093, Lanfranc's successor, Anselm, enlarged the church, which, destroyed by fire in 1174, was rebuilt and repeatedly remodelled throughout the twelfth and fifteenth centuries. The central tower two hundred thirty four feet high, known as the Angel Tower, the chief glory of the exterior, and the Lady Chapel, were among the embellishments added at this time. Some four centuries in building, the Cathedral represents both the transitional Norman and the perpendicular or Gothic style of architecture. Of the lovely Angel Tower one says: "It may be surpassed in height, but in beauty never."

Canterbury Cathedral, celebrated in both old English history and poetry, still today, in its setting of ruins of Norman castles, ancient city walls, and medieval houses with gabled ends and projecting fronts, retains many aspects of its early days and contains revered relics of its romantic past. Chief among these

[55]

is the transept called "The Martyrdom" marking the spot where Thomas à Becket was murdered December 29, 1170 by King Henry II, whose policies he opposed. It is this spot, for years the object of great pilgrimages of Christendom, which still lives in "The Canterbury Tales" of Chaucer (1340-1400), an interesting contemporary account of these religious excursions, makes Canterbury a place of considerable importance. Chequers Inn, where Chaucer's pilgrims were housed, still stands. It is said that there were some fifteen hundred yearly offerings at this shrine, each amounting to about $20,000. A mosaic pavement still remains in front of the place where Becket's shrine stood, the steps leading up to which are worn by the knees of countless pilgrims who worshipped there. This historic spot, among other ecclesiastical places and buildings of interest, suffered extensive destruction at the hands of Henry VIII during the Reformation period of 1538.

A panel above the south porch represents in curious old sculpture the altar of Becket's martyrdom. "The Gateway of Martyrdom" marks the door by which Becket passed to his doom, after having fled to the church for protection after a violent scene with the Knights of Henry, an incident faithfully and graphically described in Tennyson's "Thomas à Becket."

In the Angel or Bell Tower hangs the mighty Dunstan bell, weighing three tons, three hundredweight. Originally the gilded figure of an angel was poised on the pinnacle of the tower. The tomb of the Black Prince, boy hero of Crécy (1346), with black armor above; St. Gabriel's Chapel and the Chained Bible are other relics of interest.

SANTA MARIA NOVELLO, FLORENCE. *(See page 57)*

The beautiful stained-glass windows of the choir date from the thirteenth century. The cloisters are decorated with arms of Kentish families.

As one descends into the crypt, he sees St. Augustine's chair of Purbeck marble, which tradition says is the throne on which kings of Kent were crowned, given by Ethelbert to Augustine. Upon it every Archbishop for the last six hundred years has sat when admitted to his metropolitan functions.

Canterbury boasts an unbroken record of bishops from St. Augustine, first Archbishop of Canterbury (597), to Sir Frederick Temple (1896).

In a sense it is the most important church structure in England. Chief interest is due not so much to its arcihtecture as to its vastness of scale, wealth of monuments, rare store of thirteenth century glass, and memories of historical scenes enacted within its walls.

SANTA MARIA NOVELLO
FLORENCE

Santa Maria Novello (Church of St. Mary), the great Dominican church erected in 1278, is another old Gothic structure, famous for its simple architectural grandeur. It is celebrated also for its paintings by Cimabue and Ghirlandajo's series of frescoes of New Testament stories decorating the choir. Brunelleschi carved a fine crucifix for it. Santa Maria Novello is five minutes' walk from its companion church, the Franciscan Church of Santa Croce.

WESTMINSTER ABBEY
LONDON

To the remembered dead—
The shining dead, immortal and serene,
Soul of the earth; to beauty which hath been
And ever is, and light of starry lives,
That o'er the dark unvoyaged waters led
To power that still in mightier power revives,
To the remembered dead.

—*Woods.*

Westminster Abbey, England's "Pantheon of Genius," and, in a peculiar sense, her national sanctuary, was originally the church of a Benedictine Abbey, said to have been built in 616 by King Sebert of Essex. In 1049-1065, Edward the Confessor (1042-1066), who had a palace at Westminster, built a church on the present site of the Abbey, dedicating it to St. Peter, the Abbey's official name being the Collegiate Church of St. Peter. Despite the fact that only the foundations were laid at the time of his death, Edward, who was the first king buried therein, deserves credit for the beautiful church. The fact that it was his tomb attracted the attention of the later kings to the convenience and appropriateness of having a private chapel so near the palace.

For the first five hundred years of its existence the Abbey Church was only a part of a monastery—a place used exclusively for worship, and not as a memorial of the dead. Only royal and ecclesiastical persons connected with the church were buried there. During

WESTMINSTER ABBEY, LONDON.   West Front.

these years the shrine of St. Edward remained the holiest part of the Abbey.

In the thirteenth century, Henry III reconstructed the church, and his successors added to it, with long interruptions between building, so that it was not completed until the fifteenth century. Among the notable additions were the two west towers by Christopher Wren, and the Chapel of Henry VII, begun as a Lady Chapel, but completed by his successor as a mausoleum.

Though haltingly constructed over a period of several centuries, the unity of style is remarkable. Heavily endowed and under the special protection of the kings of England, this celebrated edifice, "with its harmony of proportions, long nave, lofty ceiling, and dim religious light from magnificent rose windows, makes a grand and solemn impression larger churches fail to leave." It was disendowed as a Cathedral during the Reformation, at which time Edward's Shrine was devastated, its gold and jewels having been seized by Henry VIII, but it was restored by Queen Mary and received its present organization under Queen Elizabeth.

"Of all England's churches," says an authority, "none is so intimately connected with the national life and history as is Westminster Abbey"—England's great Temple of Fame.

The venerable Abbey has witnessed many a brilliant coronation scene. Every English sovereign with the exception of Edward V, from William the Conqueror, has been crowned seated on the famed Coronation Chair. This chair still stands in the Chapel of Edward the Confessor, and under it rests the ancient Stone of Scone, brought from Scotland by Edward I, in 1297, in token of the subjugation of Scotland, and, by tradition, the stone Jacob used as a pillow. Here the ancient regalia was kept until it was destroyed under the commonwealth.

Burial in this historic church is one of England's greatest honors, and truly many are the mighty ones who slumber as England's remembered dead in the old Gothic church by the Thames. A wilderness of tombs and monuments crowd its pillared aisles. Close about the Shrine of Edward the Confessor are sepulchers of other kings and queens. In the elaborate Chapel of Henry VII, the most gorgeous of mausoleums, stand the sepulchers of its founder, of the haughty maiden queen, Elizabeth, and the lovely and unfortunate Mary, Queen of Scots. Here rest also, remembered by statues, busts and tablets, England's famous statesmen, poets, courtiers, soldiers, scientists, men of letters, theologians, actors, musicians and artists, each group in its allotted corner. In the Poet's Corner is the tomb of Chaucer, father of English poetry, and over it a memorial window depicting the pilgrimage to Canterbury. There also is Gray's monument, with its mocking epitaph inscribed at his request:

> Life is a jest, and all things show it;
> I thought so once, but now I know it.

A bust of Longfellow is also in this corner.

In the north cloister lies the body of General John Burgoyne, whose surrender to the American Army at Saratoga won the support of France to the cause of the American Revolutionists. Near by is a memorial to Major John Andre, erected at the time of his execution in far-off America. He was buried on the banks of the Hudson, but forty years later, at the request of the Duke of York, his body was taken back to England.

THE NAVE, WESTMINSTER ABBEY, LONDON. *(See page 58)*

In the center of the nave under a plain black slate lie the remains of David Livingston, the great African missionary and explorer.

And among the myriad of distinguished dead lies one whose identity is unknown—a private, humble soldier—possibly in life one of the most obscure of the subjects of King George V, yet in death given every honor that a grateful king and country can bestow. He lies there, the representative of hundreds of thousands of British soldiers who gave their lives to their country in the mighty World War. He was the first unknown soldier to be so honored. All other nations associated with England in that terrible conflict have followed her example in this.

"On the accession of James I of England and VI of Scotland, when the Stone of Scone had become an institution at Westminster Abbey, the Scots found consolation in the fulfillment of the ancient prophecy thus Englished, 'If fate go right, where'er this Stone is found, the Scots shall monarchs of that realm be crowned.'

"In the meantime the Stone of Scone has remained in the chapel of English kings, and has only once been taken out of the Abbey since Edward I brought it from Scotland, when it was removed to Westminster Hall, and Oliver Cromwell was installed Protector of the realm enthroned upon the Seat of Majesty. The only time up to the year of Edward VII's coronation, when, in the memory of this generation, the stone was removed from St. Edward's Chapel was at the first jubilee (1887) of Queen Victoria; and she is the only sovereign since the days of the Plantagenets who has ever sat twice in the Coronation Chair."—"Roll Call of Westminster Abbey," Smith.

The oak chair made to enclose the stone by order of Edward I was completed about 1300.

————•❖•————

CATHEDRAL
SIENA, ITALY

Built entirely of red, black and white marble and overlaid with florid ornaments of exquisite design, Siena Cathedral holds a distinctive place among Italy's celebrated cathedrals. Though Gothic in style, the dome is Etruscan or Roman, and there are no flying buttresses.

Erected between 1229 and 1380, Siena is a notable example of an unfinished cathedral. Had its original plan been completed, it would have been not only the largest Gothic cathedral south of the Alps, but one of the largest of the world. As it stands, it is only the transept of the proposed building, lengthened a little, and surmounted by a cupola and a campanile. The plague which swept over Italy prevented its completion.

The west façade of this Duomo, Siena's celebrated shrine, is considered one of the finest in Italy, and is richly decorated with statues of prophets and angels. In this it rivals the Cathedral of Orvieto (1290). A remarkable feature of the interior decoration is a line of heads of the Popes, carried around the church above the lower arches. Each in its separate niche, larger than life and crowned with the triple tiara, combined they record the whole history of the church. The pavement, inlaid in tarsia work in stone, portrays the history of the church before the Incarnation.

SANTA MARIA DEL FIORE

FLORENCE, ITALY

In the Piazza del Duomo of Florence stands the world-renowned Cathedral Santa Maria del Fiore, with its accompanying campanile, Giotto's most beautiful of all bell towers, and the venerable baptistry, in which every true Florentine is baptized. The Cathedral owed its construction to the enthusiasm and generosity of the citizens, as did many another of the celebrated cathedrals. Plans were made in 1294, and the cornerstone was laid in 1298. Arnolfo, the original architect, died soon after the work was started and Giotto was made his successor. For some two hundred years the work continued under worthy direction. In 1421, Brunelleschi (1379-1446), a Florentine, began its superb dome, not only a monument to its creator, but scarcely rivaled by any other work of the Renaissance.

> "That of St. Peter's may be a prouder and a more imposing structure, but it lacks the grand simplicity of Brunelleschi's. It (Santa Maria del Fiore's) may be less stately but it is more companionable; less imposing but more intimately inspiring."*

It was Michael Angelo's inspiration for that of St. Peter's.

The façade, though in Gothic style, is modern. Its three large entrances are ornamented with many statues, bas-reliefs, and mosaics. The exterior is celebrated for its marble encrustations, the interior for its wide vaulting and bare simplicity. Among the many works of

---

* Caffin.

art which call forth admiration of its majestic solemnity, are its walls containing works of Della Robbia, Donatello, and other famous artists, and a famous fresco in commemoration of Dante, by Michelino. When Pope Pius went to Florence he said, "In St. Peter's one thinks; in Santa Maria del Fiore one prays."

Because of its superb dome, the cathedral is commonly referred to as "The Duomo." Santa Maria del Fiore (Our Lady of the Flower) alludes to the lily, the heraldic flower of Florence.

Under the imposing dome of this celebrated church lie the remains of its creator.

The campanile, Giotto's unrivalled bell tower, begun in 1334, is in pure Italian Gothic. Its exterior is composed of marble of various colors in geometric designs. The sides of the lowest story are enriched with statues and bas-reliefs by Giotto and Luca della Robbia, the subjects forming a veritable encyclopedia of human knowledge from the Creation down to its own time. The story above this one is decorated with niches containing exquisite statuary. The windows of the last three stories, embellished with tracery corresponding to that of the Cathedral windows, are considered excellent examples of the Italian Gothic. The tower contains seven bells, the largest, cast in 1705, weighs 15,860 pounds.

A rare architectural combination of design, strength and grace, stability and tenderness, adorned by Italy's most famous artists of the fourteenth and fifteenth centuries, caused Charles IV to say of this celebrated bell tower, "The Florentines should make a glass case for the campanile and exhibit it as a gem."

How did this splendid church come to be built? Read the resolution adopted by the Council of the Municipality of Florence in 1294:

"Considering that all the acts and works of a people who boast of an illustrious origin should bear the character of grandeur and wisdom, we order Arnolfo, director of the works of our commune, to make the model or design of the building which shall replace the Church of Santa Reparata. It shall display such magnificence that no industry nor human power shall surpass it.

"A Government should undertake nothing unless in response to the desire of a heart more than generous, which expresses the heart of all its citizens united in one common wish. It is from this point of view that the architect charged with the building of our cathedral must be regarded."

Can anything better reflect the generous spirit of the Florentines?

ABBEY CHURCH
MONT ST. MICHAEL, FRANCE

Among the imposing mass of monastic buildings, capping the summit of Mont St. Michael, a rocky islet off the western coast of France, once crowned by a Temple of the Druids, is a picturesque church with lofty Gothic spire, dating from the fifteenth century. The Abbey Church, founded in 709, by St. Aubert, became a noted pilgrimage resort and in the twelfth century was famous for its library and learned monks. In 1203, it was burned by the soldiers of Philip Augustus. During the Revolution the church, rebuilt in the sixteenth century, was used as a prison.

ST. PAUL'S
LONDON

Without the Tower of London and St. Paul's what
would London be?

Westminster Abbey is the Church of the King and
Government; St. Paul's is the Church of the citizens,
the central point for the stirring events of the City of
London—its majestic dome, purple in the mists or
golden in the sunlight, the emblem of London's antiquity and present immensity.

St. Paul's, the largest and most magnificent of all
London's Protestant places of worship, and in the heart
of one of England's great business centers, marks the
site of a Christian church of 610, erected by Ethelbert,
King of Kent, and dedicated to St. Paul. From the
ruins of this church, destroyed by fire in 1087, rose a
finer edifice, the immediate precursor of the present
Cathedral, known as Old St. Paul's, and in its time the
largest church in the country and the longest in Europe.
The magnificent Old St. Paul's, which was destroyed
by fire in 1666, was of Gothic style and rich in relics
and treasures of all kinds—pictures, frescoes, vestments, gold, silver and jewels, which the wealthy citizens of London vied in giving.

From the days of King Stephen the bells of Old St.
Paul's had summoned the citizens to discuss the news
of the day, transact business and defend their liberties.
Along the fashionable walk, lords and ladies and com-
moners strolled, sometimes to stop and converse, sometimes to engage servants, and sometimes to note the
fashions, much as do strollers of today along popular
promenades.

St. Paul's. London.

Sir Christopher Wren, already entrusted with plans for the enlargement of St. Paul's and now commissioned to re-erect the ruined Cathedral, proposed the erection of an entirely new building. His design, in plan similar to Old St. Paul's, was approved by Charles II, and in 1675, he began the erection of the present structure, which was completed in 1710 under Queen Anne.

In architectural design St. Paul's is one of the most striking and best examples of English Renaissance, comparing favorably with St. Peter's. The plan is a Latin Cross surmounted by a dome, where nave and transept intercept. Over the western entrance is a two-storied portico of coupled columns supporting a pediment. The portico is flanked by two towers of diminishing stories topped by bell-shaped cupolas. The dome, in mass and outline the most majestic of the Renaissance, is St. Paul's chief glory, at once "strong, stately, and of airy lightness." St. Paul's dome, modeled after the Pantheon in Rome, was later copied in the Pantheon, Paris.

Notable among the bells of the world is "Great Paul" (cast 1881), hanging in the southwestern tower, considered the best bell in England, perfect in every respect, with soft, melodious, deep tones, sustained and continuous. It is England's largest swinging bell and rings daily at one o'clock for five minutes. It weighs almost seventeen and a half tons and four men are required to ring it. The old bell hanging in the same tower was cast in 1709.

St. Paul's organ, consisting of 4,822 pipes and 102 stops, one of the finest in the world, contains parts of the original organ built in 1697.

St. Paul's, also the burial place of heroes and men of distinction, numbers among its illustrious dead, the

Duke of Wellington, Admiral Lord Horatio Nelson, and Sir Thomas Moore. In the Painter's Corner lie Benjamin West, Sir Joshua Reynolds, Sir Edwin Turner, Sir John Millais, Sir Edwin Landseer and James Barry.

And this mighty magnificent structure also forms a fitting tomb for Sir Christopher Wren, the master architect who designed and built it. A nearby tablet reads: "Si monumentum requiris, circumspice"—(If you ask, where is his monument, look around you).

Commenting on St. Paul's, Van Renssalaer says:

> After the Norman or Romanesque period came the Gothic with its three successive styles. After these came the Renaissance period, which produced not a group or series of Cathedrals, but in magnificent isolation the great Church of St. Paul's in London—not the last Church that has been built in Great Britain, but the last which reveals an architect's genius or illustrates a genuine phase of architectural development.
>
> Everyone knows that St. Paul's is in London, as St. Peter's is in Rome and Notre Dame in Paris.

CATHEDRAL
TOURS, FRANCE

So rare was the beauty of the richly colored glass windows of this Cathedral, that Henry IV is quoted as having said that it was a jewel for which only the casket was wanting. The façade, constructed from 1426 to 1547, is a notable example of the flamboyant or waning Gothic style. Its two towers, about two hundred and thirty feet high, are of sixteenth century Renaissance style.

SALISBURY CATHEDRAL
ENGLAND

The diocese of Old Sarum was founded in 634 by St. Birinus, whose See was at Dorchester. The first church on the bleak hilltop was erected by Herman, a Fleming who went to England during the reign of Edward the Confessor. Even in the days of St. Birinus, it was an old city, with Roman roads and castles, a place of importance.

This early church was not disturbed by William the Conqueror, but was not a lasting edifice. Came in the course of time, St. Osmund as Bishop of Salisbury, and upon the site of the old church he built a new and greater one, which was consecrated April 5, 1092. Five days later it was assailed by a storm so terrific that its roof was destroyed and the entire structure damaged. So it was rebuilt.

Old Sarum was really a fortress upon the hill, surrounded by a massive wall, which protected it from marauders, but led Peter le Blois to refer to it as "the Ark of God shut up in the temple of Baal." In disgust at its location he made the suggestion which was eventually carried out: "Let us, in God's name, descend into the level."

Bishop St. Osmund died December 3, 1099, and was buried in Old Sarum. For more than a hundred years, the church he had reared stood like a sentinel overlooking and guarding Salisbury Plain. Then in the days of Richard Poore, seventh Bishop of Sarum, it was determined to "descend into the level." According to tradition an arrow was shot from a window of the church with the intention of building the new one where it fell. It must have been a stout bow that sent it winging, and a strong arm that drew the string, for the new structure was erected a full mile from the old. The same tradition, however, tells us that the arrow was guided by St. Mary, to whom the Cathedral was dedicated.

Construction of the Salisbury Cathedral was begun with the Lady Chapel, and the first stones were laid April 28, 1220, by King Henry III, whose reign exceeded half a century, and who consecrated the Cathedral thirty-eight years after he had begun its construction. With the King himself officiating, the birth of the Salisbury Cathedral attracted a most distinguished assembly, among whom was St. Edmund, later Archbishop of Canterbury.

In the Lady Chapel, a sumptuous shrine was built for the body of St. Osmund, which was removed thereto July 23, 1457, there to repose in peace until it was destroyed by Henry VIII.

The magnificent spire, the highest in England, rising 404 feet, was constructed about a century after the dedication.

Salisbury Cathedral has the distinction of having been the first great church to be built of a single architectural style, and it is strictly Early English Gothic; uniform, harmonious, even the spire added so much later conforming to the general design. By some persons it is regarded as the most beautiful of all English Cathedrals, although its interior lacks the soft colorful radiance of many, and appears, in consequence, cold. This is due to the fact that the old and beautiful stained glass windows were destroyed by the Puritans under Cromwell.

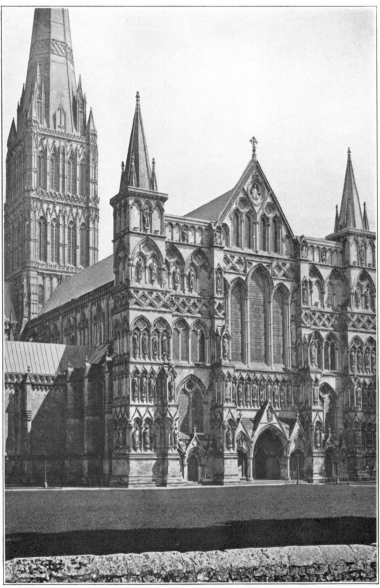

SALISBURY CATHEDRAL, ENGLAND.

With the erection of Salisbury Cathedral, Old Sarum began to disintegrate and cluster about the new church and the old town gradually fell into ruins. St. Osmund's pride disappeared, but in 1838 its foundations were uncovered, to stand a visible relic of Christian effort eight centuries before.

An old rhyme thus popularly describes the Cathedral:

> As many days as in one year there be,
> So many windows in this Church we see;
> As many marble pillars here appear
> As there are hours throughout the fleeting year;
> As many gates as moons one year does view—
> Strange tale to tell, yet not more strange than true.*

In the Lady Chapel is St. Osmond's tomb, sacred relic to the memory of Bishop Osmond and Old Sarum days.

An impressive memorial of early worship, standing on Salisbury Plain (to which Old Sarum descended to build its Cathedral) some eight miles from Salisbury, is Stonehenge, a group of huge stones arranged in circular form, suggesting a primitive place of worship. An inner circle of smaller stones formed the "inner cell," or sanctuary, where, according to Geoffrey of Monmouth (1154) ancient Celts worshipped the Celtic God Zeus. Says Rhys, in his "Celtic Heathendom," "What sort of temple could have been more appropriate for the primary God of light and the luminous heavens than a spacious open-air enclosure like Stonehenge."

A third historic place of worship in Salisbury is St. Thomas Church, founded in 1240 by Bishop Bingham and dedicated to Thomas à Becket. Church war-

---

* An "English Cathedral Journey," Kimball.

[71]

dens' Rolls preserved in this church in an uninterrupted series from the time of Henry VII to the transfer of the present system of keeping church wardens' accounts confirm its antiquity.

CHURCH OF AIX-LA-CHAPELLE
FRANCE

The Cathedral at Aix-la-Chapelle (Aachen), Charlemagne's Royal Tomb Church (796-814), was modeled after the Court Church, St. Vitale, at Ravenna. There Western Emperors were crowned and there the great founder of the Empire was buried, in his capital city and favorite residence.

The church was destroyed by the Northmen in the tenth century and its rebuilding and later restorations resulted in a combination of the Romanesque, Gothic and Classic architectural styles. Its marble, columns, pavement, and mosaics were brought from Ravenna. But the black marble stone bearing the name in brass, "Carlo Magno," no longer covers the body of the Emperor-Statesmen. Frederick Barbarossa, in 1166, caused the remains to be untombed. The church took possession of the imperial skeleton and separating it, made of each bone a holy relic. The sacristy of this church now contains the skull, arm and heart of Charlemagne; the cross he wore on his neck when the tomb was opened, and the ornate gold plates that decorated his arm chair. There also are what are reputed to be the cord which bound our Savior, the sponge given Him on the Cross and His girdle and that of the Holy Virgin. These sacred relics are exhibited every seven years.

Notre Dame, the "Queen of French Cathedrals," Paris. (*See page 73*)

NOTRE DAME

PARIS

> Harmonious parts of a great whole with their count-
> less details of sculpture, statuary and carving, power-
> fully contributing to the calm grandeur of the whole;
> as it were a vast symphony of stone, the colossal
> work of one man and one nation, a sort of human
> creation powerful and prolific as the Divine creation,
> whose double characteristic, Variety and Eternity, it
> seems to have acquired.
>
> —*"Notre Dame de Paris," Hugo.*

For eight centuries Notre Dame, the "Queen of
French Cathedrals," has stood on its narrow islet base
in the Seine River, in the center of Paris. Its foundation stone was laid in 1163, by Pope Alexander III, a
refugee in France, and the main edifice was completed
in 1240. It bears the distinction of being one of the
earliest Gothic Cathedrals in France. Chartres followed
in 1190; Rheims in 1208, and Amiens in 1220, the
three other notable Gothic ecclesiastical edifices of
northern France, further perfecting the transition of
the "lower, heavier Romanesque into the aspiring
Gothic—the medieval architects' triumph of effort for
loftiness with lightness."

This historic and most celebrated of the many
churches in France, dedicated to the Virgin, is on the
site of a Temple of Jupiter Ceranus, where a church
had been erected in 375. There is a record of two
churches on the site, one dedicated to the Virgin and rebuilt by Childebert, about 520, in Roman or Basilican
style. The earliest glass windows of France are reputed

[73]

to have been in this old church.   Fragments of mosaics and precious marbles, discovered in excavations in 1847, and now in Musee de Cluny, are supposed to be from floors and columns of the old church.   It was then considered very grand and was the scene for centuries of religious ceremonies and royal pageants.   Pillaged and badly damaged by the Normans in 857, though repaired by devoted bishops, the twelfth century found it falling into ruins.   Upon its ruins was laid the cornerstone of the present-day Church of Notre Dame.   From 1182 to the present, its naves, altars and chapels have been the scenes of most of the important religious and political ceremonies in France.   Most of the royal weddings took place there.   There were baptized the dauphins of France, and Te Deums were sung in celebration of national victories.

In 1793, the solemn and mighty Cathedral became, by order of the revolutionists, the "Temple of Reason" after indescribable devastation of its majestic façade, windows, ornaments, etc.   Bonfires were made of the mass books and Bibles. The twenty-eight statues of the kings of Israel were hacked to pieces in the belief that they were images of the kings of France.   Turret and bell tower were desecrated.   The ruin was ruthless.

For simple majesty of expression the original façade of Notre Dame is considered to have been unequalled by any other French Cathedral. Its appearance in 1830 was such an impressive though mute denunciation of its many defacements that it inspired its thorough restoration, from 1845 to 1855, under the direction of M. Viollet le Duc.

But Victor Hugo knew the old as well as the new, so let us see it through his observant eyes:

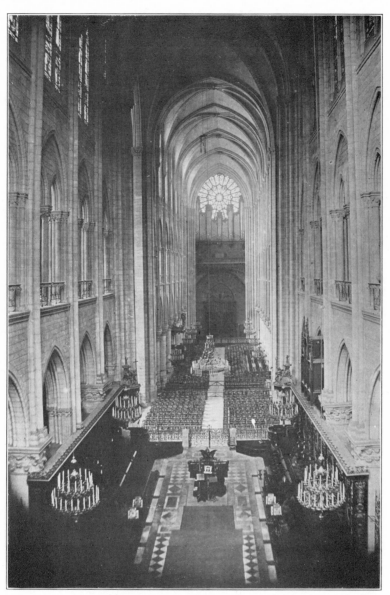

NOTRE DAME. PARIS.   Interior.   *(See page 73)*

"The façade now lacks three important things, first, the eleven steps which formerly raised it above the level of the ground; next the lower series of statues which filled the niches over the doors; and lastly the upper row of the twenty-eight most ancient kings of France which adorned the gallery of the first story, from Childebert to Philip Augustus, each holding in his hand the Imperial globe. And what has become of the delightful little steeple which, no less fragile than its neighbor, the spire of St. Chapelle, rose yet nearer Heaven than the towers, slender, sharp, sonorous and daintily wrought.

"Time yet has, perhaps, given to the church more than it took away, for it is Time that has painted the front with that sober hue of creation, which makes the antiquity of churches their greatest beauty."

Prominent among the one thousand decorative statues adorning the western façade, are those of the Virgin and Christ Child, sacred to whom are also the front left portal and that of the north transept—all exquisite examples of early Gothic sculpture. Through these massive portals passed the good King Louis IX (1226-1270) to pray before starting on his ill-fated Crusades, and through them stormed the Paris mob tearing down the Kings and Saints and setting up the Goddess of Reason. Through them in 1804 went Napoleon to his Coronation, and in 1810 to his marriage with Marie Louisa.

Among striking interior features are the magnificent rose windows of Christ and the Virgin, surrounded by the prophets and the celebrated carvings of the choir and pulpit. Flying buttresses, "delicate figures of stone," which have stood firm for eight hundred years, proof of the wonderful engineering skill of the old cathedral builders, adorn the sides. Gargoyles encircle the towers. These hobgoblins and quaint little beasts in stone are among the most fascinating features of the sculptural adornment of this Cathedral.

THE ESCORIAL CHURCH
MADRID

The Escorial (composed of a convent, palace, royal mausoleum and church), about thirty-one miles from Madrid, has a church begun by Charles V in 1563, in fulfilment of a vow to St. Lawrence to build a church because of his having been forced to cannonade one dedicated to this saint. The church was completed and dedicated by his son, Philip II, on that saint's day, the anniversary of the Spanish victory over the French at St. Quentin, August 10, 1557.

The plans of this group of massive, gray granite buildings, "the largest mass of granite in the world, and the world's eighth wonder," is a rectangular parallelogram six hundred seventy-five by five hundred thirty feet, representing the gridiron on which St. Lawrence was martyred. Four large towers represent the feet, while the church and royal palace extending to one side represent the handle. The interior buildings are placed to represent the bars. The style of architecture is severely classical, presenting a simple, bare and barrack-like appearance.

In the private apartments of the royal family was the King's cell-like bedroom, communicating with the Oratory of the church and commanding a view of the high altar, so that, unseen, the king could participate in the service of the Mass.

SEVILLE CATHEDRAL
SPAIN

Seville Cathedral, not only the largest church in Spain, but also the largest of the medieval cathedrals, stands on the site of a great mosque erected by the Moors, who captured the city in 712. For more than five hundred years it remained a Moslem city, or until it was recaptured by Ferdinand III, of Castile, in 1248.

This ancient Spanish city was the scene of the notable Church Councils from 590 to 619. Its church and political history have been of such importance that the distinction given it by its massive cathedral is well-deserved. After the discovery of the New World, Seville became the mart of the colonies and the residence of princely merchants. The cathedral was begun in 1402, and not completed until 1517. "Let us," reads the resolution adopted by the city in 1401, "erect such a cathedral that posterity will say we were madmen."

The high wall enclosing the sacred structure gives it much the appearance of a fortress. There are five naves, each of which is as large as a church, while in the central one another large cathedral could stand, so vast is everything connected with this edifice.

The interior decoration is superb, showing much extravagance in ornament and excessive detailed embellishment, a characteristic of all Spanish cathedrals. A wealth of art treasures abounds, among them famous paintings of Murillo, Spain's most beloved artist, and one of the great world-artists, and other famed Spanish artists—the chefs-d'oeuvres of some sixty-seven sculptors and thirty-eight painters. Pavements are in black and white checkered marble and the painted windows are among the handsomest in the world.

From its earlier Moorish mosque the great cathedral retains, beside its beautiful Court of Oranges, La Giralda, once a minaret, now one of the world's celebrated bell towers, designed by El Geber, inventor of algebra (1000 A. D.). Though the rest of the mosque had fallen into disrepair through the ravages of time and earthquakes, the delicately wrought minaret was so well preserved that the Spaniards kept it for the bell tower of their Cathedral. The top is capped by a small dome, on which, some three hundred feet from the ground, stands a small figure of Faith holding in one hand a palm and in the other the banner of Constantine. The dome is visible at a long distance, and glitters in the sun like an enormous ruby embedded in a mighty crown.

In one of the side aisles is a small marble casket resting on the shoulders of four elaborately dressed and ornately equipped allegorical figures, supposed to hold the remains of Christopher Columbus, brought from Havana at the close of the Spanish-American War of 1898. But this is disputed. When Columbus died at Valladolid, Spain, his body was transported according to his wishes to Santo Domingo. When this island was surrendered to the French in 1796, a casket supposed to contain his bones was taken to Havana and placed in the Cathedral there. It was these bones that were taken to Seville.

But that they were those of Christopher Columbus is strongly questioned. Many historians believe that they were those of his son Diego. While the Cathedral at Santo Domingo was undergoing extensive repairs in

1877, an ancient leaden casket was unearthed. It held human bones and upon the casket was the inscription, "These are the remains of the Discoverer of America, the first Admiral, illustrious and renowned man, Christopher Columbus." Upon this basis and on the strength of some other records, the Dominican Republic of today claims to hold the bones of the discoverer in its own ancient Cathedral.

In St. Ferdinand's Chapel, the body of King Ferdinand (1217-1252), who delivered Seville from the Arabs, rests in a crystal casket, clad in military dress with crown and royal mantle. In other chapels rest the bodies of other famous Spaniards in caskets of silver, their hands bedecked with diamonds and rubies, amid large marble altars and statues of stone, wood and silver.

THE VOTIVE CHURCH
VIENNA

The Votive Church is of florid Gothic style, exquisitely proportioned, and has delicately sculptured openwork towers three hundred and twenty-five feet high, reminding one of the Cathedral of Burgos in Spain. The church commemorates the escape of Emperor Franz Joseph from assassination in 1853. It has been called Vienna's most beautiful ecclesiastical structure.

St. Charles Church with its curious side-entrance pillars is another church of Vienna, one of the oldest and most historic cities of Europe.

ST. PETER'S

ROME

Enter; its grandeur overwhelms thee not;
And why? It is not lessened; but thy mind,
Expanded by genius of the spot
Has grown colossal . . .

But lo, the dome, the vast and wondrous dome,
To which Diana's marvel was a cell,
Christ's mighty Shrine above his martyr's tomb.

— *"Childe Harold," Canto IV.*

St. Peter's, at Rome, the largest church in the world, is a stupendous monument to the genius of Michael Angelo, Bramante, and to the genius of the Italian Renaissance. It succeeds the Basilica of San Pietro in Vaticano (Old St. Peter's), which official title it still holds, distinguishing it from other churches in Rome dedicated to St. Peter. Old St. Peter's was preserved through the Middle Ages, but in the fourteenth century began to show signs of decay. It was the ambition and intention of Pope Julius II and of Michael Angelo, as early as 1505, to whom the Pope had entrusted the commission of erecting his tomb, to rebuild Old St. Peter's to serve as a mausoleum for the Pope. Julius' successors, however, were interested only in the rebuilding of St. Peter's, putting Bramante in charge of its plan. Bramante's death in 1514 interrupted the work and also Michael Angelo's, who was again put in charge of the plans in 1546. St. Peter's was therefore nearly a century and a quarter in building (1506-1626). Raphael, too, was engaged in its construction

St. Peter's, Rome.

and decoration. There were many artists and many plans.

Michael Angelo followed Bramante's general plan of a Greek cross, but wholly re-designed the dome, which is generally acknowledged to be the surpassing grandeur of the great Renaissance Church of St. Peter's, and under which is the mystic high altar, rising over the shrine of St. Peter, the first Bishop of Rome. This vast dome, the highest in the world, measures 140 feet to the top of the cross on the ball, which to the spectator below appears small, but which would hold a dozen persons. It is said that Michael Angelo's model for this triumph in bold architectural beauty was the Pantheon. While looking at that one day he said, prophetically, "I will raise the Pantheon to the sky. I will build a church and put the Pantheon on for a dome."

Its interior plan is one of the most impressive pieces of architectural decoration in existence. Priceless mosaics represent the artistic production of mosaic workers whose ancestors for ten generations had handed the craft down from father to son. Large mosaic copies of paintings adorning the interior can hardly be told from the originals. About the walls are altars, magnificent tombs of Popes, chapels and innumerable works of art, making St. Peter's a veritable museum of the sculpture, painting and decorative work of three centuries. The total cost of the Cathedral has been estimated at $50,-000,000.

The crypt of St. Peter's, erected over the spot where it is claimed the saint was crucified, and carefully guarded throughout all the centuries of changes, contains many venerated fragments and relics from the original Basilica of St. Peter's. Michael Angelo's profoundly beautiful "Pieta," the work which raised him at the age of twenty-four to the rank of the greatest sculptor of his day, adorns the chapel.

It is St. Peter's vast cathedral, "Church of Churches," which Byron celebrates in his inimitable lines:—

Thou of Temples old or altars new
Standest alone, with nothing like thee.
     *   *   *   *
Power, Glory, Strength and Beauty all are aisled
In this eternal Ark of Worship Undefiled.

—*"Childe Harold," Canto IV.*

St. Peter's compares with other large churches as follows, the figures representing square yards of area in round numbers:

St. Peters,	18,000
Seville Cathedral,	13,000
Milan Cathedral,	10,000
St. Paul's London,	9,000
St. Sophia,	8,000
Cologne Cathedral,	7,000

The Church of St. Maria dei Cappuccini, Rome, contains Guido Reni's "St. Michael and the Dragon." In the Chigi Chapel of the Church of Santa Maria Della Pace, Rome, are Raphael's "Sybils."

CATHEDRAL
COMO, ITALY

Como Cathedral is referred to as the most perfect building in Italy, illustrating the fusion of Gothic and Renaissance styles.

ST. PETER'S, ROME. Interior. (See page 80)

COLOGNE CATHEDRAL

Cologne Cathedral, "celebrated for its immensity, beauty of proportion, and wealth of decoration," is Germany's most magnificent church edifice. Though begun in 1270, and not completed until the nineteenth century, it is yet a remarkable example of rare and admirable structural unity. The original design, derived from Amiens Cathedral, was closely followed throughout. One writer characterizes Cologne Cathedral as "French influence mixed with German peculiarities."

Cologne, originally a town of German tribes, grew to be an important city under the Romans. Under Frankish rule it retained its prominence, the Bishopric of Cologne instituted at that time having been raised to the rank of an Archiepiscopal See by Charles the Great. It contained in its jurisdiction the capital of Charlemagne's Empire, the seat where emperors were crowned. The celebrity and wealth of the Cathedral were due largely to the custom of emperors to visit it after their coronation.

An early church of the ninth century, burned in 1248, is said to have preceded the present edifice. Apropos of this earlier church, we have the interesting record:

"At the northeast end of the elevation occupied by the ancient Colonia Agrippina, in the spot where the choir of the Cathedral raises its magnificent pinnacles, there existed in very remote ages a Roman Castellum."

Work on the Cathedral was suspended by the Reformation, and was neglected until the nineteenth century, at which time funds were raised and building renewed under the king of Prussia. Its completion in 1880 (October tenth) was celebrated with great splendor by Emperor William I, attended by most of the sovereign princes. Runkart's hymn, "Nun Danket Alle Gott," the German "Te Deum," second only to Luther's "Ein feste Burg," was sung at this ceremony.

Twin towers, five hundred twelve feet high, crowned with spires of openwork tracery—a characteristic of German Gothic—are this grand Cathedral's chief glory. The "Kaiser-glocke," the great bell of the tower, was cast in 1874 from cannon taken from the defeated French. Added to this external glory are its rows of massive flying buttresses, piers, pinnacles, spires, needles, crockets, towers, mullioned windows, portals, niches filled with figures, carvings and grotesque gargoyles, which produce an astonishing effect.

The chapel, in the Church of St. Ursula, Cologne, commemorates the life of St. Ursula, the Breton maiden, and the eleven hundred other maidens massacred with her at Cologne, so the legend runs. St. Ursula became the patron saint of young girls and all women who educate and care for girls. In the Academy of Venice are a series of celebrated pictures by Carpaccio, graphically depicting the story of this saint.

It is claimed that the Chapel of St. Ursula contains, besides the bones of the massacred maidens, also one thorn from the Crown of Thorns, a piece of the True Cross, and one of its nails.

At Cologne are also the Church of the Jesuits, the Church of the Apostles (1220-1250), and the early representative Cathedrals, Spires, Trèves, and Mayence.

The Cathedral at Worms (1110-1200) is Rhenish-Romanesque, in style, similar to that of northern Italy

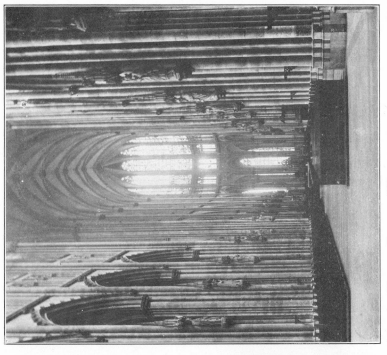

COLOGNE CATHEDRAL. Exterior and Interior Views. *(See page 83)*

but more "constructively adventurous, vigorous, and picturesque."

The Cathedral at Ratisbon ranks with Cologne and Strassburg as one of the three finest examples of German Gothic.

CATHEDRAL OF VASALI
MOSCOW

Facing the Red Square, Old Russia's famous camp-forum and place of execution, stands the Cathedral of Vasali, the Beatified, unparalleled in its curious mixture of architectural styles and glaring colors. It was built in 1554 by Italian architects for Ivan, the Terrible, in commemoration of the Conquest of Kazan. It consists of a number of buildings, under separate cupolas, differing from each other in form, dimension and coloring. The interior does not differ essentially from other churches of Moscow, being dark, close, and covered with paintings, gold and gems in great profusion.

In striking contrast with the Cathedral is the modern Church of the Saviour, Moscow's most magnificent church, consecrated in 1881 in commemoration of the destruction of Napoleon's Grand Army in 1812, and the expulsion of the French from Russia. Majesty of proportion and elegance of structure characterize this delicate, cream stone building. Its plan is a Greek cross, with five magnificent domes decorated with paintings of the Trinity, executed by Russia's ablest artists. A frieze of life-size figures adorns the walls.

[85]

MARTIN LUTHER'S CHURCH

(SCHLOSS-KIRCHE) WITTENBERG

In Wittenberg, the "Protestant Mecca," are two churches sacred to Martin Luther, known as Stadt-Kirche, in which the great Saxon reformer often preached, and Schloss-Kirche, on the wooden doors of which Luther nailed his famous Thesis on the eve of All Saints Day, November 1, 1517. Schloss-Kirche (All Saints Church, erected 1493-1499) was closely connected with the University in which Luther was Professor of Theology.

The old church was seriously damaged by bombardment in 1760, and again in 1813-14, and restored in 1885. Present interior decorations in the form of statuary, medallions, and coats of arms commemorate the heroes of the Reformation. In front of the pulpit are bronze plates with Latin inscriptions, indicating the graves of Luther (1483-1546), and his comrade in the faith, Melanchthon (died 1560). Below the gallery in huge letters are the words, "Ein' Feste Berg" (A Mighty Fortress), opening words of Luther's favorite hymn.

The famous wooden doors, burned in 1760 by the French, were replaced in 1858 by bronze doors ten feet high, bearing the original Latin text of the ninety-five Theses.

In Stadt-Kirche, the larger of the two Wittenberg churches, Luther often preached in place of the regular pastor. "It was his preaching here that made him as absolute ruler over the people at Wittenberg as Chrysostom was at Antioch and Constantinople, Calvin at

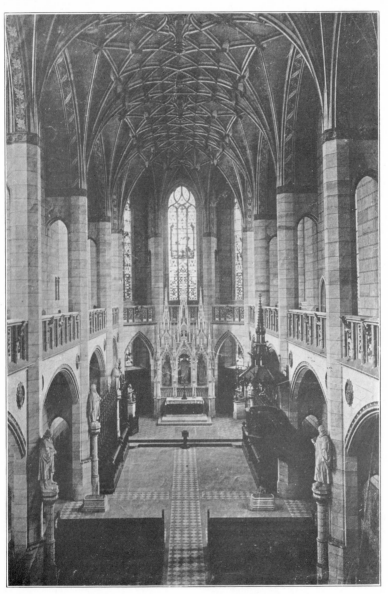

MARTIN LUTHER'S CHURCH, WITTENBERG.

Geneva, and, we may add, Knox at Edinburgh," says a historian of Luther and his times.

A nearby bronze statue, erected in 1822, occupies the site of a chapel containing a pulpit of planks where according to tradition, the Reformer sometimes preached.

"The Marseillaise hymn of the Reformation," as Heine calls Luther's hymn "Ein' feste Burg ist unser Gott," was composed by Luther for the Diet of Spires, when, on April 20, 1529, the German princes made their formal protest against the revocation of their liberties and so became known as Protestants. Luther sang it to the accompaniment of the lute every day. Nearly a hundred years later Gustavus Adolphus, the hero-king of Sweden, ordered the kettledrums and trumpets to strike up and his warriors to sing Luther's hymn as they rode into battle (November 16, 1632). After his victory, the great general thanked God that He had made good the promise, "The field, He will maintain it."

Thomas Carlyle's English version (one of the several of this celebrated hymn) is generally regarded as the best. "The hymn may have been suggested by the Forty-sixth Psalm, but it is really Luther's hymn, not David's," says one. Frederick the Great called Luther's hymn "God Almighty's Grenadier March."

In this connection it is interesting to note the great German reformer's "idea" of hymns and hymn singing:

> "The words of hymns should have a swing and a good strong meter, so that the congregation may catch up the tune to join with it. Let us bid goodbye to the music of Gregory and take the common songs of our own people, as they sing them at harvests, at village

festivals, at weddings, and at funerals, for use in our Churches. Man can as well praise God in one tune as in another, and it is a pity that such pretty songs as these should be kept any longer from the service of the Maker."

"Verzage Nicht, du Hauflein," composed by Pastor Altenburg at Erfurt, became known as "Gustavus Adolphus' Battle Hymn." It, too, was sung at the Battle of Lutzen (November 16, 1632) where victory gave fresh courage to the Protestants of Germany when their faith was thus rewarded.

> Fear not, O little flock, the foe,
> Who madly seeks your overthrow,
> Dread not his rage and power—
>   * * * *
> God is with us. We are His own,
> Our victory cannot fail.

SANTA MARIA DELLA SALUTE
VENICE

Santa Maria Della Salute, on the Grand Canal, erected 1630-1680 of Renaissance style of architecture, is a memorial to the Virgin as Our Lady of Health or Safety, in acknowledgement of the cessation of a devastating plague. It was one of the first buildings of the grotesque Renaissance, but, because of its façade, and the graceful flight of steps leading down to the Canal, it was chosen by Turner for the principal object of his well-known view of the Grand Canal. Tintoretto's "Marriage in Cana," one of his best and most highly finished paintings, adorns the sacristy of this church.

SANTA MARIA DELLA SALUTE, VENICE.   The Exterior view is from across Grand Canal.

GLOUCESTER CATHEDRAL
ENGLAND

At Gloucester, an important Saxon town, a favorite residence of Norman kings, and the seat of eight Parliaments, is a fine Cathedral, in architectural style proceeding from severe Anglo-Saxon to the richest Gothic. The assemblage of the whole, though successively erected during a period of four hundred years, is grand and harmonious. Its superb central tower, two hundred twenty-five feet high, is one of the three famous square towers in England, the others being those of Canterbury and Lincoln. This tower is its most impressive and beautiful external feature.

As early as 681 a Norman church (later developing into a flourishing double establishment for monks and nuns), occupied the site. In 1051 Edward the Confessor, while visiting Gloucester, granted Bishop Aldred land for a Cathedral similar to his Cathedral at Westminster, which he was then erecting. The Cathedral of St. Peter which Abbot Serlo, the Conqueror's chaplain, its second builder, then erected (1072-1104) was, with additions, Gloucester Cathedral, much as it stands today.

Beside the distinction of its lovely square central tower, Gloucester Cathedral has the glory of its celebrated East Window, flooding the choir with its jeweled lights, the largest in England, exceeding York's window by a few square feet of area. Restored in 1682, this window of six center and eight side lights shows window painting as executed between 1347 and 1350, the date ascribed to it because of the heraldic shields in the tower lights, apparently inserted by the survivors of the great English victory at Cressy and accounting for the name "Cressy" or "Calais" window, sometimes applied to it. The subject of the painting is the Coronation, attending figures being saints, kings, abbots, apostles and angels. Of this indescribably beautiful window one writes:

> Beautiful as a dream with its soft silvery light, faintly colored with jeweled shafts of the richest blue and red and here and there a vein of pale gold, this vast window could not be seen out of England or, at least, one of the grey and misty northern countries, where gleams of light or shafts of sunshine are exceedingly precious.

Three cherished monuments adorn Gloucester. One, a rudely sculptured figure, is a monument to Osric, ancient Saxon viceroy. The second is the tomb of Duke Robert of Normandy (the eldest son of the Conqueror), and the third, in the North Ambulatory, the tomb of Edward II. Murdered at Berkeley Castle, near Bristol in 1327, and refused burial elsewhere, Abbot Thokey gave him sumptuous burial at Gloucester. Later his son, Edward III, erected the tomb, which became a noted shrine, offerings at which greatly increased the monastery's revenues.

The Whispering Gallery, a narrow gallery seventy-four feet long, three feet wide and six high, in which the lowest whisper, if uttered close to the wall, or the slightest scratch of a pin, is heard at the other end, has this significant inscription on its wall:

> Doubt not that God who sits on high,
> The secret prayer can hear,

GLOUCESTER CATHEDRAL, ENGLAND.　Interior and Exterior Views.
(*See page 89*)

When a dead wall, thus cunningly,
Conveys soft whispers to the ear.

The lines were said to have been written by Maurice Wheeler, head master of King School.

Of the days of the suppression of monasteries and their conversion into Cathedrals by Henry VIII, one writes thus romantically and regretfully of Gloucester, and its famed Benedictine Abbey:

The Abbey which had existed for more than eight centuries in poverty and in wealth, in meanness and magnificence, in misfortune and success finally succumbed to the royal will. The last Mass was sung, the last censor waved, the last congregation knelt in rapt and lowly adoration before the altar there, and doubtless, as the last tones of that day's evensong died away in the vaulted roof, there were not wanting those who lingered in the solemn stillness of the old massive pile and who, as the lights disappeared one by one, felt there was a void, which could never be filled, because their old Abbey with its beautiful services, its frequent means of Grace, its hospitality to strangers, and its loving care of God's poor had passed away like a morning dream and was gone forever.

THE CATHEDRAL OF GRANADA

In 1492, after almost eight centuries of Moslem rule, Granada, the last stronghold of the Moor, surrendered under Boabdil, the last Moorish king. In 1520, the Cathedral of Granada was begun, "Spain's earliest and most remarkable of Renaissance Cathedrals," originally designed in Gothic style, by Enrique de Egas.

Spanish Renaissance cathedrals are also to be found at Jaen and Valladolid.

[91]

LINCOLN CATHEDRAL
ENGLAND

Lincoln Cathedral, whose Angels' Choir has been pronounced one of the loveliest of man-made works, is an example of early Gothic architecture, dating from the days when Bishop Hugh of Avalon went to England from his cell in Grand Chartreuse, where he had planned to end his days.

It is the second church to have occupied this site, the first having been built by St. Remegius, an almoner brought over and made bishop by William the Conqueror. St. Remegius (Remy) began his Cathedral in 1088 and finished it in 1092, but died two days before its consecration. He dedicated it to "The Virgin of Virgins." This first Norman church was destroyed by an earthquake in 1185, and Bishop Hugh began the present Cathedral in 1192. The western front commemorates the life of St. Remy in elaborate carvings and sculpture. Interesting parts of the original church may yet be seen in the west front and the bay of the nave. In the southwest corner is the ancient font of the founder. The Stone of Remegius marks the place where he is buried. In 1200 Bishop Hugh died, leaving as a monument to his architectural genius the plan of the Cathedral and St. Hugh's Choir, which he lived to complete.

This Choir is celebrated for its beautiful wall arcading adorned with devout sculptured angels. St. Hugh was buried in one of his chapels. He was carried to his final resting place on the shoulders of King John attended by a great body of nobles and church dignitaries.

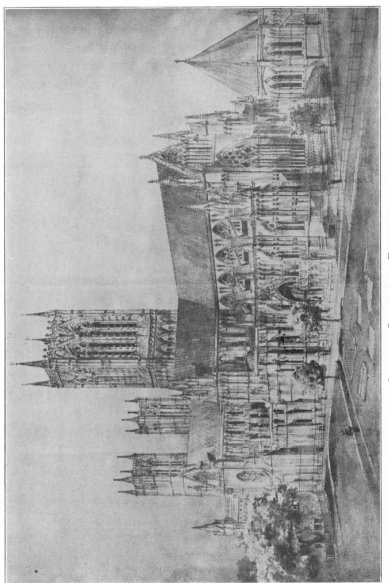

LINCOLN CATHEDRAL, ENGLAND.

The old Lincoln legend of his burial is quaintly recorded in the familiar lines:—

> A' the bells of Merrie Lincoln
> Without men's hands were rung,
> And a' the books o' Merrie Lincoln
> Were read without man's tongue;
> And ne'er was such a burial
> Sin' Adam's day begun.

In the western transept, completed after St. Hugh's death, are two early English rose windows of rare old stained glass, known as the "Bishop's Eye" and the "Dean's Eye." The glass of the latter is said to be older than that of Canterbury. The subject of this window is the Church on Earth and the Church in Heaven.

The five small lancet windows below, known as the "Five Little Sisters," contain rare grisaille of early date.

The Angel's Choir, added in 1255-1280, was constructed to contain the shrine of St. Hugh. It was on October 6, 1280, that the chest, "covered with gold and studded with pearls and other precious stones," attended by a royal pageant led by King Edward I and Queen Eleanor, his Spanish bride, was placed in this famous Choir of decorated Gothic, in which ten years later a monument to Queen Eleanor herself was erected. She had died near Lincoln and was embalmed there. From Lincoln, the King then began his long journey to Westminster for her burial, Eleanor Crosses having been erected at each halting place.

The Angels' Choir takes it name from the exquisitely sculptured angels decorating its triforium suggested, perhaps, by the angels in the original St. Hugh's Choir.

In the Central Tower hangs "Great Tom" of Lincoln, cast in 1834 and hung in 1835. "Great Tom the First" cast in 1610, was probably preceded by one or more "Great Toms," since a record of 1311 refers to ropes for two bells, and even earlier records (1173-1182) to *duas companas grandes atque sonoras.* Of the six Lady bells, taken down in 1834 to be sacrificed as extra metal for the recasting of Great Tom, three were dated 1593; one 1633, and one 1737. This remarkable bell, weighing five tons eight hundredweight, is the fourth largest bell in the kingdom. It is too heavy to ring the hours without endangering the tower, so it was chained and riveted down and is now struck by a hammer weighing 224 pounds. The name was taken, tradition says, from its original consecration to St. Thomas of Canterbury. It is thought, however, by some to have been derived from the old bell of Christ Church, Oxford (at one time in the diocese of Lincoln), bearing the curious inscription. "In Thomas Laude, resono Bim Bom sine fraude."

CATHEDRAL OF MONREALE
SICILY

Monreale Cathedral, near Palermo, overrun by the Moors in the tenth century, shows a mixture of Byzantine and Saracenic (or Moorish) styles. It is Basilican in style and is decorated in the interior with mosaics of Biblical subjects, framed in arabesque borders, whose somber richness of color and severity of design impart to the interior a solemn grandeur.

LINCOLN CATHEDRAL, ENGLAND. Interior. *(See page 92)*

DURHAM CATHEDRAL

ENGLAND

Durham is the most beautifully situated of all English Cathedrals, as it reposes on a densely wooded cliff, which gives it a peculiar picturesque charm. It marks the site of the shrine of St. Cuthbert, one of the three great English saints and the great Patron Saint of Durham. The first church was built in 995, on the spot designated by St. Cuthbert himself, as the tradition goes. This structure was of wood, "a shelter of woods and branches to protect the body of the saint." It was followed by a second one of stone, which stood until the time of William the Conqueror, about which time the old monastic congregation of St. Cuthbert, a Benedictine monastery, was established.

Foundation stones of the great Anglo-Norman Cathedral were laid in 1093. When completed, the Cathedral had much the same appearance as today.

The Nine Altars Chapel, near the Shrine of St. Cuthbert, the supreme ornament of the choir, is one of the Cathedral's chief features. High on the northwest turret is the Dun Cow, a panel of sculptured figures of a milkmaid and cow, celebrating the ancient legend connected with the selection of this site as the final resting place of the saint's bones. Borne about aimlessly on the shoulders of the monks of Lindisfarne, after resting elsewhere for two hundred years, so runs the legend, a dun cow had finally directed their final disposition at Durham.

Galilee Chapel, a most beautiful example of the transitional Norman style, whose "lightness and delicacy of structure contrasts pleasingly with the massive grandeur of the Norman Cathedral behind," also bears remembrance of the Patron Saint. At a certain spot in its pavement is a "Cross of Blewe Marble," indicating the limit of woman's approach to the altar. No woman was suffered to go beyond the cross, "because there was never woman came, where holie man Sancte Cuthbert was."

On the north door of the old Cathedral is a curious sanctuary knocker, a grotesque metallic head holding a ring in its mouth. Above this door in olden days relays of monks watched night and day. Any criminal whose hands once grasped the ring was immediately granted "St. Cuthbert's Peace," and given the protection of his shrine. Confession was taken in writing. If not pardoned within thirty-seven days, the criminal was conveyed in safety across the seas.

In Neville Chapel, rests Lord Neville, victor of the Battle of Neville Cross in 1346. In this battle the banner of St. Cuthbert (made from a cloth which the saint had used in celebrating Mass), was carried as a standard. Since then a thanksgiving hymn sung from the Cathedral tower, marks each anniversary.

In Durham, "half Church of God, half castle 'gainst the Scot," rests also the venerable Bede, monk of Jarrow, great Northumbrian scholar and historian, contemporary and friend of St. Cuthbert. From the eighth to the eleventh century, his bones reposed at Jarrow. In 1022, they were lifted and placed in St. Cuthbert's "hospitable coffin." On the tomb is engraved the well-known epitaph:—"Hoc sunt in fossa Bedae Venerabilis ossa."

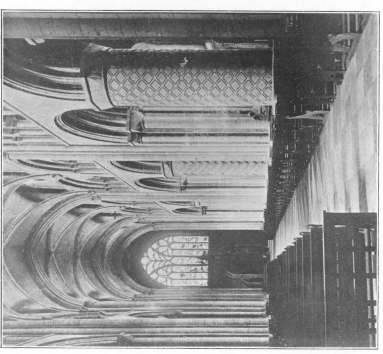

DURHAM CATHEDRAL, ENGLAND. Interior and Exterior Views.

MILAN CATHEDRAL

MILAN, ITALY

Milan, the second largest city in Italy, is particularly famous for its fine churches. Of these the principal one is the world-renowned Duomo of Milan, the most important example of the Gothic style in Italy, and an ecclesiastical structure ranking favorably with St. Peter's of Rome and the Cathedral Santa Maria del Fiore in Florence. Begun in 1387, Milan Cathedral required fifteen generations of builders, and is not yet complete.

This vast church, constructed entirely of white Carrara marble, is distinguished not so much by structural grandeur or historic interest as by decorative richness, adorned as it is by some one hundred thirty-five pinnacles and more than two thousand statues, a variety of carvings of unsurpassable beauty. More than sixty-seven hundred sculptured figures have at one time adorned the Cathedral, a marble population that given life would make an important city.

In contemplating this magnificent Cathedral, with its splendid, towering spire designed by Brunelleschi in 1440, one is awed by the myriad of statues, figures, groups and pinnacles in marble, each of the latter surmounted by a figure of life size; and high above them all the figure of the Mother of Jesus, a veritable labyrinth of human art.

The design of the façade, in Renaissance style, is simple. It is pierced by five doors and eight windows and delightfully embellished with canopied niches holding statues and delicate lace-like decorations. A notable feature of the façade is the great door with its sculptural panels representing the creation of Eve. Other events are depicted in stone on the side panels.

In the interior the general impression is that of a simple and religious majesty. Immense columns twelve feet in diameter are adorned above their capitals with statues in niches. The great windows of the choir, said to be the largest in any Gothic cathedral, are of stained glass of 1844. In the center of the cross. through an opening surrounded by a balustrade, one looks down on the crypt holding the remains of St. Borromeo, most revered saint of the district, reposing in a crystal coffin covered with plates of silver. His virtues during the plague in Milan keep his memory alive.

In 1805, Milan Cathedral sanctified the coronation of Napoleon with the Iron Crown—a broad plain hoop of gold set with precious stones and containing on its inner side a flattened nail reputed to be of the True Cross brought from Palestine by St. Helena, the mother of Constantine. Forty-three monarchs are said to have had this circlet of the Longobardi kings placed on their heads; the German emperors from the thirteenth century having been crowned with it as kings of Italy.

With the completion of the Cathedral of St. John the Divine, New York City, Milan Cathedral will yield to this new world house of worship its present rank as the world's third largest Christian church.

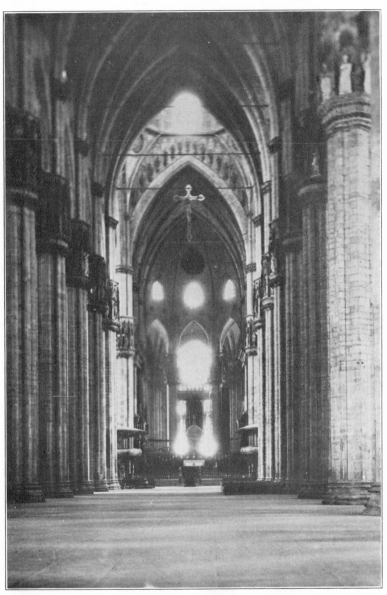

Milan Cathedral, Italy. Interior.   *(See page 97)*

ST. GERVAIS

SWITZERLAND

It has been aptly said that the Reformation, like the Rhine, had its source in the mountains of Switzerland; derived its tributaries from France and Germany, and then flowed on to fertilize the plains of Holland.

In Geneva, Switzerland, home of the Reformation, and City of Refuge, within whose walls the distressed and afflicted of all peoples have ever found shelter, are two historic churches. In St. Gervais, said to be the oldest, is a tablet bearing the names of the eighteen brave citizens sacrificed to the repulse of the Escalade, that last attempt of the Duke of Savoy to bind once more politically and spiritually the people of Geneva, which event Geneva celebrates every year on the twelfth of December, as the "Feast of the Escalade."

St. Pierre is another of Geneva's celebrated churches, and in it some pages of history were written. In bygone days a bishop presided at its altar. It was the scene of disputations over the Reformation, and in it colleges held their graduation exercises. Even today the newly elected Councillors of State repair to it to take the oath of allegiance to the Constitution.

Near the choir, in a chapel, is a massive sarcophagus and statue, marking the resting place of Henri, Duc de Robah; Marguerite de Sully, his wife, and their son Tancred. They were Huguenot refugees who found in Geneva a sanctuary where they could live in peace and safety. There is also a tablet on the wall of the nave which notes the death in exile of Theodore Agrippa d'Aubigne, marshal and admiral of France.

[99]

As the old year wanes people throng to the Cour de St. Pierre to hear the ancient bell in the tower "ring out the old, ring in the new" year and exchange happy New Year greetings.

Another celebrated monument in Geneva, closely connected with church history, is the Reformer's Statue. Prominent figures in it are Calvin and Knox. Close by stands that of Roger Williams, and near him the graven words of the Mayflower Compact together with a relief of William Brewster, John Carver, Miles Standish and William Bradford.

In Geneva is also a simple Council Chamber, known as the Alabama Room, where the arbitration treaty between the United States and Great Britain, settling what is known as the Alabama Dispute, was signed in 1878. This quiet room is hallowed also as the birthplace of the Red Cross, for here was signed in 1864, at the Convention of Geneva, the compact that carries the transposed cross of Switzerland over all the world, bringing relief to the wounded and comfort to the dying.

JERUSALEM CHURCH
BRUGES

Jerusalem Church at Bruges, erected in 1435, is a quaint church, said to have been built at the expense of two devout families who wished it to be an exact reproduction of the Holy Sepulcher. Although they made two journeys to the Holy Land for this purpose, the similarity of the two churches is not striking.

St. GERVAIS, GENEVA, SWITZERLAND. *(See page 99)*

ST. PIERRE, GENEVA, SWITZERLAND. Interior. *(See page 99)*

CATHEDRAL

PISA, ITALY

The Cathedral of Pisa, consecrated in 1118, stands a votive offering of the Pisans in commemoration of a naval victory near Palermo in 1063. At that time six vessels of materials were sent home and appropriated to the building. The Cathedral, thus erected as a monument of gratitude, represents a high development of the Romanesque (1000-1200) style of architecture, which began with imitation of the Roman Basilica and was at first exceedingly bare and somber. As the style developed, vaulting took the place of the flat ceiling of the Basilica and transepts were introduced, forming a Latin cross. By the eleventh century the Romanesque architecture of Italy was strongly influenced by the Byzantine type of decoration.

The Cathedral is constructed of white marble ornamented with black and colored bands. Two of its pillars were souvenirs from the Temple of Diana at Ephesus.

Two other celebrated buildings complete the trio, of which the Cathedral is one part,—the Baptistry and the Leaning Tower, both also Romanesque. The Tower, or campanile, was begun in 1174 and finished in 1350, and was intended to rival that of Venice. It is of white marble, and has walls thirteen feet thick at the base, and rises in eight stories to a height of one hundred and eighty feet. A stairway of three hundred steps leads to the top.

It has never been determined whether this campanile being out of perpendicular was intended or accidental.

In any event it slants so that for centuries it has been more than thirteen feet out of plumb. To this fact it owes its fame and its inclusion among the Seven Wonders of the World. Galileo, a Pisan, used it for his experiments to determine the velocity of falling bodies.

In recent years the tower has been leaning farther and farther, until now it is more than fourteen feet out of line, and in danger of falling. The government has appointed a commission to replace the foundations and anchor it, a delicate piece of engineering.

In the Cathedral which, at the transept is three hundred and eleven feet long and two hundred and thirty-seven feet wide, hangs a celebrated lamp, known as Galileo's lamp, because, it is said, its swaying suggested to the distinguished scientist the swinging of a pendulum.

HOLYROOD CHAPEL
EDINBURGH

In Edinburgh is Holyrood Chapel, which, next to Melrose Abbey, is perhaps the most familiar of the ancient church buildings of Scotland. Of this one-time extensive Augustinian monastery (established by David I in 1128), with its great church, spacious cloisters, and far-reaching cluster of ecclesiastical buildings, nothing is left but a part of the church to recall its romantic days, "when its forests, well stocked with all kinds of game, offered excellent opportunities for the chase and so became a favorite resort of its royal founder."

Leaning Tower and Cathedral of Pisa, Italy. *(See page 101)*

TOLEDO CATHEDRAL

SPAIN

A cathedral; majestic, beautiful of exterior, the pride of the city, yet whose greatest glories lie within its walls, is that of Toledo, the ancient Moorish Capital of Spain. It is one of the three renowned cathedrals in that country so rich in history, that typified the middle period of Spanish Gothic architecture (1225-1425).

The Toledo Cathedral was begun in 1227. It was modeled after French cathedrals, but designed to surpass them. It is built entirely of milky-white stone from quarries in the vicinity. It excels in area the structures that served as models, but its interior is not so high as are those of the cathedrals of Amiens, Rheims and Beauvais.

But it is a massive building. Eighty-eight pillars, each composed of sixteen spindle-shaped columns, support its roof. A soft, mysterious light that comes from the blending of the sun's rays as they stream through windows of vari-colored glass stirs the heart and mind to solemn thought and religious emotion. There are sculptured figures and paintings of superb art and immense value, while gold and color blend in a harmony of magnificence.

Among Toledo's forty chapels is the famous Mozarabic Chapel, noted in Ibanez's "In the Shadow of the Cathedral," adorned with frescoes celebrating the combats of the Toledans and Moors. Lateral frescoes record in picture the story of the ships which brought the Arabs to Spain. In the "Chapel of the Virgin," resplendent in a richness of polished porphyry, jasper,

[103]

yellow and violet breccia, surpassing the splendors of the "Thousand and One Nights," is preserved the famous statue of Our Lady of Toledo. For her wardrobe the cathedral treasures inimitable brocades, cloth of gold, silver, damasks, marvelous laces, priceless jewels, and gem-bedecked robes, together with gigantic candlesticks, exquisitely embroidered banners, and monstrances of diamonds, sacred to the celebration of her Holy Mass. Among the treasures are also many of El Greco's masterpieces, "The strange Byzantine Greek, who drifted to Toledo and in his forty years there became more Spanish than the Spaniards."

In this old Cathedral at Toledo, Spain's ancient "hundred-towered city on the golden Tagus" convened (400-701 A. D.) eighteen Church Councils of great political and ecclesiastical influence.

ST. ROCH'S
PARIS

St. Roch's, another of the historic churches of Paris, was erected by Louis XIV, in 1653, upon the site of three earlier chapels, one of them named St. Roch's. The other chapels were dedicated to the five wounds of the Savior and to St. Suzanne. On the steps of this old church, Napoleon and his troops, on October 5, 1795, faced the insurgent sectionnaires. Its walls still show holes made by grapeshot from Napoleon's cannon, some of the first grapeshot to be used. In its old churchyard are buried La Notre, renowned gardener of Versailles, and Abbe d'L'Espee, inventor of the deaf and dumb alphabet, on whose monument the alphabet is engraved. The church holds special services for the deaf and dumb in his memory.

TOLEDO CATHEDRAL, SPAIN.   *(See page 103)*

CHARTRES CATHEDRAL

FRANCE

I gaze round on the windows, Pride of France,
Each the bright gift of some mechanic guild,
Who loved its city and thought gold well spent
To make her beautiful with piety.

Thus Lowell eulogizes Chartres Cathedral, "The House of Prayer," and its celebrated windows, whence he went "to feed his eye" and give to fancy one clear holiday in the "Minister's vast repose." To this, another of the great Gothic churches, which, "like gigantic carved jewels dot the surface of northern France," belongs the distinction of having some of the most beautiful stained-glass windows to be found in Europe. Its one hundred and forty-six windows (originally some one hundred and sixty of perfect form, says Larned), of prevailing blue and violet tones in cycle form, represent the thirteenth century's most perfect stained glass. In this respect Chartres vies with Sainte Chapelle, whose rare windows have been so remarkably restored, as also to give an excellent idea of the best period of the stained glass of medieval cathedral fame.

Chartres Cathedral was begun in 1190 and consecrated in 1260. The magnificent choir screen, with over forty sculptural groups of representative scenes in the life of the Madonna and Christ, was begun in 1514 and completed two centuries later. Its exquisite sculpture has been likened to point lace in stone. The celebrated windows, alluded to by Lowell in his poem, each commemorate some guild or trade—armorers, shoemakers, weavers, etc.,—whose workers are thus remembered by their gifts to the Cathedral. Some thought or characteristic emblem of each trade was worked into the design. During the World War (1914-1918) the windows, like other treasures, suffered. Chartres Cathedral was one of the historic churches of Europe included in the official report which estimated the destruction of 264 villages, with 38,230 houses and 225 churches.

In the Cathedral of Beauvais, the choir of which is the loftiest in the world, are also stained-glass windows executed at the very best period of the art. The glass adorning the roses or wheels in the north and south ends of the transept is believed to have been the work of John and Nicholas Lepot. In the north window the glass is exceedingly brilliant, representing the sun diffusing its rays in the middle of a deep-blue sky studded with stars. In the lights beneath this rose are placed figures of female saints.

ABBEY CHURCH
ST. DENIS, PARIS

St. Denis, a suburb of Paris, is noted for its beautiful Abbey Church, one of the finest examples of Gothic architecture in France. It stands on the site of a church built in the seventeenth century by Dagobert, used as a mausoleum for rulers of France until the Revolution. In 1793, the church was badly damaged and the bodies removed from the royal tombs. Later it was restored to its former grandeur. Napoleon founded in St. Denis an institution for the free education of women related to officers of the Legion of Honor.

CHARTRES CATHEDRAL, FRANCE.   Interior and Exterior Views.
(See page 105)

RHEIMS CATHEDRAL

FRANCE

Rheims bears the distinction of being the place of coronation of the French kings from Philip Augustus (1179) down to Charles X. Religious interest has centered about Rheims since 496, when it was the scene of the baptism of Clovis and his chief officers by Bishop St. Remy, the Cathedral having been built upon the traditional site of the event. The most prominent place in the sculptural work of the façade is given to a pictorial representation of this historic incident, repeated in smaller figures and detail elsewhere. In 1429, Jeanne d'Arc conducted the Dauphin, young Prince Charles VII, to Rheims, for coronation at the altar, another incident in French history adding richly to the romantic associations of the Cathedral of Coronation, "Best Beloved Shrine in France." A statue of the Warrior Maid of Orleans, commemorating this event, stands before the entrance.

Its elaborate west façade is exquisitely decorated with statues of kings and queens, an original band of five hundred. Because of its arcaded niches of rare delicacy and beauty and a matchless rose window, Rheims vies with Amiens as the "Parthenon of Gothic Architecture." Its Gallery of Kings at the highest part of the façade is justly celebrated. Says Larned in "Churches and Castles of Medieval France":

"The figures of these monarchs are so majestic in their expression, so grandly conceived, so imposing in form, so perfectly placed in their towering niches crowned by pinnacles most richly ornamented, that they do succeed in bringing to the mind an almost irresistible conviction that kings are nearer Heaven than other people. This is not the most inspiring thought a church could give, but it was well to suggest it here over the entrance to the place of the coronation of the kings of France."

Scarcely less beautiful is its north porch with its equally remarkably wrought sculptures and the procession of saints and angels extending all around the exterior of the Cathedral "like the frescoes of Flandrin in St. Germain des Pres.". In the center of the pavement is a narrow intricate way made of stones winding in and out, called the "Jerusalem Road," because representing the pilgrimage of Crusaders.

Rheims, like other Cathedrals of France and of northern Europe, has suffered sorely from the destruction of war. The town was damaged during the campaigns of 1814 and 1870, and in the World War, the Cathedral was greatly damaged, in some respects irreparably. The rose window and many of the statues adorning the façade were heartlessly destroyed by the Germans. Americans, however, generously provided funds for their restoration.

SAN MINIATO
FLORENCE

San Miniato is a notable and beautiful example of the use of Italy's rich vari-colored marbles for embellishing both interior and exterior with bands and geometric designs, a method of decoration carried to perfection, and worthy to be called a style.

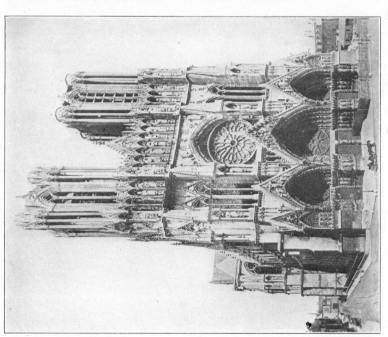

RHEIMS CATHEDRAL, FRANCE. (*See page* 107)

AMIENS CATHEDRAL
FRANCE

Amiens, the "Parthenon of Gothic architecture," is a celebrated example of the perfect French Gothic style, and, like Notre Dame, is Basilican in type, but "more splendid and less massive, possibly less stately, but infinitely alive and wholly freed from the comparative, ponderous tendency toward the Romanesque style noticeable in Notre Dame."

Amiens Cathedral was begun in 1220 and, completed as planned in 1288, was added to later. It represents sixty-eight years of work of the two Bishops, Everard, who founded it, and Godfrey, who completed and consecrated it. The façade, "a development of the Romanesque twin towers, connected by an arcade with rose or wheel windows above the central recessed door," represents west-front exterior decoration at its best—a distinguishing feature of all French Gothic Cathedrals. Larned says of the Amiens façade: "It stands quite alone, in my mind, among all Gothic façades I know, easily surpassing all the others. Here is the very essence of the Gothic builders' art." Three very high and deeply recessed portals grace the front. The central figure is an eminently majestic statue of Christ, "Le Bon Dieu d'Amiens," who welcomes all who enter the portals and gives them His benediction. At the base of the group is David, with crown and scepter, sculptured as the root and ancestor of Christ. The Apostles appear at His right and left. In the central portal are also statues of the four major prophets, and medallions interpreting their prophecies. The twelve minor prophets appear in groups on the piers of the façade. Ruskin, in admiration of the Amiens west-front statuary, aptly refers to it as "the Bible of Amiens."

Colossal statues of twenty-two kings of France, each holding the scepter, adorn the gallery of the façade. The other portals are dedicated to the Virgin and to St. Firmin, the first Christian missionary to Amiens and the first bishop and patron saint of Amiens.

Noteworthy among the magnificent interior ornamentations of this vast Cathedral is the decoration of the hundred and ten choir stalls, "whose wood carving is equalled by no other in Europe, except that of Cordova—more than three thousand figures, beautiful, delicately quaint and always suggestive of the story they tell about what happened in Jewish days in the time of Christ."

Amiens was the birthplace of Peter the Hermit, prominent in the early Crusades.

Ruskin, who said that he could never look unmoved upon a French Cathedral, "lifting its fair height above the purple crowd of humble roofs," says of that of Amiens:

> It has nothing like the artful pointing and molding of the arcades of Salisbury, nothing of the might of Durham, no Daedalian inlaying like Florence, no glow of mythic fantasy like Verona, and yet, in all and more than these ways, outshone or overpowered, the Cathedral of Amiens deserves the name given it by M. Viollet le Duc, "The Parthenon of Gothic Architecture."

AMIENS CATHEDRAL, FRANCE. *(See page 109)*

STRASSBURG CATHEDRAL

LUCIFER: Hasten! Hasten!
        O ye spirits
        From its station drag the ponderous
        Cross of iron, that to mock us
        Is uplifted high in air.

VOICES: O we cannot
        For around it
        All the Saints and Guardian Angels
        Throng in legions to protect it;
        They defeat us everywhere!

        —*Longfellow "The Golden Legend."*

So begins that celebrated poem by America's great poet, depicting the struggle of Lucifer and his demons for the possession of the Cross that tops one of the world's most famous Cathedrals. Two eminent composers, Sir Arthur Sullivan and the Rev. Henry Edward Hodson, have set this poem to music, converting it into a cantata, and the Hodson version was presented once as an opera in Philadelphia.

Strassburg, capital of Alsace Lorraine, is one of the most famous cities of the Old World, and its Cathedral is known to every traveler. The province of Alsace was for centuries the bone of contention between France and Germany. It was wrested from the former in 1870 to help form the newly created German Empire, and was restored in 1918 as one result of the World War when that same empire tumbled to ruins. Around Strassburg has been woven much of history, romance and legend, and its celebrated Cathedral rears its majestic spire that bids the fabled defiance to the demons of darkness.

The Cathedral was founded, it is believed, about 600. The remarkable façade by Erwin von Steinbach, with its lovely rose window, and noble porches and galleries in which are recorded in stone the history of the Creation and the Redemption, was completed in 1365 with the exception of the upper part, which was not finished until 1440. "A poem wisely composed," Victor Hugo says of it.

The Romanesque Choir dates from 1176 and the Gothic Nave from 1250. The Cathedral is built of red sandstone. The height of the north tower, which rises four hundred and sixty-five feet, is exceeded only by that of the Cathedral of Rouen. It treasures magnificent Gobelin tapestries, and cups which are shown during the feast of the Corpus Christi.

Among the Cathedral's practical ornaments is its celebrated tower clock, the original of which was built in 1352 under the directions of John, Bishop of Lichtenberg, and twice reconstructed. The present clock of marvelous mechanism is thirty feet high and fifteen feet wide at the base. A statue of Apollo points out the day of the month. Figures drawn in chariots indicate the day of the week—Apollo, drawn by horses, indicating Sunday; Diana, drawn by stags, Monday; etc. Above these figures is a dial, with figures on each side telling the time of day. One holds an hour-glass and turns it every sixty minutes. Moveable figures in succession strike the quarter hour. The first, an infant, strikes the bell with a rattle. The second is a youth, the third an old man, and fourth Death, who strikes the bell with a bone. In the highest compartment is a

THE CLOCK IN STRASSBURG CATHEDRAL. *(See page 111)*

figure of Christ. Each day at noon a procession of Apostles passes before Him, while a cock perched above, appears, flaps its wings, and crows three times. The cock is the clock's truly historical feature preserved since the fourteenth century, since when it has daily amused and astonished successive generations for five centuries. Lyons Cathedral has a less celebrated but similar tower clock.

CHRIST CHURCH CATHEDRAL
OXFORD

Oxford Cathedral was never a church of first rank, but a twelfth century priory church, turned five hundred years later into a Cathedral. It is a beautiful specimen of late Anglo-Norman architecture, although its original plan was disturbed by Wolsey's dream of a Cardinal College, never realized, one of several attempts to convert monastic institutions into places of education. The magnificent plan was cut short by the Cardinal's disgrace in 1529, but later taken up by the King on a small scale. The college was first called King's College and then Christ Church. The church fills the twofold purpose of a Cathedral and a College chapel.

Five windows from designs by Sir Edward Burne-Jones are among its notable interior decorations.

King's Chapel College, Cambridge, in Gothic perpendicular style, is the chief architectural ornament of King's College, founded by Henry IV in 1446. It contains remarkable stained-glass windows, fan vaulting and a wooden organ screen.

ST. ALBAN'S

ENGLAND

St. Alban's, a stern old Norman church, marks the scene of England's first martyrdom. The original church of 313 was erected on the wooded hill where St. Alban, Britain's proto-martyr met his death under the persecutions of Diocletian. This church was destroyed by the Saxons and a second church was built by Offa in 793, in penance, the tradition goes, for having murdered King Ethelbert. The present church, vast sections of which are said to be constructed of the Roman brick of the original church, was begun by the Norman Abbot Caen in 1077. Thus this old church, which at the time of the Conquest was the most important Abbey Church in England, both in site and building, has received the consecration of nearly sixteen centuries of continuous dedication. In architectural style plain, and representing all phases of architecture from Saxon to Perpendicular, it boasts the longest nave in England.

From St. Alban's Caxton issued the first historical work printed in England, in 1480. The first battle of the War of Roses raged about it in 1455. Five years later the victorious King and Queen knelt at its shine to return thanks.

The Abbey is virtually a town in itself. The church services were celebrated with a splendor and magnificence that challenge comparison with the ritual as observed by any of the famous churches and cathedrals of England. Daily the long aisles resounded with the psalmody of hundreds of voices at the Seven Hours of

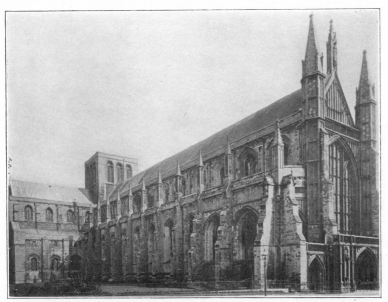

WINCHESTER CATHEDRAL, HAMPSHIRE, ENGLAND. *(See page 116)*

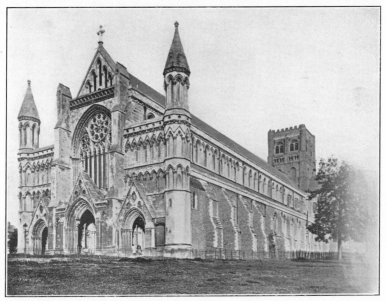

ST. ALBANS, ENGLAND.

Prayer. The festival processions brought forth crowds of novices and professed brethren in surplice and robe and cape. From early dawn until noon the venerable abbot celebrated a succession of Masses and implored the blessings of God upon the Order, the Church and the Nation.

One pictures old St. Alban's at its "Seven Hours of Prayer" and their solemn significance in the quaint lines:

> At mattins bound, at prime reviled,
> Condemned to death at tierce;
> Nailed to the Cross at sixts, at nones
> His blessed side they pierced;
> They take him down at vesper tide,
> In grave at compline lay;
> Who thenceforth bids His Church observe
> The sevenfold hours alway.
>
> —*Neale. "Essays on Liturgiology."*

ST. GUDULE'S
BRUSSELS

In the Church of St. Gudule, Brussels, is a curious oak pulpit carved in 1699 by Henry Verbruggen. It represents an enormous tree which supports the pulpit in its boughs, while among its leaves are birds and animals. At its base appear Adam and Eve pursued by a sorrowful angel, followed by Death, triumphant. At its top are the Cross and the Infant Jesus, His foot resting on a wounded serpent.

The windows of the church are pictures that resemble the paintings of the masters.

[115]

WINCHESTER CATHEDRAL

HAMPSHIRE, ENGLAND

"In the fair valley of the Itchen, where the downs on either hand grow near together," stands Winchester Cathedral, begun in 1079 by Bishop Walkelyn, cousin and chaplain of William the Conqueror. A seventh century Saxon church and a tenth century Church of St. Peter and St. Paul had preceded it. In the latter was the choir dedicated to St. Swithin, Bishop of Winchester, who died in 862, and the patron saint of the church from the tenth to the sixteenth century. The legend that the removal of his body to the shrine prepared for it was delayed for forty days by rain has been immortalized in the popular jingle:—

> St. Swithin's day, if thou dost rain
> For forty days it will remain;
> St. Swithin's day, if thou be fair,
> For forty days 'twil rain na mair.

St. Swithin's iron grill in the north nave aisle dating from 1093, is reputed to have four panels taken from the original grill protecting the shrine of the saint and to be the oldest iron work in England.

Bishop Walkelyn, we are told, built the Cathedral at his own expense, out of stone from the Isle of Wight and wood from the Hempage Forest.

In Winchester, where early kings lived, and whose Cathedral was their chapel, Egbert, crowned *"in regem totius Brittaniae,"* issued an edict ordering that the island should thereafter be called England and its people Englishmen. There, Alfred the Great, in 871, es-

ST. ALBAN'S, ENGLAND. (*See page 114*)

WINCHESTER CATHEDRAL, ENGLAND.

tablished his capital, making it the literary center of the country, and there he was crowned, lived, died, and was buried. There William the Conqueror often went and there were crowned Edward the Confessor, Henry II, and Henry IV. To Winchester went Mary for her ill-fated marriage to Philip of Spain.

Though somewhat plain and uninviting in exterior, this old Cathedral has a rich and beautiful interior. In no English Church, save Westminster Abbey and St. Paul's, lie more men of note—among these the unpretentious but revered Isaac Walton, who loved the banks of the "sweet and fitful Itchen."

To Winchester went Jane Austin, to die and be laid at rest in the spot where, though sorely ruined by the heartless ravages of the Commonwealth, today "sleeps amid the trees the tranquil grey building in the heart of one of the most charming of all south-of-England cities."

CHURCH OF ST. GENEVIEVE
PARIS

The Church of St. Genevieve (1755-81), better known as the Pantheon, also represents the classical or revival style of architecture. It has a Greek cross ground plan and four halls surrounding a central hall surmounted by a dome. It takes its name from the pictorial panels executed by Puvis de Chavannes in commemoration of the life of St. Genevieve. Mural decorations by other French artists of renown also adorn this church.

[117]

ELY CATHEDRAL

ENGLAND

For exterior effect Ely Cathedral, the Cathedral Church of St. Etheldreda and St. Peter, is surpassed only, if at all, in England by those of Durham and Lincoln, which have the advantage of finer natural settings. Nevertheless it ranks high among the celebrated Cathedrals of England, standing fourth in length and fifth in area, exceeding in these respects the Cathedrals of both Durham and Canterbury.

Ely has many distinctive features; among them a massive castellated tower, and a central octagon aptly termed the "glory of Ely," and pronounced by many artists and architects to be without a rival in the world.

Until 1081 there stood on its site the Abbey Church of Etheldreda, who left the Court of her husband, Egfrid, King of Northumberland, to devote her life to religion. With her riches she built and endowed a monastery and became its first Abbess. It was of those early days that the old English poet sang:

> Merie sungen the Muneches binnen Ely
> Tha Cnut Ching rew ther by.
> Rowe ye cnites noer the lant
> And here we thes Muneches saeng.

> (Merry sang the Monks of Ely
> As Cnut, the King rowed by;
> Row, knights, near the land,
> And hear we the monks sing.)

The erection of the present Cathedral was begun in 1082. It is chiefly in the Norman style but has de-

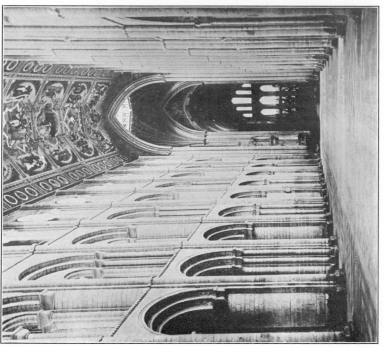

ELY CATHEDRAL, THE CATHEDRAL CHURCH OF ST. ETHELDREDA AND ST. PETER.

cided early English and later decorated architectural features. The Galilee Porch, built 1200 to 1215, is early English, while the Lady Chapel, constructed 1321 to 1349, and the Octagon Lantern (1322), celebrating in the corbels, eight scenes from the life of St. Etheldreda, are late decorated.

The Cathedral is picturesque and imposing, nestling in a rolling fen country, and to the southward, like a thickly wooded park, lies the main part of the Close, with many fragments of the ancient convent buildings. Around it all cluster a myriad of historical associations and memories.

CATHEDRAL
MURANO, ITALY

At Murano, which since the thirteenth century has been famous as the center of the Venetian glass and imitation gem industry, is a twelfth century cathedral, San Donato, The Mother Church of Murano. Doge Domenico Michele in the Second Crusade, tradition has it, obtained possession of the body of St. Donato, Bishop of Eurola, which treasure he presented to Murano's Basilican church, consecrated in 957, and henceforth called the Church of St. Mary and St. Donato. This church, says tradition, had been erected on the spot designated by the Virgin in response to the prayers of Emperor Otho, the Great, lost in a storm on the Adriatic. If saved, he vowed to build a church to the Virgin. Appearing in a dream, the Virgin designated her chosen site by a covering of red lilies.

PETERBOROUGH CATHEDRAL

ENGLAND

Peterborough Cathedral, officially known as the Cathedral of St. Peter, St. Paul and St. Andrew, was originally an Abbey Church of the seventh century, and was rebuilt by the Benedictines at the close of the tenth century. The present structure was begun in 1117. Its dedication to St. Peter gave the town its name, Peter's Borough. Like Durham Cathedral, Peterborough represents the Norman style of architecture at its best.

Says Van Rensselaer in "English Cathedrals":—

> "Its western portico is conceded to be the most famous in any of England's famous Churches—as beautiful as it is striking—the work, it seems to me, of some exceptionally brilliant Englishman, who had seen the great portals of France and had wished to surpass them, but, led on by the imagination that was more poetic than architectural in quality, ended by creating something entirely new."

Although Henry treated this ancient Church kindly, under the Cromwellites it was almost ruined along with the monastic buildings, which in their glory covered a space four times as great as that occupied by the church itself. Glass, monuments, carvings and much splendid interior furniture such as the great silver-mounted reredos, were ruthlessly destroyed. The vast picture of Christ and the Apostles on the ceiling of the choir was used for target practice and the soldiers did their daily exercising in the nave.

PETERBOROUGH CATHEDRAL, ENGLAND.

Two famous tombs are in this Cathedral, those of the two ill-fated and discrowned Queens—Catherine of Aragon, the unhappy queen of Henry VIII, and Mary, Queen of Scots. The latter was beheaded at Fotheringay Castle in February 1587, and buried at Peterborough August 1. Twenty-five years after, her son, James I, removed her body to the Chapel of Henry VII, in Westminster Abbey. The fame and wealth of this monastery was so great that it was called the "Golden Borough"; and a Pope had said that if any "Islander" was prevented from visiting St. Peter's at Rome, he could obtain the same indulgence by visiting this St. Peter's. So the spot grew in sanctity so that all pilgrims, even those of royal blood, removed their shoes under the western gateway of the Close.

LORNA DOONE'S CHURCH
DEVONSHIRE

In Exmoor still stands Lorna Doone's Church, celebrated in Blackmore's classic of the Doone Country.

> "Then Lorna Doone came out of a pew half way and took my left hand in her right. Her dress was of pure white, clouded with faint lavender and as simple as need be. . . . Her eyes, which none on earth can ever equal or compare with, told me such a depth of comfort yet awaiting further commune. . . . The sound of a shot rang through the Church and those eyes were filled with death—Lorna fell across my knees, a flood of blood came out upon the yellow wood of the altar step. It was now Whit-Tuesday and the lilacs all in bloom. I laid my wife in my mother's arms and went forth for my revenge."

—*"Lorna Doone—A Romance of Exmoor."*

[121]

WELLS CATHEDRAL

ENGLAND

The Cathedral Church of St. Andrew at Wells, marks the historic spot of springs, or great wells, which led King Ian's house of secular canons to establish their church there, and "which perhaps rendered the site a sacred spot in the days of the Druids, as in those of early Christianity." It is, perhaps, the third church on the site—the first a Saxon Church of wood, and the second the Church of St. Andrew, erected in 909 near the fountain of St. Andrew, when Wells became the seat of a bishop. The present Cathedral was begun in 1174 by Reginald de Bohun, who when thirty-three years old, accompanied Richard the Lion Hearted on a Crusade. To Bishop Jocelyn (1206-1242), "great maker of Wells," who spent his entire fortune on the Cathedral, is accredited the famous west front with its "stone population of some three hundred life-size figures only equaled by that of Rheims and Chartres."

In plan, the Cathedral is a double cross, inverted arches making St. Andrew's cross, a beautiful architectural feature. Its façade is one of the few English façades adapted to sculptural decoration.

Among other noticeable features is Wells Chapter House, "famous among these beautiful adjuncts to English Cathedrals." Its vaulting ribs, branching out from sixteen Purbeck shafts, clustered around a central pillar typify the diocesan church with all its members gathered around the common father, the bishop. Its ruby and white windows are magnificent and the crypt is unusually high because of the many springs. The

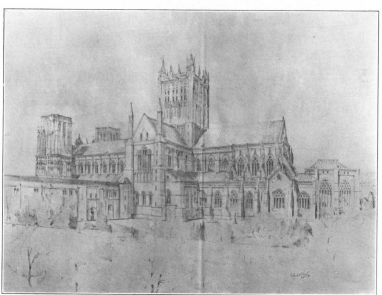

THE CATHEDRAL OF ST. ANDREW, AT WELLS, ENGLAND.
Interior and Exterior Views.

sixty-four Misericordes from the old choir stalls are considered among the best examples of medieval wood carving. The Jesse window above the high altar, telling in soft, beautiful lights the story of the Babe of Bethlehem, takes high and just rank among famous windows.

Until recently the famous Glastonbury clock hung in Wells Cathedral Tower. It was made by Peter Lightfoot, a Benedictine monk in 1325, and taken to Wells at the Dissolution. With its "multitude of instructive functions and stiff little manikins to strike the hours," this clock, one of the most wonderful in the world, is now in the Kensington Museum.

Wells, like Salisbury and Durham, is a city which has grown up around its Cathedral, with its Close and group of ecclesiastical buildings.

In size and some other respects, Wells Cathedral cannot measure up to some of England's other Cathedrals. Compared detail by detail, it falls short, but there is an exquisite harmony about every feature that gives it a charm all its own.

CATHEDRAL
VERONA, ITALY

This Romanesque structure of the twelfth century numbers among its cherished possessions the famous "Assumption," by Titian. Rude relief sculptures of Roland and Oliver, the famous paladins of Charlemagne, adorn the main portal.

YORK MINSTER

There is a Primate of All England, a title born by the Archbishop of Canterbury; and there is a Primate of England in the person of the Archbishop of York, the capital of Britain in the days of Roman rule. There are reasons for the distinction conferred upon the ecclesiastical head of this See.

Away back in the seventh century what is now England was divided into several little kingdoms. The King of Kent had a daughter, Ethelburga, who was sought in marriage by King Edwin of Northumbria. But the Princess Ethelburga was a Christian, and her suitor a pagan. She accepted him, but stipulated that she take with her to her new northern home a chaplain of her own faith. King Edwin agreed, and she took Paulinus, a Roman missionary, who was later consecrated Bishop of York. King Edwin became converted, and with his court and ten thousand others, he was inducted into the church, the entire number being baptized in one day.

York was an important settlement even before the Roman occupation during the first century of the Christian era; quite naturally becoming a military post.

Since there is a record of a bishop of York in 314 A.D., this church must have been preceded by an earlier house of worship. We read, also, that King Edwin was baptized in a small wooden church on the present site of York, an ancient Roman camp, which makes such conclusion certain. The present Cathedral (1189-1474), of such majestic proportions and great area as

YORK MINSTER, ENGLAND.

in the latter respect to exceed any Cathedral north of the Alps except Cologne, according to Pratt, is supposed to be the fifth house of worship on the spot.

Edward I made York his capital during his wars with Scotland. In 1318, Parliament assembled there. By the end of the fifteenth century, York Minster, representing the temporal power of the church and nobly supported by Archbishops who were not only military leaders, but great builders and benefactors of the Cathedral, appeared much as it does now.

The west front with its immense, magnificent windows, beautifully decorated, rivaled only by those of Carlisle, and the Twin Towers, is conceded to be the best façade in England—in this respect an exception to the prevailing rule that English façades have not the splendor of the French.

The central tower, the largest in England, and one of the finest in the world, has impressive dignity. In expanse of interior, York vies with St. Peter's and St. Paul's.

In its windows, York contains perhaps more original early English stained glass than any other building, fortunately left from the heartless general destruction of the sixteenth and seventeenth centuries. Much of its historic glass is seen in the beautiful rose window of the south transept, in admiration of which one writer says, "How delicate, how rich, how chaste, how unrivaled! All the colors seem to be intertwined in delicate fibers like Mechlin lace." "The Five Sisters" in the north transept, the largest lancet window in England, is of incomparable beauty, with its original glass of grayish-green tones, of sea-green purity, and simple early English design. Wherever York is known,

her "Five Sisters" are known. This glass is believed
to date from the thirteenth century.

Two other famous windows are the Bell Founders'
Window, reputed to be the gift of Richard Tumac, a
bell founder of York and its representative in Parliament in 1327, and St. Cuthbert's Window, celebrating
in detail the life, miracles, death, burial and translation of this saint. In the north tower hangs one of the
largest bells in the kingdom, "Great Peter," weighing
ten tons and costing, in 1845, £2,000 ($10,000).

CHURCH OF ST. BASIL

At one extremity of the Kremlin is the Church of
St. Basil, erected by Ivan, the Terrible over the grave
of Basil (the Imbecile). In the crypt of the Church
are the heavy chains and crosses which the saint wore
for penance and the iron weights worn by St. John
(the Idiot). This fantastic church is painted in the
colors of the rainbow, decorated in gold and silver.
Eleven towers, each over a tiny chapel, simulate vegetables, one an artichoke; others pineapples, onions, etc.

In Moscow is also the Cathedral of St. Michael the
Archangel, the former burial place of the Russian monarchs. It dates, in present form, from the beginning
of the sixteenth century. The walls are covered with
the portraits of the Russian monarchs buried there.

The Cathedral of the Ascension, also in Moscow
(founded in 1397), has walls and thick pillars covered with portraits of saints and Greek philosophers.
The floor is made of semi-precious stones of various
colors.

TELL'S CHAPEL, LAKE LUCERNE, SWITZERLAND.
(See page 128)

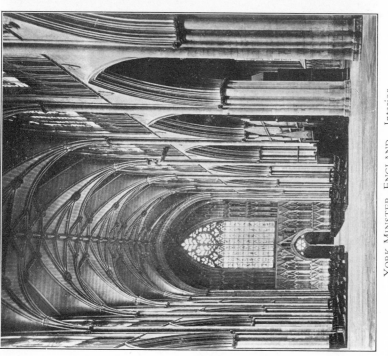

YORK MINSTER, ENGLAND. Interior.
(See page 124)

EXETER CATHEDRAL
ENGLAND

Exeter Cathedral had its beginnings in a Saxon Abbey erected by Athelstan, who reigned from 925 to 941. Canute, first king to reign over all England, and who also was King of Denmark, Sweden and Norway (reigned 1014 to 1036), replaced it with another church, and in 1107, under William the Conqueror, the present edifice was begun. It was consecrated in 1328 in virtually the form in which it stands today.

No finer example of medieval architecture exists in England. Although pure Gothic it is different from others of that style. It has no central or western tower. There is a unity of design and a harmony of proportion that appeal to the eye seeking the beautiful and artistic. It is broad rather than high, massive, solid, built for the ages. It has magnificent marble piers and wonderful contrasts in color and ornate window tracery, bewildering in its diversity. Its splendid carvings and glorious vaulted roof combine to give it a place exclusively its own in early English architecture.

Among other unique features of this Cathedral is its Minstrels' Gallery, decorated with fourteen beautiful canopied niches, containing figures of exquisitely wrought angels playing on musical instruments. The lovely and celebrated great east window of nine lights displays in rich and varied colors figures of saints, which are distinguished by their emblems. St. Helena holds the True Cross.

The great clock on the wall of the north transept, dating from the time of Edward II, strikes the hours on the Great Peter bell, brought by Bishop Courtenay from Llandaff. It was cracked on November 5, 1611, perhaps by too violent ringing in celebration of the Gunpowder Plots, and recast in 1676. It is now not rung, but struck by a hammer.

Another curious treasure of Exeter is an old baptismal font of white marble, decorated with cherubs and a dove, prepared for the baptism of Henrietta Anne, youngest daughter of King Charles I and Queen Henrietta Marie, born in 1644 at Exeter, where the Queen was in hiding from Cromwell's soldiers.

In Exeter is a tablet to and a bust of Richard Blackmore (1825-1900) of "Lorna Doone" renown.

TELL'S CHAPEL

Tell's Chapel, erected in the fifteenth century on the picturesque shores of Lake Lucerne, Switzerland, marks one of the many spots immortalized in Schiller's "William Tell." Appropriate frescoes, representing the exploits ascribed to this national hero of Switzerland, adorn the walls, while opposite the doorway is an old altar at which religious services are held.

"At such a time," says Stoddard, "this tiny shrine may be considered part of the sublime Cathedral of the Mountains, whose columns are majestic trees, whose stained glass is autumnal foliage, whose anthems are songs of birds, whose requiems are the moanings of the pines, and whose grand roof is the stupendous arch of the unmeasured sky, beneath which the snow-clad mountains rise like jeweled altars, lighted at night, as if with lofty tapers, by the glittering stars."

—"Switzerland," John L. Stoddard's Lectures.

EXETER CATHEDRAL, ENGLAND. Interior and Exterior Views.
(See page 127)

ST. GEORGE'S CHAPEL
WINDSOR CASTLE

St. George's Chapel is one of the principal features of the ancient castle that has been the principal home of the Kings and Queens of England since the days of the Conqueror. Ages before Duke William crossed the channel, a Saxon king built a hunting lodge in the forest on the river bank, and his successors used it. It is easy to imagine that King Arthur and his Round Table Knights assembled there upon occasion to hold revel and to hunt the hart and the bear, with which the forest abounded. William found the lodge and carefully preserved it, while building his keep upon the hill nearby. This keep was the beginning of Windsor Castle, so rich in historical associations, in romance and in legend.

King Edward III, "Edward of Windsor," revived the Round Table and introduced the patron saint St. George to whom he erected this chapel. He also established the Sons of St. George, later to be made Knights of the Garter, when he founded that Order. He installed these Knights in St. George's Chapel, establishing a custom that has been followed by all his successors. The chapel was added to by Edward IV and Henry VII.

It is of particular interest to recall that George V, when his country clashed with Germany in the World War, discarded his own German surname of Wettin, and decreed that thenceforth the family name of the Kings of England should be Windsor.

Prominent decorations in this Royal Chapel are memorials to King Edward the Confessor (who, tradition says, "lisped his prayers and cured the halt and the blind" near Windsor's ancient Saxon lodge), and to St. George and the Dragon. The tomb of Edward IV and his beautiful Queen, Elizabeth Widville, and a memorial window to them are also prominent features. There are also the tombs of Henry VI, Henry VIII, Charles I, George III, George IV and William IV.

Albert Memorial Chapel, another royal chapel, adjoining St. George's Chapel, erected by Henry VII as a royal mausoleum for himself, was later restored and beautified by Queen Victoria as a memorial to Albert, the Prince Consort. This chapel was at one time known as Wolsey Chapel.

W. D. Howells, in writing of Bath Abbey Church, refers thus poetically to the perpendicular Gothic style of which this chapel is so notable an example:

> It is mostly of the Perpendicular Gothic, which, I suppose, more mystically lifts the soul than any other form of architecture, in gracious harmony with itself through its lovely proportions. From the stems of its clustered columns, the tracery of its fans spreads and delicately feels its way over the vaulted roof, as if it were a living growth of something rooted in the earth beneath.

SANTA MARIA FORMOSA
VENICE

In this church is Vecchio's celebrated masterpiece, "St. Barbara," Patron Saint of Soldiers, and in Santa Maria dei Frari, one of the largest and most beautiful churches in Venice, is Titian's wonderful painting, "The Madonna of the Pesaro Family."

ST. GEORGE'S CHAPEL, WINDSOR, ENGLAND. *(See page 129)*

MELROSE ABBEY

SCOTLAND

If thou wouldst view fair Melrose aright,
Go visit it by pale moonlight;
For the gay beams of lightsome day
Gild, but to flout the ruins gray;
When the broken arches are black in night,
And each shafted oriel glimmers white;
When the cold lights' uncertain shower
Streams on the ruined central tower;
When buttress and buttress alternately,
Seem framed of ebon and ivory
  *   *   *   *   *
When distant Tweed is heard to rave,
And the owlet to hoot o'er the dead man's grave,
Then go—but go alone the while—
Then view St. David's lonely pile;
And home returning soothly swear,
Was never scene so sad and fair.

—*Sir Walter Scott "The Lay of the Last Minstrel."*

Melrose Abbey, originally the home of old Cistercian or "White Monks" (founded 1098) and today preserved as a part of the estates of the Duke of Buccleuch, was founded and liberally endowed by King David I in 1136. In 1322 it was destroyed by the English, rebuilt by David Bruce, and again effaced at the time of the Reformation. Its ruins are Scotland's finest example of Gothic architecture and sculpture. The stone of which the Abbey was built has resisted the weather for many centuries, retaining such perfect shape as to have preserved almost intact most minute ornaments of sculpture. The buttresses ranged along the sides of the ruins are richly carved and fretted, containing niches for statues of saints and labeled with scrolls bearing appropriate texts of Scripture. Much of the exquisite stone tracery of the windows and most of the statues have been demolished.

James, Earl of Douglas, and gallant Chief of Otterburn, slain in the battle of Otterburn on August 15, 1388, was buried at Melrose beneath the high altar. A keystone decoration represents the head of Michael Scott, the famous wizard, buried in the east corner of the south chancel chapel, according to the "Lay of the Last Minstrel." The heart of Robert Bruce is interred near the high altar.

"Whatever else of beauty or interest," says one writer, commenting on Scotland's ruined Abbeys, "Melrose, quaint and ancient village, may possess is completely eclipsed by the stately grandeur of this massive ruin."

GLASGOW CATHEDRAL
GLASGOW

Glasgow Cathedral, though often rebuilt, stands to-day in memory of the first Cathedral (dedicated in 1197) in pure Norman style. It was completed in the middle of the fifteenth century. Its high altar, placed over the shrine of St. Kentigern, "Apostle to the Scots," marks the site of the altar of this saint's little wooden church on the south side of which he was laid to rest. This ancient Celtic church, we are told, was built on the banks of the Molendivar as early as 560, by St. Kentigern, sometimes called St. Mungo (543-603), who established Christianity in Scotland, which, upon the withdrawal of the Romans from Britain early in the fifth century, was given over to anarchy; Saxon and Briton, Pict and Scot, striving for mastery. Nothing is known of the town for more than five hundred years after St. Stephen's time, until David, Prince of Cumbria, the future David I, in 1116, re-established the See of Glasgow and began to rebuild the church, under Bishop Jocelyn's direction. It was added to by Bishop Blackader.

The Cathedral is rather gloomy and massive, lacking the elegance of many other old Cathedrals. It is 319 feet long, 63 feet wide, with a central spire rising 217 feet. Formerly there were two western towers, but these were removed, one in 1846, the other two years later, which removal has been pronounced a "grievous error of judgment." In the vicinity were the residences of the thirty-two canons, but all have disappeared except the manse of the prebendary of Provan.

[133]

Some of its ancient splendor was destroyed during the Reformation, but its stout walls withstood all assaults. This fact is quaintly accounted for by Andrew Fairservice, in Scot's "Rob Roy."

> Ah, its a brave Kirk. Nane o' yere whigmaleeries and curliewurlies and open-steek hems about it—a solid, well-jointed mason work that will stand as lang as the world keep hands and gunpowther off it.

In memory of the damage done during the Reformation, the Memorial of the Nine Martyrs of the Covenant, one of the Post-Reformation monuments executed in 1666-1688, may be seen in the Chapter House. On the memorial are these lines:

> Years sixty-six and eighty-four
> Did send their souls home into glore,
> Whose bodies here interred ly,
> Then sacrificed to tyranny
> To Covenants and Reformation,
> Cause they adhered to their station.
> These nine with others in this yard,
> Whose heads and bodies were not spared
> Their testimonies foes to bury
> Caused beat the drums then in great fury,
> They'll know at resurrection day
> To murder Saints was no sweet play.

The church belongs to the Crown, but the choir is used as one of the ten city churches belonging to the Corporation of the Municipality.

ST. PATRICK'S
DUBLIN

St. Patrick's Cathedral, dating from 1190, is said to stand on the site of a church founded by St. Patrick himself (372-461) whose life from slavery to priesthood and sainthood is depicted in the Cathedral's west windows by Wales of New Castle. The Cathedral was burned some two hundred years later, but raised with new splendor, and the building as it now stands, though it has undergone restorations, follows in its main features the original design. In its nave hang the old Colors of various Irish regiments. Tradition has it that the church was set on fire in 1316 by the citizens in order to check the advance of Edward Bruce, brother to King Robert Bruce.

The tower, unrivaled in Ireland and unsurpassed as a belfry in the United Kingdom, is the work of Archbishop Minot. It is 147 feet high from the floor to battlements, 30 feet square at the base, and has walls 10 feet thick. The granite spire 101 feet high was built in 1749.

In St. Patrick's Cathedral are buried many persons intimately connected with Irish history, among them Jonathan Swift, Dean of the Cathedral for more than thirty years. His pulpit still stands. His marble bust adorns the wall with the characteristic epitaph composed by himself:

> Here lies the body of
> Jonathan Swift,
> Dean of this Cathedral,
> Where bitter indignations

Can no more lacerate his heart.
Go, Traveller, and so far as thou art able
Imitate this strenuous advocate of liberty.

Close by his grave is that of Stella, the woman he loved.

In the door of the Chapter House is a hole through which, tradition says, the Earls of Kildare and Ormond shook hands. Cromwell and James II are both said to have used the church as barracks.

Near St. Patrick's is Christ Church Cathedral, said to be slightly the older of the two Cathedrals, marking the site of an ancient hill fort and original church attributed to a Danish King of 1038.

St. Patrick's bell in Dublin Museum may be seen in a beautiful metal bell cover of the eleventh century, magnificently ornamented in gold and silver, gems and crystal, a sacred relic of the life and labors of the saint who laid a foundation which made Ireland the center of religious influence in northern Europe. St. Patrick's remains are supposed to lie in the Cathedral of Downpatrick.

TRONDHJEM CATHEDRAL
NORWAY

Trondhjem Cathedral, the most northern in Europe, occupies the site of the first Christian church in Norway. In 997, Olaf Trygvesson founded a city at the mouth of the river Nid, and called it Nidaros. In the course of time it became the city of Trondhjem. The founder built a palace and a church, and dedicated the latter to St. Clement. King Olaf Haraldsson established an episcopal See there and installed the Monk Grimkell as Bishop.

The first church was virtually rebuilt in 1020; but in 1066 King Olaf Kyrre began the construction of a Cathedral upon the site, as a monument as well as a tomb for St. Olaf, Norway's Patron Saint. All that was mortal of him was entombed in the high altar. Around this tomb the national and religious life of Norway centered. To it as a shrine went pilgrims from far and near. It was the most sacred spot in Norway.

The dome was enlarged in Orgival style by Archbishop Eystein (St. Augustine), and the Cathedral was finished in 1248 by Archbishop Sigurd Sim. In 1299 the Cathedral had its first coronation, that of King Haakon "The Longlegs," and it then became the place of coronation for Norway's kings.

Repeatedly the Cathedral lost its fine dome by fire, and as fast as one was burned another arose in its place. In 1521, Archbishop Eric Walkendorf was exiled, as Lutheranism spread, and his successor under royal command, turned it into a Lutheran church. The reliquaries of St. Olaf and St. Augustine were taken to Copenhagen and melted, and the bones of St. Olaf were buried under the Cathedral. The place was virtually forgotten and neglected until 1814, when, once more a Catholic place of worship, the dome was again rebuilt and the Cathedral restored.

From the ambulatory behind the choir opens a tiny chamber containing St. Olaf's Well, of rugged, yellow stone with holes remaining in the pavement through which the tripping rain ran away when the buckets were set down.

In the graveyard, acres in extent, are hundreds of graves, all kept like gardens, with roses and honeysuckle clambering over the tombs, and each grave holding a vase in which fresh cut flowers are placed daily. So this city of the dead is prettily and poetically known as the Cathedral Gardens.

SANTA CROCE (Church of the Holy Cross) FLORENCE, ITALY.
(See page 139)

SANTA CROCE
FLORENCE

St. Francis of Assisi and St. Dominic, two great religious powers and reformers of the medieval church, both established large and influential church orders bearing their names: the Franciscans, or Black Friars, founded in 1212, and the Dominicans, or White Friars, founded in 1220. Says Ruskin: St. Francis taught the Christian man how to behave and St. Dominic what he should think. One, the apostle of works and the other of faith, each had his band in Florence."

Santa Croce (Church of the Holy Cross), erected in 1294, is the most perfect little Gothic chapel in Italy. Its Pazzi Chapel is Brunelleschi's choicest ecclesiastical design. Over its altar is what is said to be the only authentic portrait of St. Francis of Assisi, founder of the Franciscans, taken from life by Giotto's master, Arnolfo. Beside it are its celebrated companion pieces, St. Francis' "Commanding Angels"—Poverty, Obedience, and Chastity, fitting decoration for the Church of St. Francis, whose simple creed upon which he founded his great Franciscan Order was, according to Ruskin,

> You must work without money and be poor,
> You must work without pleasure and be chaste,
> You must walk according to orders and be obedient.

Among the celebrated remains buried within and distinguishing this church, sometimes referred to as the Florentine Pantheon, are those of Michael Angelo and Galileo, to whom Byron thus pays tribute:

[139]

In Santa Croce's holy precincts be
Ashes which make it holier dust which is
Even in itself an immortality.
There repose
Angelo's, Alfieri's bones and his,
The starry Galileo with his woes.

—*"Childe Harold," Canto IV.*

ST. ISAAC'S
LENINGRAD

During the building of this "first shrine of all the Russias," from 1819 to 1858, the city that boasts its possession was St. Petersburg. Early in the World War the ill-fated Czar Nicholas II, Russianized its name to Petrograd. After that monarch had been deposed and murdered, and the Bolshevists under Lenine and Trotzky ruled, the capital was transferred to Moscow. And when Lenine died, his followers wrested the name of the great Peter from his capital and called it Leningrad.

The steps of St. Isaac's are rose granite, and the porticos are supported by massive columns of the same material, sixty feet high, seven feet in diameter, with a mirror-like polish. They are the largest columns ever quarried and fashioned except Pompey's Pillar in Egypt and Alexander's Column in Leningrad. The inlaid walls are richly adorned with mosaics, portraits of the saints and jeweled shrines of gold. There is a portrait of Christ studded with diamonds, the largest of which is valued at $35,000.

The Cathedral cost $14,000,000, a quarter of which was required to construct the foundations. Into the Holy of Holies, shielded by a veil of gold, malachite, lapis-lazuli and agate, people rarely enter.

St. Isaac's Cathedral, Leningrad.

CATHEDRAL OF ROUEN
FRANCE

In Rouen, ancient capital of Normandy, where Jeanne d'Arc, the nineteen year old girl warrior of France, was kept for months in a gloomy prison and which afterward became the scene of her martyrdom, is a Cathedral which, says a critic, "would be wholly Gothic if its central spire did not dip into the zone of the Renaissance."

Rouen Cathedral was erected between 1200 and 1220. Its twenty-five highly ornamented chapels contain numerous monuments of historic interest. One of the old side chapels contains much of the finest of sixteenth century stained glass. The cast-iron spire on the central tower (four hundred eighty-five feet) is the loftiest in France. Except for the highest story, the St. Romain Tower at the left, dating from the twelfth century, is the oldest part of the building.

Rouen is noted for its old ecclesiastical structures. In addition to the Cathedral, it contains the Church of St. Ouen, built in the fourteenth and fifteenth centuries, and which is as large as the Cathedral. In its restored state it presents a pure and elegant example of Gothic architecture. The first stone of St. Ouen was laid in 1318, and the principal part of the church was finished before 1500. During the French Revolution the church was used as an armory and stable.

The town figured early in ecclesiastical history as the seat of Bishop Rollo, who with his Norsemen, settled in Rouen at the close of the ninth century. Later it became a Huguenot stronghold. St. Ouen marks the early stages of the decline of Gothic Cathedral building (1150-1500), when "structural expression became subordinate to decorative elaboration."

CATHEDRAL OF THE ASSUMPTION
MOSCOW

In the large court of the Kremlin, the Acropolis of Russia, we find ourselves in the midst of the most bewildering conglomeration of palaces, Churches, and monasteries of which the imagination can dream.

—*Theophile Gautier*.

The Cathedral of the Assumption, (Uspensky Sober) is Russia's most sacred edifice and is one of the most ancient and characteristically Russian Cathedrals in the Kremlin, Russia's center of religious and political life. It was built by an architect of Bologna in the fifteenth century on the site of a church founded in 1326. Its style (Lombard-Byzantine) is severely plain, and its plan almost square. Four enormous tower-like pillars, as massive as the Egyptian columns, support a central cupola. Its impressive interior decoration is, in the main, Byzantine. Paintings on gold backgrounds cover the walls from floor to ceiling like a tapestry of gold. Its pillars are decorated with thousands of figures. Gems and precious metals of great antiquity abound, among them one attributed to St. Luke.

The treasury of the Cathedral contains many relics of saints, valuable Bibles, and manuscripts, and is one of the richest in Russia. Ivan IV (the Terrible) was crowned in this Cathedral in 1547, and this custom has been followed by every Russian Emperor since.

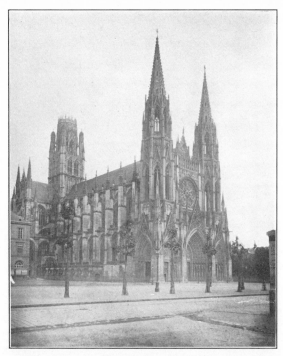

CATHEDRAL OF ROUEN, FRANCE. *(See page 141)*

CATHEDRAL OF THE ASSUMPTION, MOSCOW.

BURGOS CATHEDRAL

SPAIN

At Burgos, for a long time first city of Castile, is one of the most richly ornate Gothic edifices in the world, founded in part by an English bishop in 1221. It is not a large church as cathedrals go, but has one of the finest exteriors in Gothic architecture. The western towers are crowned with open-work spires that recall Cologne, and the beautiful octagons above the Chapel at the eastern end, make a harmonious grouping.

A famous treasure of Burgos is the relic of the Cid, Spain's national hero. There is a great chest fastened to the walls by iron clamps, probably the oldest chest in the world, on which is inscribed, "Cofre del Cid." The story is that Ruy Diaz de Bivar (Cid Campeador), hero and simple author, once lacking money, had the chest filled with sand and stones and carried to the house of an honest Jewish money lender, who accepted it as security for a loan, obeying the command not to open the mysterious coffer until he was reimbursed.

At Burgos is the celebrated Christ, so revered that no one is permitted to see it except by candlelight. It is reputed to be made of human skin, with real hair and eyelashes, and the thorns of the crown upon his brow are real. The skin, now a brownish yellow showing great age, is streaked with what appears to be real blood, and there is a legend that it bleeds every Friday. This Christ wears a white garment embroidered in gold, falling from the waist to the knees. At the foot of the Cross are three ostrich eggs, presumably alluding to the Trinity.

ST. CHAPELLE
PARIS

St. Chapelle (1242-1247) or Royal Chapel, in Paris, remains a monument to good St. Louis of France. It was erected by him as a fitting shrine to contain the relic of the Crown of Thorns. The tradition is that Baldwin, son-in-law of Jean de Brienne, Emperor of Constantinople, had promised the Crown of Thorns, preserved in the Treasury of the Byzantine Emperors, to St. Louis. But on his return to Constantinople, Baldwin found his father-in-law dead, and the relic in the hands of the Venetians, who held it as a pledge for some 100,000 francs, lent to the Emperor. This sum St. Louis paid. In August, 1239, the Crown of Thorns reached Paris and was first deposited at Vincennes, whence the monks of St. Denis took it first to Notre Dame and later to the Chapel of St. Nicholas.

Three years later, according to tradition, Baldwin sent St. Louis the famous iron top of the lance that had pierced the Savior's side, the Holy Lance of Antioch—the chief glory of the First Crusade; a piece of the true Cross, and other relics to induce him to undertake another Crusade. During an illness, St. Louis made a vow to go, but not until he had provided a place for the relics. St. Louis completed this undertaking in three years, the result being that exquisite building in pure Gothic, St. Chapelle, from the stairway of which he and many succeeding kings of France, at stated times, exhibited the sacred relics to the people gathered in the chapel below.

NOTRE DAME, ANTWERP. *(See page 145)*

NOTRE DAME

> Who has not seen the Church under the bell? Those
> lofty aisles, those twilight Chapels, that cumbersome
> pulpit with its huge carvings, that wide grey pave-
> ment, flecked with various lights from the jewelled
> windows, and those famous pictures between the vol-
> uminous columns over the altars, which twinkle with
> their ornaments.

Thus Thackeray, in his "Roundabout Papers," refers to Notre Dame, "latest, most spacious and most
magnificent cathedral of the Netherlands," and one of
the most remarkable churches of Europe. The original
was a chapel built for the miraculous image of the
Blessed Virgin.

One of Notre Dame's highly prized treasures is
Rubens' "Descent from the Cross," ranking among
the world's greatest pictures. Among others are Leon-
ardo da Vinci's "Last Supper"; Raphael's "Sistine
Madonna"; Michael Angelo's "Last Judgment," and
Rembrandt's "The Night Watch." Rubens' "Assumption," adorning the lower part of the altar piece, is an
excellent example of the artist's comprehension of religious decorative art. It is said to be a higher conception than Titian's "Assumption," at Verona.

To the celebrated Antwerp Cathedral's clock, sounding its half hours, and the chimes of which can be
heard many miles, Thackeray thus fancifully refers,
"Day and night the kind little carillon plays its fantastic melodies overhead."

In St. Jacques' Chapel, Antwerp, Rubens' "Holy
Family" adorns the altar of the chapel in which the artist himself is buried.

CATHEDRAL OF MALINES

(MECHLIN) BELGIUM

At Malines, Belgium, is a Cathedral in whose tower hangs a set of forty-five bells called a carillon, after the great Flemish musical instrument, an incidental feature of the Flemish Renaissance. Carillon is tuned to the chromatic scale and played from a manual keyboard. Most of these bells were cast in the seventeenth century by Hemong, of Amsterdam. They surpass in volume and tone even the famous chimes in the belfry of Bruges, set up in 1743, which inspired Longfellow's celebrated poem, "The Belfry of Bruges."

In this connection it is worth noting that according to report the Park Avenue Baptist Church, New York City, possesses the largest carillon in the world, consisting of fifty-three bells. In Canada the best known is the set of twenty-three bells in the Metropolitan Methodist Church, Toronto. The largest carillon so far on this continent is that of St. Peter's Church, Morristown, N. J., which recently installed a set of thirty-five bells.

At Malines is also the Cathedral of St. Rombold, the spire of which is referred to as the greatest projected during the Middle Ages. The tower part alone is three hundred and fifty feet high, and had it been completed as projected the cupola would have been six hundred and forty feet from the ground.

St. Rombold, Metropolitan Church of Belgium, became a Cathedral in 1559. Napoleon, discovering that religion was necessary for the welfare, peace and prosperity of a country, and that without the blessings of

Christianity, nations could never achieve greatness or preserve their stability, restored the churches in France and Belgium. They became a "leading principle" in the policy of the first Consul and his famous Concordat of 1801.

———•❖•———

CHAPELS OF ST. PETER AND ST. JOHN
TOWER OF LONDON

Half a mile below London Bridge on ground which was once a bluff commanding the Thames stands the Tower, a mass of ramparts, walls and gates, the most ancient and most poetic pile in Europe—white with age and wrinkled with remorse.

—*William Hepworth Dixon.*

In this grim old Tower, England's oldest and most romantic building, are two historic chapels—St. John's Chapel in the White Tower, and St. Peter's Chapel in the Tower of Green. The former, a beautiful example of Norman architecture, belongs to the earliest date of the Tower (1078), having been built by William the Conqueror, probably upon the site of some ancient Saxon stronghold or Roman fortress. The White Tower was originally called "Caesar's Tower." It was probably his sanctuary of worship. In St. Peter's Chapel, "musical with bells," the remains of Anne Boleyn, Katherine Howard, Lady Jane Gray and the Duke of Monmouth lie buried beneath the altar.

In the Tower of London, with its "eight hundred years of historic life and nineteen hundred years of traditional fame," Sir Walter Raleigh, English seaman and favorite of Good Queen Bess, wrote his "History of the World," while one of its eminent prisoners.

ST. STEPHEN'S CATHEDRAL
VIENNA

St. Stephen's Cathedral, Austria's finest Gothic edifice, a chapel to St. Stephen, was begun in the twelfth century. The present edifice, completed in 1506, was founded by Duke Rudolph, to whom also Vienna is indebted for its university.

The spire is four hundred and fifty feet high, only a little lower than those of Cologne and Strassburg, and is covered with artistic stone carving and Gothic ornamentations. At times, when the fate of the Austrian capital was trembling in the balance, the belfry was used as an observation station. There the Viennese officials stood to watch the movements of the 200,000 Turks under Kara Mustapha, who threatened it in 1683. The principal bell in the tower commemorates the victory of the Cross over the Crescent, since it was cast from the bronze of the hundred and eighty-eight cannon taken on that occasion from the Moslems.

From the tower can be seen, adorning the steep roof of brilliantly glazed tile, the monster double-headed eagle of the Hapsburgs, measuring one hundred and eighty feet from tip to tip of wing, each eye composed of four large, gilded tiles.

It was in this Cathedral that hundreds of mail-clad soldiers knelt before the great high altar to receive the sacrament of consecration before departing for the Holy Land to wrest from Moslem hands the sepulcher of Christ. Some who fell in such sacred expeditions were carried back to find eternal rest there.

The Cathedral contains, besides its extensive catacombs and old imperial burial vault, many fine paintings and memorials. Its treasury is rich in antique vestments, finely carved reliquaries, and other relics. The high altar, built in 1647, of black marble has a famous painting of the "Martyrdom of St. Stephen," by Anton Bock. The famous old bell, cast in 1711, the largest bell in Europe west of Russia, was first swung in honor of the entry of Emperor Charles VI into Vienna in 1712. It requires twelve men to put it into motion.

SAN AMBROGIO
MILAN

San Ambrogio, a Lombard church erected on the site of one that had dated from the ninth century shows, in the older part of its exterior, curious sculptures in which grotesque Scandinavian animals are mingled with Byzantine features. These correspond with sculptured ornaments found on some of the Rhenish churches, which would seem to indicate that Lombard workmen engaged in its construction had been employed in Germany, and had there imbibed a taste for symbolic ornamentation.

In the ancient crypt of this Romanesque church, in a silver shrine, rest the three saints, Ambrogio, Gervasio and Protasio. The column at which they suffered martyrdom stands near. Behind the high altar, the canopy of which is borne by four porphyry pillars from a pagan temple, is a severe and stately marble chair, said to have been the coronation seat of emperors and kings.

LICHFIELD CATHEDRAL

ENGLAND

Lichfield Cathedral, England's "Queen of Minsters," a small but beautiful red sandstone church, holds this title by virtue of its exquisite proportions, graceful outlines and rich ornamentation. Its three symmetrical spires, by which it is preeminently distinguished, are styled "The Ladies of the Vale." In them the beauty-loving eye sees rare feminine grace. Lichfield, a Cathedral of the thirteenth and fourteenth centuries, is an excellent example of decorated Gothic architecture.

Tradition records the site of Lichfield as the spot upon which a thousand Christian martyrs were put to death at one time, during the persecutions of Diocletian and Maximian at the beginning of the fourth century. A field in the neighborhood still bears the name "Christian Field." Lichfield, etymologists say, means in Saxon, the "Field of the Dead."

Of the numerous beautiful objects enshrined in Lichfield perhaps none is more generally inquired for or holds more fascination, than does Sir Francis Chantrey's "Sleeping Children," an exquisite group of modern sculpture, celebrated alike by the poems of Mrs. Hemans, Jean Ingelow, and Sir William Lisle Bowles. The beautiful lines of the latter read:

> Look at those sleeping children! Softly tread,
> Lest thou do mar their dream; and come not nigh,
> Till their fond mother, with a kiss, shall cry,
>
> "'Tis morn, awake, awake! Ah! they are dead."

Yet folded in each other's arms they lie—
So still—oh, look! So still and smilingly,
So breathing and so beautiful they seem,
As if to die in youth were but a dream of Spring and
       flowers—
Mothers shall gaze with tears upon this monument,
And fathers sigh with half suspended breath,

"How sweetly sleep the innocent in death."

ST. DAVID'S CATHEDRAL
WALES

St. David's Cathedral, quite removed from the beaten track, "a magnificent relic of the past, with which the living seems strangely at variance," lies in a deep moorland glen on a rocky peninsula jutting into the Atlantic, near a rude village grouped around a stone cross on steps. To all true Welshmen, St. David's was the most sacred spot in Britain and two pilgrimages to the Pembrokeshire coast were considered equal to one to Rome. The old road which led to the Cathedral was called the Meidr Saint or Sacred Way. The barren coast is still studded with ruins of chapels or hermitages which once served to remind the sailors and fishermen of the sacredness of the soil they were passing. Ships lowered topsails as they floated silently by.

Records of 812 refer to a predecessor of the present St. David's as having been plundered and burned by the "Pagans." The present Cathedral, erected probably in 1180, was remodeled by Bishop Gower (1328-1347) in Middle Pointed Style.

LLANDAFF CATHEDRAL
WALES

In Llandaff, South Wales, is another Cathedral, entitled, like St. David's, to interest, as Bumpus says: "as the representative of that mysterious British church of which no man can tell who was the founder—a church which was teaching Christian doctrine and discharging holy offices centuries before Gregory the Great made his memorable puns in the Roman Slave Market, or Augustine and his monks bore their silver cross along the road from Ebbsfleet to Canterbury."

It stood neglected and in ruins for three centuries and was restored in 1697.

A painted triptych, "A Nativity," of 1861 by Dante Gabriel Rosetti, adorning this Cathedral pictures David as ancestor of Christ. Its Madonna presents for the first time the face of the woman who inspired much of the artist's later work, Miss Bowden, afterwards Mrs. William Morris.

The celebrated "Great Peter" bell of Exeter is said to have hung originally in this Cathedral.

CHURCH OF THE MADELEINE

PARIS

In Paris, city of beautiful churches, is another church
fashioned in imitation of a Roman Corinthian Temple
and dedicated to Glory. In 1763, Louis XV signed
the letters patent for the erection of a church undertaken by the Empire for the accommodation of an over-
flow from a smaller Church of the Madeleine. The
Revolution prevented its completion, however. Work
upon it was renewed in 1806, with the intention of
making it a library or Pantheon. The Emperor Napoleon, however, discarded the original plan except that
of the façade, and ordered its erection as a Temple of
Glory, a gift from himself to his soldiers of the Grand
Army. Again came delay, with 1814, so that the
building was not completed until 1842. In architectural style, the Church of the Madeleine is a notable example of the classic.

PART II
NEW WORLD CHURCHES

EARLY MISSIONS, CATHEDRALS
AND CHURCHES

CATHEDRAL, MEXICO CITY, MEXICO. (See page 159)

CATHEDRAL

MEXICO CITY

Many of the Churches of Mexico are architectural
gems of the first water, that compare favorably with
the noted Cathedrals of Europe, and he who forgets
this overlooks one of the most important factors in
Mexican history and civilization.

—"The Old Franciscan Mission of
California"—James.

In Mexico City, founded around 1325, and one of
the most ancient cities of the New World, successively
the capital of the Aztecs, Spanish vice-royalty of New
Spain, and Republic of Mexico, a small church was
erected as early as 1524. It stood on the site of the old
Aztec Temple of Tenochtitlan (1446), the ancient
name of Mexico City, it having been the royal command to destroy all vestiges of heathen worship and
build missions and churches in their stead. The first
church on this historic spot, founded by Charles V,
was replaced by a Cathedral in the reign of his successor,
Philip II, of Spain. The present Cathedral Church of
the Ascension de Maria Sanctissima, was erected over
the spot where from the high altar of the Montezumas
once ran the blood of human sacrifice, and is one of the
largest and most sumptuous church buildings in the
New World. It was commenced in 1573 and dedicated in 1667, but not completed until the early part
of the nineteenth century at an expense of $2,000,000.
The foundation of this massive structure of basalt and
gray sandstone is said to be composed almost entirely
of sculptured Indian images and some of the remains

[159]

of the great Aztec altar, or Temple of Sacrifice, which stood near. Its exterior is impressive, having a fine tower 176 feet high and two massive open towers each over 200 feet high, containing bells exposed to view, the most conspicuous landmark of the city. The plan is a cross 426 feet long by 203 feet wide, with numerous side chapels adorned with magnificent altars profusely decorated in gold, marble and precious stones. The façade, having three entrances flanked with the two tall towers, is an attractive blending of Ionic, Doric, and Corinthian orders in Spanish Renaissance.

Built at a time when the church was a treasure house of wealth, the Cathedral commanded the best art of the world in both architecture and decoration. Priceless vases, images and ornaments of silver, gold and precious stones adorned it. In 1857, the gold and jeweled statue of the Assumption was seized to provide funds for the new Republican Party. Its value was estimated at over $1,000,000. The balustrade on each side of the central altar, with a top rail decorated with human images, is composed entirely of an amalgam of gold, silver and copper, for which an offer was made to replace it with silver and pay $1,000,000 additional.

Among its treasured paintings are several of Murillo's best works, and those of other celebrated Spanish artists. Its church bell, Santa Maria Guadalupe, is, except for the great bell of Moscow, said to be the largest in the world.

The Altar of Kings, made entirely of highly wrought and polished silver, is profusely decorated with crosses and ornaments of pure gold. In nearby aisles are buried many closely associated with the history of Mexico. Here before the altar on May 22, 1822, the

CATHEDRAL, MEXICO CITY, MEXICO.   Interior.   *(See page 159)*

first emperor of Mexico was crowned, and two years later he was buried beneath it. Here also the ill-fated Maximilian was crowned. He was shot in 1867 and his widow, Charlotta, went insane and in that state was still living in 1925.

Hernando Cortez conquered Mexico about 1521, and after remaining for several years to consolidate his conquest, made a voyage back to Spain assured that Spanish sovereignty had been firmly established in the land of the Montezumas. Both Spain and the Church were quick to see the possibilities of Cortez's achievement and acted promptly. First of the Holy Orders of the Church to arrive were the Franciscans in 1524. They were followed first by the Dominicans and then by the Jesuits, and the Archbishopric of Mexico was established in 1545.

While the nation colonized the church converted, winning many natives to Christianity. Schools, hospitals and asylums were established, and missions built around which have clustered many romances and legends.

COLUMBUS CATHEDRAL

Le Cathedral de la Virgin Maria de la Concepcion, commonly known as Columbus Cathedral, erected in 1724, is one of Havana's chief monuments of historic interest. It is a large quaint structure in Spanish-American style, built of native limestone, with a large dome and "stumpy" towers flanking the entrance. It occupies the site of an older church said to have been built by the Jesuits in 1704. Two of the old bells in the tower are dated 1664 and 1698.

The interior effect, rich in frescoes and pillars of marble, is impressive of age and spiritual grandeur. The floor is of variegated marble unencumbered by seats, the worshippers kneeling. The high altar is a magnificent piece of workmanship, consisting of a base of various kinds of harmoniously blended marble, and supporting a dome and pillars of porphyry, under which is a statue commemorative of the Immaculate Conception, which gives the Cathedral its official name. Side altars of old Spanish mahogany are richly carved and gilded. Pillars highly polished, strikingly relieved by gilt bronze capitals, give the semblance of deep red marble. Fine paintings of old Spanish masters make impressive decoration.

The massive dome is decorated with paintings of Moses, the Prophets, and the Evangelists. A painting, said to be by Murillo, represents the Popes and the Cardinals celebrating Mass preparatory to the sailing of Columbus. Above the altar San Cristobal (St. Christopher), the Patron Saint of Havana, bears the

COLUMBUS CATHEDRAL, HAVANA, CUBA.
(See page 162)

SAN DOMINGO CATHEDRAL, SAN DOMINGO. *(See page 163)*

Christ through flood. A famous side chapel is that of
Santa Maria de Loretta, a reproduction of the shrine of
Loretta in Italy, one of the famous shrines of Christendom. The bones of Columbus, according to tradition
first interred at San Domingo, and transferred to Havana almost three hundred years after his death in
Valladolid, Spain, in 1506, were enshrined in this
Cathedral for more than a century. After the close of
the Spanish-American War (1898) they were supposedly taken back to Spain.

A mural tablet of white marble in the choir, bearing
in high relief the bust of the "Great Discoverer," and
appropriately decorated with grouped nautical instruments, indicate the place where Columbus' bones long
rested. Accompanying the tablet is the following inscription:—

> Oh, remains and image of the great Colon,
> Endure for a thousand years guarded in this urn,
> And in the remembrance of our Nation.

Under Spanish rule the Roman Catholic Church
was the established church of Cuba. Since the Spanish-
American War, Protestant denominations have been
established there.

San Agustin, formerly a monastery, built in 1608,
is the oldest church in the city of Havana.

Santa Catalina, built in 1698, contains the bones of
the Martyrs Celestina and Lucida, brought from Rome.

Santo Domingo was a Dominican monastery,
founded in 1578 by Count and Countess of Casa Bay-
ona, whose portraits adorn the sacristy of the present
church.

La Merced, built in 1746, is the wealthiest and
most aristocratic church. It is embellished with rich

marble altars, handsome chapels, and fine paintings, among which is the curious old painting giving it its name—"Our Lady of Mercy." It represents a group of Indians being slaughtered by the Spaniards in 1493, and saved through the intervention of the Virgin, seated on a wooden cross with the Christ Child in her arms. A Spanish inscription in the corner relates the incident pictured in the painting.

Belen Church, officially Santa Maria de Belen (Our Lady of Bethlehem), built in 1704, was originally a Franciscan church and monastery given over by the government in 1853 to the Jesuits, who set up an observatory said to be the best in Latin America; a library of Cuban history, and a museum of native wood and natural history specimens.

All the above churches are in Havana.

CATHEDRAL, HOLY TRINITY
QUEBEC

Franciscan monks were the former proprietors of the land on which this edifice stands. On it they built Notre Dame des Anges. In 1629, Quebec was captured and the monks went back to France. Not until 1670 did they return to erect another chapel, which in 1760 became an English church, succeeded in 1800 by the present English Cathedral.

The exterior of Holy Trinity is substantial and plain. It stands in a well-kept Close. Its plan is considered one of the best designs of Sir Christopher Wren, and similar to St. Paul's, New York City. Its communion plate was a gift of the king.

CATHEDRAL, HOLY TRINITY, QUEBEC.

MISSION OF CONCEPCION, SAN ANTONIO, TEXAS. *(See page 165)*

MISSION OF CONCEPCION
SAN ANTONIO, TEXAS

The missions of Texas, like those of Alta California, were almost exclusively Franciscan. Early records say that in 1690, Alonzo de Leon and Padre Manzanet were sent to found missions, which were to serve the double purpose of holding the country and of converting the natives to Christianity. The primitive Mission, San Francisco de los Texas was founded not far from the Neches River, but abandoned because of pestilence, famine, drought and the continual raids of hostile Indians, who like the Indians of New Mexico, were less readily civilized than those of the Californian coast. For this reason the Texas missions were grouped, instead of separated by a day's journey, as were those of California.

San Antonio de Bexar, the first important settlement by Spaniards in Texas, and one of the several missions founded in 1716, became the center of the most prosperous Texan missions. Prominent among these was the Mission of the Conception (Concepcion La Purisima de Acuna) some two miles from San Antonio, the shrine of early Texan history, and capital during virtually all the time of Spanish and Mexican occupancy. Situated on an elevation of some 700 feet, and supplied with an abundance of pure water, it is not strange that the "helmeted Spanish explorers and cowled Franciscan monks" selected it as a promising site for the permanent and more successful labors of their garrison and mission.

[165]

It was built in honor of Juan de Acuna, Marquis of Casa Huerta, Viceroy in 1722, and was established March 5, 1731. It is a stately structure, with two towers and simple, dignified front, and is considered to be the first mission in San Antonio. It is more familiarly known to Texans as "Old Conception Mission."

San Jose de Aguayo, founded in 1720, in honor of the governor, was on an elevated site overlooking the river below San Antonio and, we are told, surpassed in magnificence every mission east of the Rio Grande. It was of the Moorish style of architecture, and its great glittering dome was visible for more than a hundred miles. Its interior was resplendent with richly carved and beautiful statues and decorative paintings, the work of a Moorish artist in Seville, whose ancestors, it is said, had decorated the halls of the Alhambra. This kingly mission of Texas, its dome fallen, its sculptured figures and decorations of outer walls mutilated by barbaric hands, stands today in solitary but grand ruin, a monument to the tireless efforts of Texan padres.

The Alamo, Texas, "restless and movable shrine," Texas' most historically noted mission (founded 1700), was located originally on the Rio Grande, under the name of San Francisco Solano. It was transferred finally in 1744, after occupying other locations, to its present site. Until 1793 it was a parish church for the populace, and as a mission fortress witnessed the massacre of "Davy" Crockett and 178 other heroes of Texas, on March 6, 1836. This church has been characterized as "noted for history rather than sanctity."

The Alamo, Texas' Most Noted Mission.

The Cathedral of San Fernando, built around a chapel of 1730 and amplified into a Cathedral in 1868, marks the center of San Antonio. The oldest part of the Cathedral takes the form of an apsidal chapel, with stunted buttresses and a low, flat dome painted blue, giving it a decidedly Moorish effect. The façade of pointed arches and limestone walls has been so modernized as to leave one in doubt as to its original appearance. The interior, with its vari-colored images, pictures, candles, statues, and its incense, still preserves a strong Latin-American church impression.

TEOCALLI
GUATUSCO, COSTA RICA

The Teocalli (House of the God) of Guatusco in Costa Rica suggests the appearance of the Teocalli of Tenochtitlan destroyed by the Spaniards, part of its site now being occupied by the Cathedral of Mexico City.

It was a truncated pyramid 86 feet high with base 325 x 250 feet. One passed five times around it by a series of terraces to reach the top. On the platform were ceremonial buildings and the terrible image of the god Huitzilopochtli (supposedly now in the Museum of Mexico City), and the sacrificial stone upon which it is estimated no fewer than 70,000 human victims were slaughtered at the dedication of the temple to appease his bloody appetite.

[167]

OLD FRANCISCAN MISSIONS
CALIFORNIA

Before me rise the dome-shaped Mission towers,
    The white Presidio,
The swart commander in his leather jerkin,
    The Priest in stole of snow.

The story of the old Franciscan missions of California reads like romance. Lower California, too, had its missions, thirty-three in all, monuments to the God-fearing, humanity-loving, and self-sacrificing Jesuit padres, Kino and Salviaterra, as were the upper (or Alta) California Missions of the Franciscan Padre Serra. The result of some hundred years of effort, their glory began to wane with the removal of the Jesuits by Charles III, in 1767. The missions of Lower California were continued for a few years under the Franciscans, with Father Serra as Superior, assisted by his boyhood friend, Father Palou, and sixteen priests from the College of San Ferdinand, Mexico City. But the missions were finally left to the Dominicans, and by 1825 had virtually disappeared.

It was with the transfer of Padre Junipero Serra (1713-1787), to Alta California, that the Franciscan missions of that State-to-be came into existence. It had been the intention of Spain to colonize Alta California even as early as 1542, but not until 1769 had "the fullness of the time arrived." From that time to 1822, California, like Mexico, was under the rule of Spain, but when Mexico gained her independence, she made California a part of her own territory. It was during that half century that the California missions enjoyed their most prosperous era uninterfered with by Spanish rule. Linked with the name of Father Serra, founder and first padre president of Franciscan Missions in California, is that of Don Jose Galuez, Visitador General of New Spain, the practical head of the first Franciscan missionary expedition and a man of remarkable wisdom and force of character. He was true to his orders to "occupy and fortify San Diego and Monterey for God and the King of Spain."

San Diego, "the Plymouth of the Pacific Coast" was, in 1769, the scene of Father Serra's earliest mission, the first of the twenty-one Franciscan missions erected, a day's journey apart, along "El Camino Real" (The King's Highway) from San Diego to Sonoma, the last and most northerly mission, founded in 1823. During these some sixty odd years, the mission acquired great wealth. The Indians were induced to lead a settled life and become proficient in farming and other civilized pursuits. Once the second leading mission, San Diego is now a ruin. Palms one hundred and thirty-six years old stand as silent guardians of its past glory and present desolation. Nearby is an abode house, called "Ramona's Marriage Place," where lived Father Gaspara, "a friend of the Indians," immortalized in Jackson's "Ramona" as the padre who married Ramona to her Indian lover.

San Carlos Borremo, founded at Monterey, June 3, 1771, bears the distinction of being the second mission, and for seventeen years the home mission of Father Serra. It was the scene of his death in 1784, and his final burial place. Virtually an abandoned mission at the time of the Decree of Secularization (separation of the church from the State), it stands today one of the most faithfully restored missions, with façade complete, bells still hanging in the belfry, interior in excellent repair. With an organ in its shallow transept and the high altar in its shallow apse, it is one of the finest types of Mexican architecture. Among its cherished possessions is the processional cross borne on feast days by Padre Serra.

San Gabriel the Archangel, the fourth mission established, and because of its great wealth and power called the "Queen of Missions," is today perhaps the most noted of all the missions, because of its location between Pasadena and Los Angeles, and its famous Mission Play. It was founded September 8, 1771. A few years later it was chosen by priests from the College of San Fernando, Mexico, as the site of a leading mission to the Archangel. A generation or so later (1806) under Father Jose Maria Zalvidea, the padre so popular in "Ramona," it entered upon its period of great prosperity. Today it is in good repair and is visited by tourists, who view among other things of historic interest its famous "Old Mission Grapevine," planted one hundred and thirty-four years ago and now covering a framework of sixty feet square. In the immediate vicinity eastward is the famous ranch of "Lucky Baldwin." The San Gabriel Campanile, or bell tower, and its exterior stairway, are well known in picture, song and story.

America's "Passion Play," enacted at San Gabriel in the Mission Play House, tells in accurate and fascinating pageant-drama, the romantic story of California's old Franciscan Missions and their ruin. An ancient mission bell announces the end of each intermission. The actors, native Californians, descended from old

SAN GABRIEL CAMPANILE, OR BELL TOWER

SAN GABRIEL MISSION, CALIFORNIA.

Spanish families, and Indians descended from converts under Franciscan fathers, live in quaint bungalows and old adobe homes in San Gabriel. The Franciscan monks, Spanish soldiers and Indian singers and dancers are natives, "to the manner born," and also actors trained to the highest degree of perfection. Stage properties are treasured heirlooms of old Mexican days. The première of this famous pageant-drama, written by John Steven McGroarty, a California poet and historian, took place on the evening of April 29, 1912. In 1914, it was taken to San Francisco and San Diego, but it has never been performed outside of California.

Picturesque Santa Barbara, founded in 1786, with its refectory, dormitory and quaint old garden, still occupied by Franciscan monks, one of the most important and best preserved of the California missions, is celebrated as the only one whose ministrations have not ceased since its founding which was in 1786. In the days of its prime, its prosperity was so great that its wealth was coveted by both Spain and Mexico. Among its treasured relics are paintings with which Indians decorated the walls and the old mission bells of which one writer in poetic fancy says:

> Bells of the Past, whose long-forgotten music
> Still fills the wide expanse
> Tingeing the sober twilight of the Present,
> With color and romance
>
> I hear you call and see the sun descending
> On rock and wave and sand,
> As down the Coast the Mission voices blending
> Girdle the heathen land.

San Luis Rey de Francia, founded June 13, 1798, in the days of its glory and wealth the pride of all the missions, was known as "The Kingly Mission." It possessed more than 200,000 acres with much more subject to its control. It owned and pastured an annual average of 20,000 cattle and nearly as many sheep under the care of some three thousand Indian converts. In the year 1834, this mission had thirty-five hundred Indians to support and more than 25,000 head of cattle, 10,000 horses and 90,000 sheep. It raised and harvested from its arable lands annually, in the zenith of its prosperity, more than 60,000 bushels of grain, and from its vineyards many barrels of wine.

Other celebrated missions were San Juan Capistrano, built in 1776, and in construction and decoration one of the finest examples of mission building, and Santa Clara and Santa Inez, which last two speedily fell into ruins after the Decree of Secularization.

This Decree, so disastrous to many early missions, was issued from Spain September 13, 1813, which, however, was not fully effective for twenty years. Spain never acknowledged the title of the priests to the lands, and decided to turn the mission estates into administrative districts. The Decree directed that all missions in America which had been founded ten years, should at once be given up to the Bishop "without excuse or pretext whatever." Despite the grace of twenty years, the scramble for the property and possessions of the missions immediately began and soon the missions were abandoned.

SANTA BARBARA MISSION, CALIFORNIA. *(See page 171)*

SAN JUAN CAPISTRANO MISSION, CALIFORNIA.

SAN MIGUEL

SANTA FE, NEW MEXICO

Santa Fe, "City of the Holy Faith," is the site of the oldest church in the United States. For years after 1606, when the Spaniards first settled there to work gold and silver mines, Santa Fe, the second oldest city in the United States, continued to be the heart of the great province of New Mexico, the Spanish capital, founded thirteen years before the Pilgrim Fathers landed at Plymouth Rock. Old records say that in 1617 there were eleven mission churches there. (However, even though in 1680 they catered to a population of 25,000, yet in importance, wealth, or influence, the New Mexico missions never compared with the other great missions of the eighteenth century in other provinces of Mexico.)

In the oldest part of Santa Fe stands San Miguel Church. The original edifice was an adobe mission, erected by the Spaniards in 1540, with walls extremely thick in an effort to withstand attacks of Indians. The present church was built in 1636. Twelve years of desecration and desertion followed the Pueblo Indian revolt of 1680, in which the padres of some fifteen missions were killed, and the church and the mission mercilessly mutilated. In 1682, De Vargos, vowing vengeance on the Indians, conquered them and set about repairing San Miguel, whose massive adobe walls were still standing. These walls, a part of the church restored in 1710, stand in Old Miguel today. A copper bell cast in 1350 hangs in the belfry. Inside the church are many highly prized relics, statues and paint-

[173]

ings, among them St. Michael and the Dragon, and the "Annunciation." Several of the paintings bear holes made by Indian arrows shot during the Pueblo insurrection.

The pictorial reredos was the artistic feature of the church, the plan of which is a coffin-like design seen in many Pueblo shrines, with walls narrowing toward the altar to form the apse and to provide space for the reredos.

Other spots of historic interest in Old Santa Fe are the Rosario Chapel, marking the spot where De Vargos made his vow to conquer the Indians, and an adobe hut, said to be the oldest house in America. In the "Palace" (an adobe one-story structure, a block long, built early in the seventeenth century), until 1909 the residence of Spanish, Mexican and United States governors, General Lew Wallace finished "Ben Hur." It now houses the Historical Society of New Mexico.

St. Anne de Beaupre, Quebec.   *(See page 175)*

ST. ANNE DE BEAUPRE

QUEBEC

In 1620 some Breton mariners, escaping from death in a terrible storm along the St. Lawrence River, in gratitude founded a little village and erected a rude church to St. Anne. In the course of time the rude little building decayed, and in 1658 a more substantial structure was built to take its place, on land donated by Etienne Lassard, a pious farmer. This church stood as the revered village shrine until 1776, when a third church was erected. This church stood for a century, and in 1876-1878 it was rebuilt and elaborated into the present fine structure. By Papal Decree, St. Anne had been named the Patron Saint of Quebec, and the name was reverently bestowed upon the great church that had been begun by the simple Breton sailors. In 1887, the Pope created it a Basilica.

In its reconstruction the old plan of the church was closely followed. Most of the materials therein were used again, and the original tower and bells were retained. Above the foundation near the entrance to the chapel is a statue of Bonne Ste. Anne de Beaupre. There are eight large altars, gifts from as many Canadian bishops, and in the chancel are some beautiful stained glass windows.

But it is not to its age or appearance that Ste. Anne de Beaupre owes its great and extended fame, but to its rare and sacred relics—bones purporting to be those of the Sainte herself, to see which miraculously cures "the sick and the lame, the halt and the blind."

[175]

Early in its life the attention of royalty was attracted to the church sitting shyly back in the country about twenty miles or so from the city of Quebec, and rich gifts were lavished upon it. One of its most treasured possessions is a chasuble embroidered in gold and silver, made by Anne of Austria, Queen of France and mother of Louis XIV, "Le Grande Monarque." Another is a crucifix of solid silver, the gift of the great French explorer of 1706, Lamoine d'Imberville.

For many generations pilgrims have journeyed to this shrine from all parts of Canada and the United States and even other lands, seeking cure for their ills, and many are the tales told of such cures. More and more persons journey thereto every year,—there have been viceroys and nobles, soldiers and sailors, proud aristocrats and humble laborers, Indians and fisher folk. One of the most celebrated of those who have made the pilgrimage was the first Bishop of Quebec, who, though a scion of an ancient and mighty race, the Barons Montmorenci de Laval, turned his back upon the glitter of the court to become a humble apostle among the Indians in the new world.

The Basilica was burned in 1922. The corner stone of the new one was laid with imposing ceremonies July 26, 1923, in the presence of more than fifteen thousand pilgrims, and five of these, sorely stricken, were reported to have been completely cured by the magic touch of the bones of Ste. Anne.

Every year devout visitors swarm to this famous church for the Novena, or nine days' devotions ending on Ste. Anne's Day, July 26.

RUSSIAN ORTHODOX CHURCH, SITKA, ALASKA. *(See page 177)*

RUSSIAN ORTHODOX CHURCH
SITKA, ALASKA

Who would think in his search for ancient churches, to look in a part of the world which so lately was looked upon as a land of ice and snow, and of no particular use except to trappers who would dare to penetrate its wilds to snare the animals whose rich, furry pelts would keep milady warm, or venturesome mariners who sought the seals along the coastal islands for the same purpose?

When in 1867 the United States bought Alaska from Russia for $7,200,000, it was regarded as a sort of donation to the Czar, relieving him of an incubus and fattening his treasury. Its vast wealth, of which even now we have only glimpsed, was unsuspected. And yet it is in Alaska that we may still find a church that dates from about a century and a quarter ago— St. Michael's, Sitka.

The Russia-America Company charter of 1799 stipulated that the Government should establish a church and maintain a military force in this distant possession. So the church came into being. At the zenith of Russia's occupation there was a Greek Catholic bishop and fifteen ordained priests in Alaska, besides many deacons and missionaries, and the industry of bell making flourished, the bells going to missions and churches from Behring to Mexico.

With the purchase of Alaska by the United States and the removal of the higher church executives, the church, dedicated by the Metropolitan of Moscow, waned. When in its glory, this church, its interior "highly decorated in white and gold," possessed superb treasures of jeweled caskets, chalices of gold and silver, and richly illuminated magazines and books. There were massive silver lamps and chandeliers, censers and candlesticks. Vestments and robes were of velvet and old damask and the bishop's cap was rich with rubies, pearls and amethysts. An enamel cross set with diamonds was taken to San Francisco when the bishop left Alaska.

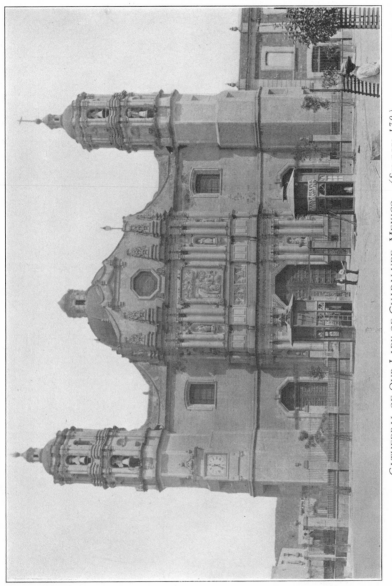

CATHEDRAL OF OUR LADY OF GUADALUPE, MEXICO. (*See page 179*)

CATHEDRAL OF OUR LADY OF GUADALUPE

MEXICO

A less pretentious place of worship than the Cathedral, but a much venerated church of Mexico, is the Shrine of Guadalupe, at the foot of the hill Tepeyac, two miles from the city of Mexico. This church is officially known as the Cathedral of Our Lady of Guadalupe (Church of Nuestra Senora de Guadalupe).

The legend of its origin is that, on December 12, 1531, the Holy Mother appeared to Juan Diego, a humble Indian shepherd boy of the neighborhood while he was resting at the foot of the hill on his way to Mass in the city. Following her summons from out the cloud enfolding her, the lad went nearer and she told him to tell the Archbishop that she wanted a church built to her on the spot. The Archbishop, discrediting the Indian lad's story, demanded a sign, sending his servant along to bear witness. Again the Virgin appeared. As a sign she told the shepherd boy to go to a certain barren rocky place where he would gather beautiful Spanish roses. The roses, which he carried in his blanket to the Archbishop, resulted in the erection of a chapel to enshrine the blanket, on which appeared miraculously the Virgin's picture as the roses dropped out of it, while the shepherd boy again gave the Virgin's message. The Shrine of Our Lady still treasures the old blanket as its chief relic.

At the base of the hill is the Holy Spring, traditionally created by the tapping of the Virgin's foot on the ground as she gave her command.

In the graveyard of this old Cathedral lie buried many of Mexico's honored dead, among them General Santa Anna.

On December 12—celebrated as the feast day of the Virgin of Guadalupe—the Cathedral, chapel, and hillside teem with devoted worshippers.

OLD MISSION CHURCH
MACKINAC ISLAND, MICHIGAN

The church on Mackinac Island, Michigan, was the outgrowth of a mission station established in 1823, when Mackinac Island was a strategic point in missionary as well as military affairs and trading interests. It was built in 1829.

Its motley throng, including Indians, Jesuit Mission pupils, fur traders, officers and soldiers, is vividly portrayed in Washington Irving's "Astoria."

It is the same today as the day it was dedicated, even the gray weatherworn exterior is purposely left unpainted. It has a high pulpit, plain, square pews with doors, small panes of glass in the windows and the old-fashioned gallery at the entrance end.

A favorite of lovers of old sanctuaries, Old Mission Church is now preserved "as an historic relic of the island and a memorial of early mission work and, secondly, as a chapel for union religious services when summer tourists crowd the island." It is said to be the oldest Protestant church in the northwest.

It was on the veranda of the quaint hotel which was once the main mission building, known as the Mission House, that Dr. Edward Everett Hale begins his famous story of "The Man Without a Country."

[180]

ST. JOSEPH'S, ST. AUGUSTINE, FLORIDA.   *(See page 181)*
Interior and Exterior Views.

ST. JOSEPH'S
ST. AUGUSTINE, FLA.

St. Augustine, the oldest city in the United States, contains several historic structures dating back to the first century of its existence. Prominent among these is St. Joseph's Cathedral, which, with its quaint architecture, vies with the most impressive churches of Latin America. In its belfry hangs a bell bearing the inscription, "Sante Joseph Ora Pro Nobis Do 1682."

From the eventful day—August 28, 1565—St. Augustine's Day—on which Pedro Menendez de Aviles reached the coast of Florida, St. Augustine saw some two centuries of tempestuous history, with Indian depredations and buccaneering, evidences of which are the ruins of the old wall erected as a protection against Indian incursions, and Fort Marion, begun in 1656, as the Fort of San Marco. Among other pioneer vicissitudes was the destruction of the shrine of Nuestra Senora de la Leche, erected on the spot where Menendez and his explorers knelt in solemn Mass on the day they entered the harbor. In 1586 a parish church of wood was built. In 1646 another edifice was constructed and named Church of St. Augustine. This church was replaced by a stone edifice which was used until the completion of the Cathedral of St. Joseph in 1799.

The old residence of the Spanish governors, now used as a Post Office, is reputed to be the oldest building in the United States.

SAN XAVIER DEL BAC

ARIZONA

In Arizona, where on all sides one views reminders of a historic past, "ruined cliff dwellings, aqueducts, fortifications of a still older civilization and quaint missions of Spanish priests," stands the venerable mission church, San Xavier del Bac, twenty miles from Tucson. This old church, built about 1654, is probably one of the earliest shrines of the Jesuits, who as far back as 1540, with their proverbial zeal, energy and daring, had penetrated the hot and forbidding wilds of Arizona and New Mexico. Many who traveled hundreds of miles on foot through deserts, over mountains and sun-seared plains, enduring untold hardships, died, some at the hands of savages, leaving no permanent monument behind.

In the interior of the present church, the façade of which reveals the obscure date of 1768, may be seen the domes and half domes of the old church, decorated with frescoes of angels and Bible characters. Painted and gilded lions on chancel rails recall St. Mark's in Venice, appropriate to this old church of an architecture suggestive of Venetian-Byzantine style.

Not far beyond the old church is the Papigo Indian Reservation, the most prosperous and fertile in the country.

MISSION DOLORES

So it is popularly known everywhere, although it is properly San Francisco de Asis Solano. From the correct name was derived that of the California City at the Golden Gate, where the ancient mission stands. The popular name is due to the fact that the site was chosen by Padre Palou, near a spring and creek which, in honor of the day he named the Arroyo de los Dolores.

The mission was founded October 9, 1776, the year that marked the creation of so many missions in the far west while in the far east, the British colonies were waging a successful war for Independence, which was declared on July 4th, marking the birth of the new nation, which in time was to absorb the then disinterested Spanish lands on the Pacific.

The Mission consisted of a church fifty-four feet long and a house fifteen by thirty feet, both of wood, plastered with clay and roofed with tiles. The next year, Father Serra paid his first visit to San Francisco and said Mass on the titular saint's day, and then he stood and gazed out upon the limitless sea and said: "Thanks be to God that now our Father St. Francis, with the Holy Cross and procession of the missions has reached the last limit of California. To go farther he must have boats."

COLONIAL CHURCHES

One of the elements of beauty in churches is association. The church of old, in village, town or city, was the heart of the community. There the people went to pray, to hear the Word of God expounded. In the church the babe was baptized or christened, the bridegroom received his bride, the funeral sermon was preached and in the yard, ashes were returned to ashes and dust to dust.

The community church was a place of joy and sorrow, life and death, misery and comfort, turbulence and peace. It is so today in small towns and in quiet country villages, while the rush and bustle of modern city life has changed some of these characteristics. The churchyard burial ground has given way to the cemetery, but the church itself still functions otherwise as of old, and no doubt ever will.

The old-fashioned church was the Colonial church. It was in many cases enriched not only by local and personal associations but memories of national import. It was reared amid the testing vicissitudes of pioneer days, and so it is a revered landmark of national birth, development and achievement, and a milestone in spiritual progress.

Born of the changing order of things and adapting themselves valiantly to it, the Colonial churches have been the struggle and victories of seekers after truth. To them, Lowell might well have written his challenging lines:

HISTORIC CHURCHES

New occasions teach new duties,
　　Time makes ancient good uncouth;
They must upward still and onward
　　They would keep abreast of Truth.
Lo, before us gleam her camp fires,
　　We ourselves must pilgrims be;
Launch our Mayflower and steer boldly
　　Through the desperate winter sea.
Nor attempt the future's portal
　　With the past's blood-rusted key.

RUINS OF FIRST PROTESTANT CHURCH IN AMERICA, JAMESTOWN, VA. (*See page 187*)

FIRST PROTESTANT CHURCH IN AMERICA

JAMESTOWN, VA.

Only a picturesque ruin, a tower now remains of the first Protestant church in America, at Jamestown, Va., a monument to those early English colonists whose first act after debarkation on May 14, 1607, was to engage in the worship of God. The first service, however, was not in the church, but under Virginia's blue sky, before a reading desk formed by nailing a board between two trees. In the words of John Smith: "This was our church until we built a homely thing like a barne set on crocketts covered with raftes, sedge and earth." This primitive house of worship, with its canvas canopy for rude shelter and seats of unsawn timber, continued to serve the colonists until the fort and some cabins were built. The services were conducted by the Rev. Robert Hunter, appointed chaplain of the Virginia Company by the Archbishop of Canterbury after the ritual of the Established Church of England— "two services each Sabbath Day and communion every three months."

The church, a rude structure, erected by Captain John Smith, after his first exploration trip, was soon destroyed by fire. A new building was immediately begun, but the work was interrupted by the departure of Captain Smith for England and by destructive Indian raids. The arrival of Lord de la War as Governor encouraged the completion of the House of Worship. It was fitted and furnished with the choicest woods that

America's forests could provide. The Communion table and altar were constructed of black walnut. Pews, pulpit and shutters were of cedar. The altar was decorated for its dedication with the wild flowers of Virginia. The baptismal font, later known as Pocahontas Font, now at Bruton Parish, at Williamsburg, Pa., "was hewed out like a canoe." Two full-toned bells from England called the worshippers to Sunday services and on week days to morning work and evening rest. Lord de la War appeared regularly in "full dignity of velvet and lace with bodyguard in rich attire and scarlet cloaks." In April 1614, the native Princess Pocahontas, was baptized in the Christian faith and in this same little Church later was married to John Rolfe. There assembled the Council of Burgesses (1619), records of which make the following quaint note:

"For as much as men's affairs do little prosper where God's service is neglected, all the Burgesses took their places in the quire till a prayer was said by the minister that it would please God to guard and sanctify all our proceedings to His own glory."

In 1639 the little wooden church was succeeded by a solid brick structure, fifty-six by twenty-eight feet, adorned by a square tower forming the entrance. In 1676, occurred Nathaniel Bacon's rebellion against Governor Berkeley. During this strife Jamestown was burned and nothing was left of America's first Protestant Church save its tower,—today's picturesque ruins of "this first and most ancient landmark of the Protestant Church in America," in whose adjoining churchyard lie buried the Governors of Virginia who died in office and the Rectors who served the little parish.

CHURCH OF THE PILGRIMAGE

PLYMOUTH, MASS.

The heavy night hung dark
The hills and waters o'er,
When a band of exiles moored their bark
On a wild New England shore.

What sought they thus afar?
Bright jewels of the mine?
The wealth of seas, the spoils of war?
They sought a faith's pure shrine.

Ay, call it holy ground,
The soil where first they trod,
They have left unstained what there they found,
Freedom to worship God.

—*"Landing of Pilgrim Fathers," Heman.*

The Mayflower Pilgrims, "these being about a hundred souls" so said William Bradford in his "History of Plymouth," halted at Plymouth Rock, on the shores of Cape Cod in 1620 to worship God, "before fearlessly setting forth to conquer the unknown." Among the number was William Brewster, at whose manor house in the little village of Scrooby, in Nottinghamshire, they had met to worship before leaving the Church of England and going to Holland (1608) to worship according to the dictates of their consciences.

The first sermon preached in this country before any church was erected was delivered by Ruling Elder William Brewster. On December 21, 1621, he preached the first Thanksgiving sermon, celebrated because of "our harvest being gotten in." Soon at the top of the hill alongside Leyden Street, running parallel to the

[189]

water front and named in honor of the Dutch city that had given them refuge, the first Meeting House was erected, also used as a fort. It was here that Governor Bradford and Captain Miles Standish worshipped with the other Pilgrim Fathers, invoking Divine blessing upon "this work which God of his goodness hath hitherto blessed." In Pilgrim Hall (erected 1824) today may be seen Captain Standish's sword and Governor Bradford's Bible.

The site of Plymouth Pilgrim Meeting House was acquired in 1637 "somewhat" by virtue of an inheritance from one of the Colonists. At this time the first church was erected on the north side of Town Square according to an old deed. The church was without a pastor for fifteen years, from the time Elder Brewster died in 1644, because of its inability to pay a minister of education and ability. The membership, therefore, dwindled in numbers and enthusiasm until George Whitefield's "great awakening" which led to the building of a new church in 1776. The present Church of the Pilgrimage was erected in 1840 by another congregation near the site and in commemoration of the original Meeting House of the Pilgrims,—the fourth to house the descendants of the First Congregational Society in America,—at which time the name "Church of the Pilgrimage" was adopted.

The church of 1776 had a bell taken from the old church, into which it was put at least as early as 1679. Church records of that time record an order "by the Towne for the Constable to take course for the sweeping of the Meeting House and the ringing of the bell," and to pay an Indian for the "killing of a wulfe."

The first Thanksgiving in New England was celebrated in Plymouth. The celebration occupied three days, the English exploiting themselves for the entertainment of the Indians, who in return played their native games and sports, and in other ways entered into the spirit of the occasion, to the delight of the colonists.

In spite of the friendliness of the Indians, however, there was always some danger of an outbreak, hence Captain Standish marched with his armed guard to church and took his position at the left of the preacher.

The Sabbath day in New England in those days was a bit severe. Men were required to be good by statute whether they felt like it or not. It is on record that a man was fined for carrying grist home on the Lord's day, and the miller who let him take it was held equally guilty. Elizabeth Eddy, a cleanly soul, was fined ten shillings for wringing and hanging out clothes on that day, the austere judges not believing that cleanliness is next to Godliness. In 1658 James Watt wrote a business note in the evening. He could not wait until midnight, possibly because it had to be done and he was getting sleepy, but it brought him the humiliation of public reproof. In Dunstable, a soldier suffered with chilblains, so he wet a piece of an old hat and put it in his shoe to ease the pain. As this happened on Sunday it cost him forty shillings, and history fails to tell us whether or not the chilblains were eased.

It is difficult to reconcile such drastic measures with old Plymouth's record of "exemplary generosity rather than severity," in the application of theological doctrine.

OLD NORTH CHURCH

BOSTON

He said to his friend,
"If the British march
By land or by sea from the town tonight,
Hang a lantern aloft in the belfry arch
Of the North Church tower, as a signal light,
One if by land and two if by sea,
And I on the opposite shore will be
Ready to ride and spread the alarm
Through every Middlesex village and farm
For the country folk to be up and at arm."

—*"Paul Revere's Ride," Longfellow.*

Old North was Boston's second church, given imperishable fame because of the lantern signals which were flashed from the belfry to Paul Revere when he started on his ride that aroused the New England colonists to oppose the march of King George's troops and to fire the "shot that was heard 'round the world."

This church was actually founded upon the spirit that brought independence to the colonists. Its organizers had withdrawn from the First Church in 1650 because of a difference of opinion among the congregation over the beheading of King Charles I the year before. The new church stood for political and religious independence. Because of their locations the churches were designated North and South.

A British Army officer referred to Old North as a "nest of traitors." Had he said "rebels," the title would have been warranted, when one considers the number of political mass meetings held under its roof, and the

OLD NORTH CHURCH, BOSTON.
Made famous by the Midnight Ride of Paul Revere, April 18, 1775.

famous and fearless early pastors who presided over its religious, political and social life.

Among these were Increase Mather, and his son Cotton, under whose pastorates it is said the church exercised more influence than any other in the country. The "free, strong, thinking, vital" Emerson, whose bust adorns the present church as one of its chief monuments to a celebrated past, was another of its influential pastors. The first crusade against intemperance was presented in its pulpit by Henry Ware in 1840. From its pulpit were set forth relentlessly the duties of members as citizens and patriots as well as Christians. It was under Ware's ministry, says Wallington, that the congregation separated from the orthodox Congregationalists.

The original building of 1652 was a square wooden structure having a high pulpit and stiff, high-backed pews, some with private entrances leading out into the street. The church served also as a fire house and public arsenal. This building, destroyed by fire in 1673, was replaced in a year by a larger one, which served as the house of worship until 1775, when it was torn down and used for firewood by the British.

In 1779 a union was formed between Old North Church and the "Brick Church," an offshoot from it.

Commenting on the Old North Church, Thomas Van Ness wrote:

> The Second Church has never stood for creed or dogma. It is now classified as Unitarian, yet its original covenant has never been altered or erased from the membership book. Just when the change in thought took place no one can determine.

[193]

Longfellow in his poem gave Paul Revere undying fame, which was his due; but he was not the only one that rode forth that night upon seeing the signal flash from Old North Church. There was another staunch patriot with him, William Dawes; and while both planned to go to Lexington and Concord, they were to ride by different routes. Both reached Lexington, but it was Dawes who reached Concord.

When the United States entered the World War, President Wilson wanted a business man and financier to purchase supplies for the Army, and summoned a Chicago banker, Charles G. Dawes, a direct descendant of William, to assume the task, giving him the rank of Brigadier General. The President was a Democrat; the banker a Republican; but both were Americans to the core and actuated by a single purpose. When after the War, narrow partisan politicians in Congress sought to discredit the administration, and summoned General Dawes as a witness, he so picturesquely and contemptuously discredited them that he ended their efforts, and won the love of the whole country.

In 1924, the American people elected him Vice President, without any effort on his part, and the following April, 1925, when the one hundred and fiftieth anniversary of the Battles of Lexington and Concord were celebrated, he, with General Pershing, Commander of the American forces overseas in the World War, attended, the new Vice President being the guest of honor. And on April 20 a cavalryman, impersonating William Dawes, rode again over the route accompanied by Vice President Dawes and General Pershing, in modern motor cars.

OLD SOUTH CHURCH
BOSTON

"Old South" Church was the Meeting House in which some of the finest legislation in America took place. Within its walls in Colonial and Revolutionary times were spoken some of the boldest words of patriotism and from its rostrum went up the strongest of appeals that fanned into flame the fire which drove the British from the revolting colonies.

Though the First and Second Churches (Old North) were already in existence, Old South was the first to stand out for the "new order of things." At its town meeting, "the backbone of Colonial Legislation" were passed some of the wisest laws of history. Old South is sometimes called "The Church of the Town Meetings."

"It is one of the many glories of Old South Church," says Wallington, "that with it originated the initial struggle to separate Church and State in our country." The story of its origin bears this out. Some twenty-nine of the members of the First Church contended that citizenship should not be dependent upon church membership (the policy of the mother church holding that none could be freemen except church members and none but freemen voters) and formed a separate congregation. They were denied the right to do so by both the Church and the Governor, and so they appealed to the selectmen of Boston, who granted their request. Then it was (1690) that there came into existence the "Meeting House of cedar, two stories high, with a picturesque steeple, standing on the green, amidst buttonwood trees." In this church, with its modest interior, lofty pulpit and high-back pews, Benjamin Franklin was baptized in 1706. In 1729 this building was destroyed and a more substantially built brick edifice erected in 1730, by the now strong congregation, and to whose spiritual life much fervor had been added by the preaching of the noted evangelist George Whitefield during the "Great Awakening" of 1740.

Dr. Joseph Sewall was pastor of Old South for several decades. In the original church Chief Justice Sewall, his father, made public confession and repentance for the part he had taken in the notorious Salem witchcraft. It was in this second church convened the series of town mass meetings, both before and during the Revolution, which have made Old South so historically famous, It became the "overflow-meeting" room for Faneuil Hall. From the largest mass meeting Boston had yet seen (June 14, 1768) over which John Hancock presided, went the petition to the governor, asking that the British frigate be removed from Boston Harbor. From Old South Church its assembly of citizens marched to the Boston Massacre. From another meeting in the church, equally eventful in American history, went many of the first citizens of Boston, dressed as Indians, on December 14, 1773, to participate in "The Boston Tea Party."

The old church was desecrated by the British in the ensuing war. Burgoyne used it as a riding school during the winter of 1774-1775, appropriating the pews, gallery and pulpit for his camp fires and converting Deacon Hubbard's "beautifully carved pew with its silken hangings" into a pig sty. But today the church

OLD SOUTH CHURCH, AND WASHINGTON STREET, BOSTON. (See page 195)

stands much as repaired in 1776, and now serves as a Museum under the supervision of the Massachusetts Historical Society.

The first preacher of Old South was the Rev. Thomas Thatcher, who came before the cedar Meeting House. It received its name "Old South" in 1817, when a new church, built near the old church became known as "New South."

There is a tablet upon the Old South Church, as follows:—

Church gathered	1669
First House built	1670
This House erected	1729
Desecrated by British troops	1775-6

ST. MICHAEL'S
MARBLEHEAD, MASS.

St. Michael's occupies the site of a church the corner-stone of which was laid in 1714. Wallington says that of the thirty-three persons contributing to the original building fund, twenty-nine were sea captains who brought over in their boats most of the material and equipment for the church. From the ceiling hangs a handsome brass chandelier, presented in those early days by the Collector of the Port of Bristol, England. The first organ, bought from St. Paul's, New York City, is said to have been the one on which the inaugural march was played when the Father of His Country became the first President of the United States. It was Captain Blackler, of St. Michael's, we are told, who commanded the boat on which Washington crossed the Delaware to fight the Battle of Trenton.

OLD SHIP CHURCH

HINGHAM, MASS.

Old Ship Church at Hingham, Mass., a quaint, religious landmark dating from 1681, exemplified the severe taste and substantial workmanship of the early New Englanders' Church architecture. This church underwent virtually no material change in more than two centuries. Rectangular, two stories high, and having a belfry, which served also as a lookout station, its peculiar appearance has given it its name, "Old Ship." The massive pulpit, covered by a canopy, which also served as a sounding board, was reached by a steep stairway. Its rafters were uncovered. Its seats were plain wooden benches without backs. Not until 1817 did stoves take the place of foot warmers. Separate pews were assigned to elders, deacons and the widow of the first pastor, and in 1763 to persons "skilled in music." In 1802 orchestral instruments (bass viol, violin, flute, bassoon, clarinet) were added as "an aid in service," and in 1866 an organ.

All town meetings and village gatherings were held in the old meeting house, in which on Sundays the Rev. Peter Hobart preached against the sin of hoopskirts and women's millinery, and in which on weekdays "the congregation assembled to discuss means of avoiding Indian depredations."

In Hingham of old one member was taken to court for "common sleeping during public exercises on the Lord's Day and for striking him who waked him. Since he was not sorry, he was sentenced to be severely whipped," a favorite means of discipline. Not even

"Old Ship" Church at Hingham, Mass., Dating from 1681. Oldest Meeting House in the United States.

aristocrats were exempt from it, though it was legally forbidden that "any true gentleman be punished with a whip, unless his crime be very shameful and his course of life vicious and profligate." Speaking against the parson made one liable to have his ears cut off.

"Old Ship" is the oldest Meeting House in the United States that is still used for the purpose for which it was erected and still remains on its original site.

There was a still earlier Meeting House at Hingham, built soon after its settlement in 1635. It was the proud possessor of a belfry and bell, probably the first in the colonies, and was surrounded by a stockade to protect it from marauding red-skins, and perhaps, other possible enemies. Its nearest neighbors were the Pilgrims of Plymouth, and the two communities exchanged visits by way of a trail through the forest. To erect a successor to this House of Worship in 1671, one hundred and forty-three persons were assessed a total of £430, an amount equal to about a third of the personal property in the Plymouth colony.

"THE LITTLE CHURCH OF ENGLAND"
NEWPORT, R. I.

"The Little Church of England" in Newport, R. I., later known as Trinity Protestant Episcopal Church, was erected in 1702 under the sponsorship of Sir Edmund Andros, representative of King James II in the New England Colonies, New York, and New Jersey. At that time it was considered the finest structure of its kind. Today it remains much the same, with its "big high-backed pews, the same pulpit raised high on its pedestal, and the original sounding board."

FIRST CHURCH
BOSTON

Boston's First Church, presided over in its beginning by John Winthrop, one of the four men originating its organization, numbered among its early leaders John Eliot and Roger Williams, respectively characterized "The Faithful" and "The Progressive." The latter left Boston for Salem, from which he later was also banished because of his too liberal views. Later John Cotton was called to the pulpit of the First Church.

John Eliot, "Apostle to the Indians," a Puritan of Puritans, educated in Cambridge, "an acute grammarian," realizing the limited opportunity there for a nonconformist school teacher, migrated to the "Wilderness of the West," as our forefathers were accustomed to term the New World.

The welfare of the Indians soon became his chief concern. He came in close contact with them in his Roxbury Church, and took an Indian belonging to Long Island into his family, who served as his interpreter and taught him "words." From the Indian interpreter he learned to say the Ten Commandments, the Lord's Prayer, and various passages from the Bible in the Indian tongue.

With his pupils Eliot finally translated the whole English Bible into the language of the Massachusetts Indians, the English Society paying the expenses of printing and publishing it. The language of the Massachusetts Indians was chosen for the translation, since it belonged to the language of the Algonquins,

FIRST CHURCH, BOSTON.

the branch of their race most widely dispersed in North America. Two hundred copies of this Bible, known as "John Eliot's Bible" the first printed in the Western World, were issued in strong leather binding for the Indians. A fine copy was sent to Charles II, now the treasure of Jesus College, his Alma Mater at Cambridge, which erected a brick building called the "Indian College."

The Bible was set up by an Indian named John Printer and was six years on the press. It was followed by an Indian grammar, Psalter, Baxter's "Call to the Unconverted," and "The Practice of Piety."

The zeal of the English Church for the Christianization of the Indians is suggested by the following old record:

> That the settlers maie wyne and incite the natives of the Country to the knowledge and Obedience of the onlie true God and Savior of Mankinde and in the Christian Faythe, which is our Royall Intencion and the Adventurer's free Profession, is the Principall ende of this Plantacion. (Extract from first Royal Charter granted by Charles I to Massachusetts Colony.)

UNITED CHURCH
NEW HAVEN, CONN.

The United Church, New Haven, Conn., with the Old South Church of Boston was among the first churches to separate State and ecclesiastical interests. Jonathan Edwards was associated with its pulpit.

KING'S CHAPEL
BOSTON

King's Chapel, the fifth house of worship erected in Boston and the first Protestant Episcopal Church in New England, has been aptly characterized as the first missionary church on Puritan soil, persecuted by the Puritans and founded by force. This suggests the story of its origin.

Some sixty years had passed and there had been as yet no congregation of the Established Church of England in the Colonies, so in 1686, one day there appeared from the British frigate "Rose," the Rev. Robert Ratcliffe, "an established minister of the Church of England, together with the other members of a commission appointed by King James II to preside over the Church in America." The Puritans refused to permit him to occupy any of their pulpits until they were roughly compelled by Governor Edmund Andros to do so. Ratcliffe was unable to buy from them even a plot of ground for his church, and so Governor Andros set aside a corner of a burial ground for his use, upon which in 1689 arose the first King's Chapel, a small edifice of wood, enlarged in 1710. This building was found in a state of decay in 1741 and was succeeded in 1753 by the present structure. During the building of this church the congregation worshipped in Trinity.

The original King's Chapel was attended by the royal governors until after the Colonies gained their freedom, at which time the church almost lost its name. It was known as the "Stone Church" for a time and it is said that it again took its name King's Chapel at

KING'S CHAPEL, BOSTON, the first Protestant Episcopal Church in New England.

the timely suggestion of one that it be considered the Chapel of "The King of Kings." The governor's pew was twice as large as the others and gorgeously canopied. The bill of lading for the organ installed in 1756, which Handel is said to have selected, is still preserved.

The Boston Gazette and Country Journal of August 30, 1756, announced its installation "with sermon suitable to the occasion, prayer to begin at four o'clock." The Bible in use today in King's Chapel was given by King James II, who also presented a valuable communion service.

With the coming of the Rev. James Freeman to King's Chapel in 1782, to serve as lay reader, King's Chapel was reborn Unitarian—with "less of ruffled sleeve, powdered wigs, velvets, chariots and liveries" than the chapel had witnessed in its pre-Revolutionary days. This was the first official acceptance of the Unitarian faith on the part of a congregation in the United States.

Not far from King's Chapel is Boston's famous "Liberty Tree," which was at a later time doubtless ornamented in effigy by many who sat in King's Chapel. In its nearby burying ground, said to be the oldest cemetery in Boston, dating back to 1630, lie the remains of the Winthrops and numerous other Colonial celebrities.

The luxurious interior of King's Chapel when compared to the rude simplicity of the Puritan Meeting Houses "was regarded," says Wallington, "as a blot upon the soil of Massachusetts." Banners, escutcheons and coats of arms of the King, the Governor of Massachusetts, noble families of England whose members occupied pews, adorned the walls. The Ten Commandments, the Lord's Prayer, and the Creed were painted on the east wall, and the hourglass in an elaborate brass stand, stood on the pulpit.

FIRST CHURCH
HARTFORD, CONN.

The original congregation of this church were emigrants from Braintree, Essex, England. Four years after their arrival in 1632 they migrated from Massachusetts to Hartford, "through the trackless land, driving cattle before them, living upon milk and avoiding wild beasts and savages as best they could." They took with them their pastor and teacher, the Rev. Thomas Hooker, eminent among New England divines. Their first meeting house, built in 1638, was succeeded ten years later by a better edifice. In 1739 a third house was erected near the site of the present building and was dedicated in 1807. This Hartford Meeting House, unlike other New England churches, made no selection of seats for the rich and powerful. No collection box was passed; each left his contribution in the box on the "Deacon's Table" in front of the high pulpit. Among its members was Horace Wells, celebrated as the discoverer of the principle of anaesthetics in surgery.

With its early adoption of the "perfect equality," so boldly preached by its leader, the Rev. Thomas Hooker, the influence of the little Church of Hartford is said to have been "more far reaching than that of any other church of Connecticut."

FIRST BAPTIST CHURCH

PROVIDENCE, R. I.

The First Baptist Church of Providence had its first Meeting House in 1700, though the Baptist Society had been in existence since Roger Williams' settlement of the town in 1639. For some sixty years the congregation had been meeting in homes or out under the trees. The church was composed mainly of Williams' friends, who had followed him from Salem, from which "the Welshman" had been ordered by the authorities of the Massachusetts Bay Colony to leave and "not draw others to his opinion." Members of the Puritan societies of Massachusetts joined him. Elected its first pastor, Roger Williams soon resigned to preach to the Indians, which he did for some forty years.

Tradition tells of a cabin Meeting House in which Roger Williams began to preach when he first went to Salem, used for twenty-six years. It was "the shape of a haycock, with fireplace in the center, with smoke escaping from a hole in the roof."

The Meeting House of 1700 resulted from the labors, generosity and devotion of Pastor Pardon Tellinghast, who was its donor and builder and who served some thirty-six years without salary. In 1726 another building was erected and used until 1774, when the present building came into existence, "a wooden building 80 feet square with graceful steeple at the west end (196 feet high) built after the design of Sir Christopher Wren" and quite similar in appearance to the present church.

The lofty pulpit and sounding-board are gone, however. Seats are modern and the gallery for slaves has been replaced by a square loft. In 1850 the progressive congregation, with pride in their enterprise, replaced candles and oil with gas.

The inscription on the bell of this church recalls with significance former days when fashions were unhampered in this church, and when men and women were privileged to wear what they chose. At that time Cotton Mather was regulating fashions in Boston "according to what he thought godly."

Its quaint inscription reads:—

> For freedom of conscience this town was first planted,
> Persuasion, not force was used by the people;
> This church is the oldest and has not recanted,
> Enjoying and granting bell, temple and steeple.

The bell was later recast and the inscription changed to read, "This church was founded A.D. 1639, the first in the State and oldest of Baptists in America." It also records Roger Williams as the first Pastor.

Another tablet bearing the inscription "Built for worship and to hold Commencements in" suggests the close connection between Roger Williams' Church and Rhode Island College (now Brown University) which it has long sponsored with a fine spirit of liberality, scholarship and culture.

FIRST BAPTIST CHURCH, PROVIDENCE, R. I. *(See page 205)*

ST. JOHN'S

St. John's Church marks the site of an earlier house of worship called Queen's Chapel, so named in honor of Queen Caroline, wife of King George II of England. It was a wooden building erected on a site given for the purpose. In 1807, the present brick church was built. Longfellow has immortalized one of its former rectors in the "Poet's Tale" of his "Tales of a Wayside Inn." Near the town is located the old home of another of the characters celebrated in this poem, Governor Wentworth.

Among the cherished relics of this church are a prayer book, a silver communion service, and a Bible (one of the four "vinegar" Bibles extant) sent by the Queen.

The Vinegar Bibles are so called on account of a typographical error. They were published in 1717 by John Basket, "King's Printer," of Oxford, England. The compositor set up "vinegar" instead of "vineyard" in the phrase "the parable of the vineyard." Some volumes got into circulation before the mistake was noticed and corrected. The other three of these faulty Bibles are owned by Christ Church, Philadelphia, Christ Church, Boston, and the Lenox Library, New York City.

The Credence Table is made from the wood of Admiral Farragut's flagship, the U. S. Frigate "Hartford," on which he captured New Orleans. In 1836, after its varying vicissitudes, old St. John's acquired the "Brattle Organ" imported from London, 1713, another cherished relic, as is also the old bell, which summoned the ancient parish to church, taken from the French Cathedral of Louisburg, Cape Breton, successfully stormed by Pepperell, April 4, 1745. Twice re-cast, once by Paul Revere and later by his successor, the bell still rings the New England curfew from out its pleasing inscription:

> From St. John's steeple
> I call the people
> On holy days
> To prayer and praise.

Washington's visit to St. John's, recorded in his diary of November 1, 1789, enriches the history of this church. On this occasion he is said to have been "clothed in black velvet ornate with jewelled buckles, and to have sat in Governor Wentworth's pew, newly equipped with red plush cushions." Washington's note of this event concludes with "and in the afternoon I went to one of the Presbyterian or Congregational Churches."

At Portsmouth is also the Old North Church whose original meeting house was built in 1657 and served for fifty-six years with its first pastor, the Rev. Joshua Moody, a Congregationalist, and one of New England's ablest divines. Governor Cranfield, a staunch Episcopalian, taking advantage of the Conformity Act of King Charles II, we are told, sent Mr. Moody to jail in Newcastle in 1683, because of the pastor's public attack on a matter of civil injustice. He was released only upon consent to leave the Colony, much to the sorrow of his loyal parishioners. For ten years he preached in Boston, after which he returned to his old church, four years before his death.

ST. JOHN'S CHURCH, PORTSMOUTH, N. H. *(See page 207)*

MEETING HOUSE-ON-THE-GREEN, LEXINGTON, MASS. *(See page 209)*

MEETING HOUSE-ON-THE-GREEN
LEXINGTON, MASS.

Another equally historic New England church was Lexington's Meeting House-on-the-Green, also closely connected with Revolutionary War events. The original of the present building was built in 1714, when Cambridge Farms became Lexington, and costing some £500, has been referred to as a "barn-like edifice with no heat or steeple." In this church preached the Rev. John Hancock, a Harvard graduate and a man of great intellectual capacity, who expounded to the congregation two discourses with an hour between, from carefully prepared manuscript, holding that "preaching without manuscript, and good sense, seldom go together."

In 1794 the old church was replaced by a new one erected near its site, which in turn was replaced by the present building, the previous one having been burned down. A nearby flagstaff marks the site of the original Meeting House-on-the-Green, from whose bell tower sounded the alarm on the memorable morning of April 18, 1775.

The Meeting House was used as an arsenal as the clouds of war loomed, and on the fateful morning Parker shouted to his soldiers: "Every man of you who is equipped follow me, and those of you who are not, go into the Meeting House and furnish yourselves from the magazine and immediately join the company."

The first Meeting House, built soon after separating from the mother church at Cambridge (1692)—a rude structure with wind and weather coming through its unchinked spaces—cost about £300, contributed by forty-three persons representing twenty-two family names. Its congregation was not gathered in the shadow of the Meeting House but scattered about the lonely farms. Near by were the stocks, ready for use in enforcing its discipline.

TRINITY CHURCH
BOSTON

While serving as rector of this church, Phillips Brooks gave to the world his "Queen of all Christmas hymns," "O, Little Town of Bethlehem." The story goes that the great basic truth, as expressed in its words, came to him on a Christmas Eve as he was standing with bowed head in the old Church in Bethlehem, close by the spot where, according to tradition, Jesus was born.

The impression was so vivid and so intense that he did not need to commit it to paper. It was with him forever, and when he reached home he wrote it down.

The hymn was first sung in Trinity Church, Boston, as part of the Sunday School service in 1868, and from that day to this, it has held its high place as a Christmas song. The music for the hymn was written at Dr. Brooks' request by the organist of Trinity Church.*

* "Great Hymns and Their History," Gregory.

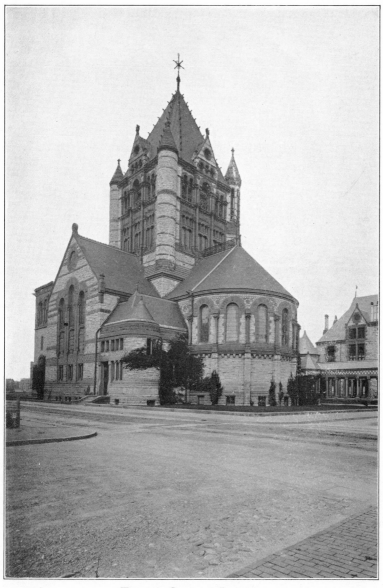

TRINITY CHURCH, BOSTON.
Where Phillips Brooks, as Rector, gave to the world the famous Christmas
Hymn,—"O, Little Town of Bethlehem."

OLD SOUTH CHURCH

NEWBURYPORT, MASS.

As early as 1635, Newburyport, Mass., held divine service beneath a majestic oak, under the leadership of the Rev. Mr. Parker, an English minister who remained pastor for forty-five years. The present meeting house bears the inscription on a memorial tablet, "Meeting House of First Presbyterian Society erected 1756."

The church records say that for some seventy years worshippers depended entirely on footstones for warmth, and a church law providing that the sexton should have twenty cents for each stone he "had to fill before service and remove after." In 1819 wood stoves were purchased at an outlay of $100. Closely connected with this church from its beginning was the Rev. George Whitefield, a devoted friend of one of its pastors, the Rev. Jonathan Parsons, in whose home the noted evangelist died on the day he was expecting to preach in his pulpit. His body lies buried in a crypt under the pulpit and the church treasures his Bible among its relics. The old church and eminent preacher are thus jointly celebrated in Whittier's lines:

> Under the Church of Federal Street,
> Under the tread of its Sabbath feet,
> Walled about by its basement stones,
> Lie the marvellous preacher's bones.
> *   *   *   *
> Still, as the gem of its civic crown,
> Precious beyond the world's renown,
> His memory hallows the ancient town.

CENTER CHURCH

NEW HAVEN, CONN.

This church (erected 1814) immortalizes in an historic stained glass window the story of its pioneer organization (1639) under John Davenport and the seven elders who with him planned the original church. The pastor is represented preaching under the wide-spreading elms to the faithful flock, which he led through the wilderness from Salem to its Connecticut home.

In the crypt of this church repose the mortal remains of the grandparents of President Rutherford B. Hayes; Mary Edwards, "the amiable and excellent consort of Jonathan Edwards," and "Margaret, first wife of Benedict Arnold, who died June 19, 1775."

On its historic green, sacred now to the three churches occupying its middle space, Benedict Arnold assembled the Governor's Guard to lead it to Cambridge to swell the patriot army. There Lafayette reviewed troops and Washington passed on his way to Trinity Church.

Pastor Davenport, we are told, "arrived at Quinnipiac (City of Elms) with twin determinations—to found a settlement which should be governed by the Church and to establish a great nucleus of learning." The latter he realized through the earnest labors of the "scholarly and gentle" William Hooke, at one time Chaplain to Cromwell at Whitehall and preacher in Center Church, who "first took practical action toward

OLD SOUTH CHURCH, NEWBURYPORT, MASS. *(See page 211)*

the establishment of Yale College." To this college John Davenport, known to the Indians as "so big study man," left $1,000 worth of books.

"OLD JERUSALEM"
PORTLAND, MAINE

This church, which has been known as "Old Jerusalem" since 1821, when a special service was held for the sailors and seafaring folk, had its first building in 1725, the members up to that time "being too poor to have a preacher and build a church." In 1740 a more substantial church was built, in the belfry of which hung its old bell of 1758, which, upon receipt of the news of the closing of Boston Harbor in 1774 rang for twenty-four hours, followed by all the other bells of the town. Since then, if there is any bell ringing to be done, the honor of starting it is reserved for "Old Jerusalem."

Enlarged and rededicated in 1761, the original church served until 1825. The present church has a chandelier, taken from the old one, suspended from a cannon ball shot from an English fleet and lodged inside its walls. The convention which formed the Constitution of Maine met in "Old Jerusalem."

QUINCY CHURCH
QUINCY, MASS.

Quincy Church, Quincy, Mass., built in 1827 of stone from President John Adams' quarries, shelters the remains of that President, his son, President John Quincy Adams, and their wives.

[213]

LITTLE DOVER MEETING HOUSE
DOVER, N. H.

The history of Dover Meeting House, erected in 1639 by sturdy Dover fishermen and today succeeded by the First Congregational Church (built in 1829), records an amusing event significantly illustrating the determination of the early colonists to submit to no "taxation without representation." In brief, a sheriff came from Massachusetts to collect taxes from Dover citizens, holding that Dover was included in his collectible territory. He was knocked down by a Bible hurled at him from the pulpit by a liberty-loving woman, who was also an enthusiastic member of the riot. The sheriff included in his report:—"We were glad to escape with our lives."

FIRST CONGREGATIONAL CHURCH
SALEM, MASS.

The First Congregational Church of Salem, Mass., organized in 1629, bears the distinction of having been the first Congregational Church entirely organized on the American Continent. Services were first held under a traditional tree, and from 1629 to 1634, in an unfinished building. Records refer to "A thatched, daubed, and patched-up little Meeting House used for services" until replaced in 1670 by another, built on land donated by the town, the old Meeting House having been set aside as a "skoole house and watch house." A third house was built in 1718 and occupied for over a hundred years. It was replaced by the present brick structure, dedicated in 1826.

OLD MEETING HOUSE
CONCORD, MASS.

In Concord's "Old Meeting House," the First Provincial Congress met on October 14, 1774, with John Hancock as President, and its village green was the scene of the assembling of troops on April 19, 1775. The present Unitarian Church near its site was built in part of its timbers. The Rev. William Emerson, grandfather of Ralph Waldo Emerson, ministered in 1743 to its congregation, the first of the preacher line of Emersons.

The General Court, in 1635, decreed that "no new building should be built more than a half mile from the meeting house." Thus according to Bacon, Concord was doubtless the first of the settlements arbitrarily to build with the Meeting House as its nucleus.

CHRIST CHURCH
BENNINGTON, VT.

Christ Church, Bennington, Vt., (dedicated 1762, served also as town hall, school and court house. In it the first State legislature met. It has been remodeled and still serves as a house of worship.

COLLEGIATE CHURCH (DUTCH REFORMED)

NEW YORK CITY

When the West India Company sent emigrants to America, it was its custom to send with them or soon afterward a pious schoolmaster, who in addition to teaching the children of the emigrants, presided at religious meetings and read sermons until a regular clergyman could be assigned. In 1623, the Dutch established a colony at the southern end of New Amsterdam, or Manhattan. Five years later the Rev. Jonas Michaelius, assigned by the North Synod of Holland, arrived to assume that post, and upon his arrival the first Dutch Reformed Church in America was organized, with about fifty communicants. Services were held in a room over a horse mill where the colonists ground their corn.

Three years later, in 1631, the Dominie Everardus Bogardus arrived to officiate as the first regular minister, and this event was marked in 1633, by the erection of the first church building of this congregation. It stood in Pearl Street on the bank of the East River, and close to it was erected a parsonage and stable.

This edifice was succeeded, in 1642, by another, erected by Governor Kieft, and named the First Dutch Church of St. Nicholas, in honor of the tutelary and guardian Saint of New Amsterdam. To this "Church in the Fort," (The Battery), as it was referred to, the several Collegiate Churches now in New York City trace their origin.

COLLEGIATE CHURCH (Dutch Reformed) NEW YORK CITY.

A bronze tablet on one of its successors carries this legend:—"Site of Fort Amsterdam, 1626. Within these fortifications was erected the first substantial church on the island of Manhattan."

"On the front wall of The Church-in-the-Fort," says Disosway, "was a marble slab with this legend:— 'An, Dom MDCXLII W Keift Dir. Gen. Heeft de Gemeente dese Tempel doen Bowen.' (In the year of our Lord 1642 W. Keift being Director General has this congregation caused this Temple to be built)."

A similar tablet on the Marble Collegiate Church (Fifth Avenue and Twenty-ninth Street), reads that its work and worship on Manhattan Island began as early as 1614 and that its first house of worship was erected in 1633. In the belfry of this church, which served for some fifty odd years, hung, it is said, the first bell in the Colony of New Netherlands, bearing the inscription:

Dulcior E nostris Tinnitibus resonat aer
P Henomy me fecit 1674.

To the "Church-in-the-Fort" came worshippers from miles around, among them for twenty years the Dutch setlters from Long Island. (See "First Dutch Reformed Church, Flatbush").

In 1693, a new brick church was dedicated in Garden Street, now Exchange Place, built upon a section of an extensive peach lot bought from Mother Drisius and "by far the most substantial and finest church yet in Manhattan." To this church was transferred the bell, pulpit and furniture of the old church. The plate, communion, and baptismal bowl were made by Amsterdam silverworkers, who hammered them from the money and silverware sent from the colony for this purpose. The baptismal bowl has been used by the succeeding congregations of St. Nicholas.

Walls and windows of the old church were decorated in vivid colors with the coats of arms of families of prominence in the congregation. For forty years or so the Garden Street Church (later called South Dutch in contradistinction to Middle and North, when they were established) was the only church of the Reformed faith in New Amsterdam. It had a quaint and interesting history from the time its nine trustees obtained the first charter ever granted to a religious organization in that colony (May 11, 1696).

The Collegiate Church of St. Nicholas at Fifth Avenue and Forty-eighth Street, descendant of the Middle Collegiate of 1729, dedicated in 1872, is one of the finest of Dutch Reformed churches, with ample endowment from fortunate real estate investments. It has a bell which had been made in Amsterdam in 1731, and had once hung in the Middle Collegiate Church in Nassau Street. During the Revolution the bell was taken to Carlisle, Pennsylvania, for safe-keeping, and the British converted the church into a riding school for their dragoons. It was rung April 11, 1775, to celebrate the election of a committee to choose delegates to the Continental Congress, and on July 9, 1776, when the Declaration of Independence was read to the Army, it pealed forth the glad tidings.

When the war was over the church was restored to its original purpose, and the bell was run again July 4, 1790, the day the church was reopened for services. It was tolled during President Lincoln's funeral in 1865; on August 9, 1885 while General's Grant's funeral was passing; at memorial services for President McKinley; on January 30, 1919 during the memorial services for Colonel Theodore Roosevelt, who had been a member of the Church of St. Nicholas, and during the funeral services of President Harding.

The Collegiate Church, as a branch of the Reformed Church of America, takes its name from the "Church-in-the-Fort" custom, whose ministers exchanged their pulpits in rotation with their colleagues.

The last Collegiate Church organized in New York City, Seventy-seventh Street and West End Avenue, has a cornerstone reading:—"Organized 1628—Dedicated 1891."

TRINITY CHURCH
FISHKILL, N. Y.

Trinity Church, at Fishkill, N. Y., erected in 1769 by the church organization of 1756 under the leadership of the Right Rev. Samuel Seabury, America's first Protestant Episcopal Bishop, enjoys the added distinction of having been the scene of the signing of the ratification of the Constitution of the United States by New York in State Convention.

Bishop Seabury's body lies in the little churchyard of St. George's, Hempstead, L. I.

The First Dutch Reformed Church at Fishkill, built in 1731 and later serving the Continental Army as a military prison, is the building alluded to by Cooper, as the prison in which Harvey Birch was confined.

TRINITY CHURCH
NEW YORK CITY

Old Trinity Church, the mother church of the Episcopal denomination in New York City, opposite Wall Street, the financial center of the world, enjoys the distinction of being not only rich in historical association but also immensely wealthy. The story of its wealth is the story of "Queen's Farm," the estate on which it is located, and a part of the Island of Manhattan purchased by Governor Minuit from the Indians in 1626 for $24. Originally this famous "farm" belonged to Anneke Jans, whose poverty until the day of her death made Trinity rich.

Anneke and her husband, Roeloff, arrived in New Netherlands in 1630 and settled at Fort Orange (Albany). In 1636 Roeloff received from Governor Van Twiller a tract of about sixty-two acres of "new land" on Manhattan along the Hudson at the site of the present West Broadway and Canal Street. On this he built a small house, intending to make it his permanent home, but his plans were cut short by death and in 1638, his farm became known as the "Dominie's Bowerie," Anneke having married Dominie Bogardus, New Amsterdam's first regular preacher, at whose church she worshipped. Her second husband was lost at sea, and the poor widow, now with eight children, moved back to Fort Orange, where she died in 1663.

The following year New Amsterdam became New York, and its language changed from Dutch to English. The "Dominie's Bowerie" became known as the "Dominie's Farm," and later, when made over to Gov-

TRINITY CHURCH, NEW YORK CITY.
Opposite Wall Street, the financial center of the world.

ernor Lovelace, as the "Governor's Farm." When it was confiscated in 1673 by the Duke of York, it was known as the "Duke's Farm," and when the Duke of York became James II (1685), it was called "King's Farm," and given over to the raising of vegetables for the royal governor, who followed. In 1697, Governor Fletcher, who greatly desired to advance Episcopacy in the province, leased the "Farm" to Trinity, at that time a little chapel at the fort called "King's Chapel." The Church paid an annual rental of sixty bushels of wheat. The chapel stood on the west side of Broadway and a slope of green land behind it ran down to the Hudson River.

In 1702, when Queen Anne came to the English throne, the property, at this time assuming the name "Queen's Farm," through the influence of Lord Cornbury, the Queen's cousin, was given to Trinity Church by royal patent dated November 20, 1705. Queen's Farm, embodying all that tract of land lying between Vesey Street on the south and Christopher Street on the north and running from Broadway to the Hudson River, soon began to bring in a handsome income, as the southern end of Manhattan at that time was increasing rapidly in value. In 1738 "Queen's Farm" was rated very valuable property, the greater part of which Trinity still possesses and appropriates to varied and extensive Christian service in the big city.

It was in 1697, while sponsored by Governor Fletcher and his lease of "Queen's Farm," that the incorporation of Trinity Parish was granted (May 6) —the third in date of formation among corporations of the City of New York and the first church known as Trinity was completed. It was a small square structure which was enlarged in 1737. The congregation occupied this edifice until 1776, when the building was destroyed by fire, after General Howe's seizure of the town. In 1788 a second building arose over the ruins and in 1841, the cornerstone was laid for the present Trinity, one of the earliest examples of revived Gothic architecture in the United States. In the adjoining cemetery are headstones carrying the names of some of the earliest settlers (one dating 1681), and heroes of Revolutionary War times. Notable among the distinguished dead are Alexander Hamilton, "that greatest of all New Yorkers" (died 1804), Robert Fulton, and Captain James Lawrence of the "Chesapeake" (1812). The bodies of those who died in the British prison ships appropriately rest in the churchyard of the first Church of England in New York City.

Among the churches which Trinity has "mothered" are Grace (1809), St. Paul's (1766), St. John's (1807), St. Mark's (1799) and St. George's (1752).

On August 23, 1756, the cornerstone of King's Chapel, now Columbia University, was laid by the Governor of the Province on that section of "Queen's Farm," "in the skirts of the city," appropriated by Trinity to that purpose.

ST. PAUL'S
NEW YORK CITY

St. Paul's, opened for service October 30, 1766, is one of the most interesting and influential chapels of Trinity Church and one of the oldest church edifices in New York City, having miraculously escaped the devastations of war and fire. When Trinity and all its records were burned in 1776, St. Paul's was saved and there, during the British occupation, Lord Howe, Major Andre, and many of the soldiers attended church. On his Inauguration Day, Washington attended church at St. Paul's, and in his diary records: "Went to St. Paul's Chapel in the afternoon." The organ that was played on the day of inauguration was afterward sold to St. Michael's at Marblehead, Mass. Later President and Lady Washington went to church in their "coach and four." Washington's and General Clinton's pews are today marked by tablets on opposite walls.

Beneath the chancel of the church lies the body of Major General Richard Montgomery, hero of Quebec (1775). A memorial window sent from France by Benjamin Franklin, faces the monument. The coat of arms of the Prince of Wales decorated the pulpit.

An interesting news note in the New York Gazette of May 14, 1764, reads:—"We are told that the foundation stone of the Third English Church, which is about erecting, is to be laid today. This church is 112 x 72 feet."

St. Paul's, of American Colonial architectural style, is one of the rare instances of a stone building at this period, the usual material being either brick from England or, more usually, wood, "both limited in carving and other enriching embellishment possibilities."

ST. PETER'S

ALBANY, N. Y.

In Albany, N. Y., in 1704, the first American service of the Established Church of England, with a settled clergyman was held. Prior to this the organization (later forming St. Peter's) had met in a small building erected on the site of Fort Frederick about 1675.

From 1712 to 1715 the parishioners met in a Lutheran Church, kindly opened to them, at which time under the patronage of General Hunter, successor to Lord Lovelace, as Governor of New York, they dedicated the first English Church of Albany, succeeded by a larger one in 1802, and in 1859 by the present St. Peter's.

Queen Anne's gift of a communion service to the "Little Chapel of Onondagas" suggests her intense zeal over the missionization of the Mohawk Indians in the interests of whom the English Society had sent out its first pastors and through whose efforts (1763-1766) the Book of Common Prayer was translated into the Indian language.

Under the chancel of St. Peter's lies buried Viscount George A. Howe, who was killed in the Battle of Ticonderoga, then Fort Carillon, in 1758.

ST. PAUL'S, NEW YORK CITY. (See page 223)

ST. PETER'S, ALBANY, N. Y.

GRACE CHURCH

NEW YORK CITY

The original Grace Church (incorporated 1809) stood on a site of an early Lutheran Church erected in 1702 and burned in 1776. In 1846, the present edifice was erected. Philip Hone, writing in his diary under the date of 1846, says of the second Grace Church:—

> A singularly pure and noble example of Gothic architecture. This is to be the fashionable Church and already its aisles are filled with gay parties of ladies in feathers and mousseline-de-laine dresses and dandies with mustaches and high heeled boots; the lofty arches resound with astute criticisms upon Gothic architecture from fair ladies who have had the advantage of travel, and scientific remarks upon acoustics from elderly millionaires, who do not hear quite so well as formerly..

St. John's also served parishioners in what was then one of the most fashionable centers of the town.

St. Mark's-in-the-Bowery, is the outgrowth of a Dutch Chapel of 1660. It contains a memorial stone to Peter Stuyvesant, Captain-General and Governor-in-Chief of New Amsterdam, on whose "Bouwerie" (country estate), the church now stands.

Prominent among other early churches fostered by Trinity are Christ Church (1794), French Church, Du Saint Esprit (1804), St. Stephen's (1805) and St. Michael's (1807).

"THE LITTLE CHURCH AROUND THE CORNER"

On December 20, 1870, while all Christendom was preparing to celebrate the anniversary of the birth of the Christ Child, George Holland, an eminent actor, passed away in his sleep in New York City. So high did he stand in the affections of his fellow players that they determined to pay him all honors. His closest friend was Joseph Jefferson, one of the greatest actors in history, and to him fell the lot of arranging for a fitting service.

Jefferson sought the rector of a fashionable Fifth Avenue Church and humbly asked him to officiate, and permit the service to be held in his church. To Jefferson's astonishment and chagrin, the rector haughtily refused, saying that he and his church could not be used for the funeral of an actor. "There's a little church around the corner that does that sort of thing," he superciliously told his visitor.

"Then," replied Jefferson, "God bless the Little Church Around the Corner."

The snobbish rector referred to the Protestant Episcopal Church of the Transfiguration, Twenty-ninth Street and Fifth Avenue. To the little church went Jefferson, and when he explained his mission to the upstanding young rector, the Rev. George H. Houghton, he listened with sympathy and understanding, and opened his doors to the player folk, who assembled in strength to pay their last tribute to their dead friend.

[226]

"LITTLE CHURCH AROUND THE CORNER," NEW YORK CITY.

It *was* a little church, low and rambling, of modest brick, poor in money, but rich in the spirit of Godliness and human kindness; but the incident brought it undying fame which extends throughout the world. It became the Actor's Church. Player folk became its members. In it many were married. From it many were buried, among the latter Edwin Booth, Richard Mansfield, Dion Boucicault, Sidney Drew and Nat Goodwin. Henry Irving, though a resident of London, became a member, as did John Drew, who still attends; and Sarah Bernhardt attended its services whenever she was in New York.

Dr. Houghton continued to preside over the destinies of his little church and to confer his kindly ministrations wherever needed for nearly fifty-three years after the Holland funeral, passing away full of years and honors in April, 1923.

In honor of the event that gave it fame and as a memorial to Jefferson and Holland, particularly the former, on February 20, 1925, a magnificent stained glass window was unveiled in the presence of a throng of distinguished players and theatrical folk as well as men and women eminent in other walks of life, and the cord was pulled by Lauretta Jefferson Corlett, the little great-granddaughter of Joseph Jefferson.

One half the window depicts Jefferson as "Rip Van Winkle," his most celebrated character, with his arms around the shoulders of George Holland; the other half shows Jesus, with his arms outstretched to welcome them to Paradise. Below are the immortal words, "God Bless the Little Church Around the Corner." In smaller lights are depicted five scenes from Washington Irving's famous legend of the Catskills upon which the play, "Rip Van Winkle" was based, and in them are included even the dog "Schneider," and Rip's tankard that he loved so well. It is one of the few church windows in the world portraying secular figures and scenes.

CHURCH OF THE BRETHREN
GERMANTOWN, PA.

The Church of the Brethren, more commonly referred to as "Dunkards," founded their mother church in America at Germantown, Philadelphia. They arrived in this country in 1719, and by 1723, were gathered together in church organization under the leadership of Peter Bicker, their first elder and pastor. For many years they worshipped in the homes of members. In 1760, they occupied a log building in front of their first Meeting House. The front part of the present Meeting House was erected in 1770 and the rear in 1897.

In Germantown is also the first Mennonite Church established in America. The first Meeting House was erected in 1683, and William Rittenhouse, America's first papermaker, was its first pastor. The first building was replaced by another in 1708, and in 1770, the present building was erected. The pews of the original church are still in use, and the communion table is the same one upon which the first protest against slavery was signed.

FIRST PRESBYTERIAN CHURCH

NEW YORK CITY

More than two hundred years ago, half a dozen persons held a series of meetings in a little house in Pearl Street which led to the organization in 1716 of the present First Presbyterian Church of New York City, whose seal bears the inscription, "The First Church in the State of New York." As they had no building, services were held in City Hall until their first church structure was erected in 1719 on the north side of Wall Street, between Nassau and Broadway, appropriated later by British troops as a riding school. In 1844 the cornerstone of the present edifice was laid. The church is of imposing fifteenth century Gothic style, its nave modeled after the Church of St. Savior at Bath, with handsome windows and west-end front tower in graceful proportions,—a copy of the Magdalen Tower at Oxford, England. The chapel was added in 1893.

Among the officers and members of the First Presbyterian Church were many prominent both in Presbyterian Church history and in city and State affairs. Princeton Seminary and the Presbyterian Hospital were founded largely through its efforts. It led in the organization of Church boards and was the mother of the "Brick Church," Rutger's Riverside Church, the Scotch Presbyterian and the Fifth Avenue Presbyterian Church. The congregation enjoys the distinction of having been the first Presbyterian Church to organize as a religious corporation under the laws enacted by the first legislature of the State.

In the vestibule is a large mural tablet of black slate, a relic of Revolutionary times, taken from the wall of the Wall Street Church. It reads:—

> Under the favor of God this edifice, sacred to the perpetual celebration of the Divine Worship, first erected in 1719, was thoroughly repaired and built larger and more beautiful in 1748. The Presbyterians of New York, founding it for their own and their children's use, in this votive tablet dedicate it to the God who gave it. May it be yet more illustriously adorned by Religion, by Concord, by Love, by Purity of Faith, of Worship and Discipline. May it, by the favor of Christ endure throughout many generations.

ST. ANDREW'S
RICHMOND, STATEN ISLAND

This church was erected in 1706 by an organization of Huguenots. It numbers among its cherished relics the original charter of the parish, old prayer books, a silver communion service, and an old bell sent by Queen Anne at the time she sent the Rev. Eneas Makenzie to serve as its first regular pastor. Previous to that the congregation had been served by a chaplain from the fort on Manhattan Island, who visited them from time to time to hold religious service in French, or for their Dutch neighbors in the language of the Netherlands, the form of worship being in either case that of the Church of England.

A second church was erected in 1713, partly through the generosity of a joint land donation from Adolphus Philipse and Ebenezer Wilson, then "Mayor of New York." The present building, also erected in pre-Revolutionary times, occupies the site of the original church.

[230]

JOHN STREET METHODIST CHURCH, NEW YORK CITY.   Erected 1758.   (See page 231)

JOHN STREET METHODIST CHURCH

NEW YORK CITY

American Methodism recognizes as one of its oldest sites that on which the John Street Methodist Episcopal Church stood, built in 1768, by Philip Embury, a carpenter from Ireland. A later building took its place. This in turn was torn down in 1818 to give place to the present building in 1848. Its extreme simplicity was in keeping with a provision in the Discipline, reading:—

> "Let all churches be built plain and decent and with free seats as far as possible; but not more expensive than is absolutely unavoidable; otherwise the necessity of raising money will make rich men necessary to us, and if dependent upon them and governed by them, then farewell Methodist discipline, if not doctrine too."

Methodism was long ago solicitous not to be known as a rich man's church.

The structure built by Embury was the first Methodist preaching house in America, but St. George's, Philadelphia, is the oldest still standing. The one to which we now refer, was of ballasted stone covered outside with stucco, and whitewashed inside, built at an estimated cost of some six hundred pounds sterling. The high pulpit, resting on a single pillar, was reached by a winding stair. The fronts of the gallery and altar were white. A plain carpet covered the altar and pulpit stairs. In the altar were two wooden benches, a few chairs and a plain table. Lamps with sperm oil provided light, and round, high stoves, heat. The book board was without cushion and the floor uncarpeted. The windows had green blinds outside and on the men's side were rows of pegs on the wall for their hats. The seats were wooden benches with narrow strips for the backs.

If a man, arriving late, entered the women's side, the sexton would order him to his own side even during the service.

What is known as the "Old Book" of John Street carries some curious and interesting facts. Among these, are items for care of Preacher Williams' horse, cost £3/16/1, and a feather bed and bolster £7/16/4; clothing for Boardman £7/10, and to carry him to Philadelphia £2. Another charge is for a top hat for the preacher.

Robert Strawbridge, Embury's associate, who like himself had come to the New World "driven not by persecution but by necessity of seeking more adequate income for his family," after putting together a cabin for his family at Sam's Creek, Maryland, next built a log Meeting House, the first place of Methodist worship in Maryland.

CHRIST CHURCH
SHREWSBURY, N. J.

This church, erected July 21, 1769, was organized by the Missionary Society of the English Church with difficulty because of the strong feeling of the independent Quakers, Presbyterians and Baptists of the community against the Established Church and remains a triumph over early parish struggles.

OLD TENNENT CHURCH

MONMOUTH BATTLEFIELD, N. J.

About 1692, a sturdy body of Scotch Covenanters erected a rough log church at Wickatunk, New Jersey, cutting the lumber for it in the forest about them. It was known as the Old Scot's Meeting House. In 1731 they deserted their first church and built another about five miles south, on White Hill, so called because of the number of white oak trees that grew thickly about it. One of these trees still stands.

The first acre of ground for this church was obtained from William Ker for "the sum of one shilling, current money of the province," and the deed is still preserved. The new church, which was destined to become one of the most historic in America, was forty feet long and thirty feet wide, with galleries. The communion table from the first church was taken to it, and it is there yet. Its pastor was the Rev. John Tennent, whose ministry was brief, for he died in 1732. He was succeeded by his brother William, who served it for forty-three years.

How William was led to enter the ministry through his visions during a remarkable trance is one of the cherished traditions of this church. He always averred that in that trance he visited Heaven and witnessed the glories of which he so ably preached for many years.

Its first charter was granted in 1750 under King George II. In 1751 the new and present building was erected to accommodate the steadily growing congregation. This building is just twice the dimensions of its predecessor, but with interior virtually unchanged. It

[233]

is of the solid and enduring white oak that grew by its side, sheathed with cedar shingles, with a high, steeply slanted roof and neat little spire of colonial design.

The Rev. William Tennent lived to see his country declare itself free from the Mother Country, but not to see his beloved church the center of a bloody and important battle. He died in 1777, and was buried under the center of the floor because it was feared that if placed in the churchyard his staunch support of the patriot cause might lead to the desecration of his grave by the British.

It was on an intensely hot day, June 28, 1778, that through Washington's strategy the British faced disaster, only to find relief and the opportunity to escape through the blundering of General Charles Lee, and it was in the shadow of Old Tennent that the Great Commander lost his temper and roundly cursed his subordinate.

The wounded of both sides were carried into the church and laid upon the pews, some to have their hurts dressed and be started on the road to recovery, and some to die. Under the cushions of some of the pews the stains of their blood are still to be seen. The dead were buried in the yard that now stretches its broad and tenderly cared-for acres in all directions. Among them was the brave young English officer, Lieutenant-Colonel Henry Monckton. Half a century later William D. Wilson, a Scotchman, who had become a school teacher in the vicinity, erected a board tablet over the grave. Later this was replaced by a tombstone by Samuel Fryer. Since 1913 his grave has been decorated by the British Flag every Memorial Day, an attention which brought forth grateful acknowledgment

OLD TENNENT CHURCH, from an old engraving.

OLD TENNENT CHURCH, MONMOUTH BATTLEFIELD, N. J. *(See page 233)*

from the 7th Viscount Galway, the dead soldier having been the second son of the first to bear that title.

Less than a mile away from the church is the well from which Molly Pitcher drew water which she carried to the American gunners, only to take the place of her husband when he fell overcome by the intense heat.

Old Tennent still carries the bullet holes made in it during the battle. One of Washington's chaplains, the Rev. Dr. John Woodhull, who participated in the battle, the next year was called to take the pulpit that had been vacant since the death of Dr. Tennent, and Dr. Woodhull remained for forty-five years, or until his death, November 22, 1824.

In 1786 the church was re-incorporated under the laws of New Jersey. In 1859 its corporate name was made "The First Presbyterian Church of the County of Monmouth." In October, 1920, the title was legally changed to "Old Tennent Church."

Until 1815 there were no stoves in the church, the worshippers keeping themselves warm with their own foot warmers, or tin-lined boxes holding pans of live coals covered with some ashes.

One of the features of this church is the New Endowment Plan, by which persons or organizations may endow a pew in honor of some friend or distinguished citizen. Among those so honored are George Washington, the Rev. William Tennent, General Bartolome Mitre, first President of the Republic of Argentina, General Ulysses S. Grant, President Roosevelt, Herbert Ward, the English explorer, Captain Louis L. Lefebvre, Governor Franklin Fort, of New Jersey, and Governor John W. Dana, of Maine.

"Old Tennent" is the Mecca of thousands of visitors every year and is well worth a visit.

OLD DUTCH SLEEPY HOLLOW CHURCH

TARRYTOWN, N. Y.

It stands on a knoll surrounded by locust trees, almost
rectangular, hip roof, small belfry, and at either end
vanes as old as itself.—*Irving*.

Conspicuous among the old buildings of Tarrytown, N. Y., made famous by Washington Irving's
"Sleepy Hollow," are the Dutch Reformed Church,
dating from 1685, and the Flypse Manor House erected
a few years earlier. This venerable church owes its
origin to Vredyk Flypse, known as the "Dutch Millionaire," a carpenter who became wealthy in fur trading, and the owner of large tracts of land along the
Hudson. The bricks in the chimney, the little flat yellow bricks around the windows, and its bell were
brought over from Holland in his own trading vessels,
the old Burgher having established a substantial trade
between New Amsterdam and England and Holland.
In 1697, the Rev. Guiliam Berthoff came from Holland
to serve as the pastor of the Pocantico Church, so called
from the river by which the church, the Manor House,
and the Flypse Mill stood.

Walls of stone thirty inches thick insured the per-
manency of the Sleepy Hollow Church. Windows
seven feet above the ground were protected from the
Indians with iron bars. The interior was simply
fitted with a huge pulpit and sounding board, and seats
without backs, except those on either side of the pulpit,
which were originally intended for the members and

OLD DUTCH CHURCH AT TARRYTOWN, N. Y.
Made famous by Washington Irving's "Sleepy Hollow"

guests of the Manor House and were later appropriated by the elders and deacons. A gallery was provided for slaves and "redemptioners," the latter poor settlers who had sold their services in payment of passage over. The historic bell bears the title "Si Deus pro nobis, quis contra nos." Services are open to visitors during the late Summer and early Fall.

A plate in the west wall of this quaint church says:—"Built in 1699," but the little bell in the belfry is inscribed "Amsterdam 1685," and coffins beneath the floor bear plates dated from 1650 to 1660, so that the conclusion is that it was built earlier or else there was an earlier church.

The First Reformed Church of Tarrytown, which now owns "Old Sleepy Hollow," has in its possession the old communion table brought from England— massive oak inlaid with ebony—solid-silver beakers, two plates, and a baptismal bowl, the gift of its founder and his wife, Frederick Phillip, "Carpenter from Friesland," and Catherine Van Cortlandt.

In the graveyard of this church, "Sleepy Hollow Cemetery," with numerous moss-covered stones inscribed with epitaphs in the old Dutch language, lies Washington Irving. There rests also an old sailor, buried in 1768, who, evidently, judging from the homely, home-made poetry on his tombstone, had navigated the seven seas in the days of the clipper ships. It reads:—

> Boisterous Winds and Neptune's Waves
> Have tost me to and fro
> By God's Decree, you can plainly see,
> I'm harboured here below.

OLD SWEDES' CHURCH
WILMINGTON, DEL.

Six days labored the folks, and when rose the sun of the
    Sabbath,
Rifle and plough were dropped, and the wheel stood
    still in its corner,
Then from near and from far, to the Churches three of
    the province,
One at Tinicum, one at Wicaco, one at Christina,
Gathered the congregation's God-fearing men and their
    households.

—*"Songs of New Sweden," Arthur Peterson.*

William Usselincx, founder of the Dutch West Indian Company, which had figured in the colonization of the New World, withdrew from that organization because, it is surmised, he was unable to contribute sufficent money to obtain a dominating share in it. He thoroughly understood the project, and in 1624 went to Stockholm and with little difficulty interested King Gustavus Adolphus in his plans. These involved organizing a trading company along the lines of the Dutch concern, and the King readily assented.

In fact, the King grew enthusiastic over the project of planting colonies on the Delaware, extending his own kingdom and influence as well as carrying the Gospel to heathen lands. He proposed the founding of a free state, "where the laborer should reap the fruits of his toil, and where the rights of conscience should be inviolate." But before he could accomplish much, Gustavus Adolphus was drawn into the Thirty Years War, and fell, in his moment of victory, at Lutzen, in 1632, leaving his little daughter Christina to reign, un-

Old Swedes' Church, Wilmington, Del.

der the guidance of the astute Chancellor Oxenstierna. One of his last acts was to urge that the colonization plan be carried out.

Oxenstierna acted promptly on behalf of his young charge and Queen. Usselincx was made director of the company and assured of a royalty of a tenth of one percent on the company's traffic, and Peter Minuet was selected to command the first expedition. Minuet passed up the Delaware and landed at the Minquas Creek, where he immediately began the erection of a fort, within which were a church, store and houses. Minuet called the colony New Sweden, the fort, Fort Christina, and the creek, the Elbe; but the people called the latter the Kristina Kill, from which is derived the name it now bears, Christiana Creek. From this center the Swedes tilled the soil of Pennsylvania, Delaware and even New Jersey, and from it grew Delaware's chief city, Wilmington.

On or near this site, some sixty years later, was dedicated on Trinity Sunday, 1699, Holy Trinity Church, "Old Swedes'", one of the three early Swedish Lutheran Churches springing from the original fort church, and claiming the distinction of being among the oldest active places of worship in the United States. The site and the glebe for the church were donated by John Jacob Statcop, one of the church wardens. The building, a notable example of early Colonial architecture, whose builder and architect was the Rev. Eric Bjork, a Swedish Lutheran priest and Provost of the Swedish Church of Christina, commemorated relationship between the church in America and in Sweden, and the leaders of the Thirty Years War.

[239]

The pews were not distributed according to worldly possession or social position, but in honor of the length of time and the importance of service given by pew holders, to the erection of the church, the pews descending from generation to generation.

With the exception of the strengthening of the walls in 1750, "Old Swedes' " remains today much as when originally constructed. The town, first known as Fort Christina, later was named Willingston in honor of Thomas Willing, and from this was evolved Wilmington. Thomas Willing was the owner of a large tract joining the church glebe, and a devout parishioner.

In 1758, when applying for a new minister from the homeland, the church requested that he "might occasionally preach in English, as Swedes and English were so intermingled that it was necessary that religious instruction be given in both languages." In 1789, it followed that "Old Swedes' ", up to that time under the jurisdiction of the Swedish Lutheran Church, became a parish of the English Church, so largely had the proportion of its English-speaking people increased since 1748, when it began alternating services in the English and Swedish languages.

In its churchyard lie the dead of many generations and of almost every religious denomination, some 16,000 persons, many of them pre-Revolutionary. The oldest tombstone is dated 1656. A whole section is devoted to graves of French refugees who fled here from San Domingo before the Revolution. Among those resting in this old churchyard is Bishop Alfred Lee, prominent in ecclesiastical history, who as a tribute to his knowledge of Holy Scripture, served on the

American Committee for the Revision of the King James Bible.

On June 15, 1924, the church celebrated its two hundred and twenty-fifth anniversary. In connection therewith a writer in the Philadelphia Evening Bulletin on June 12, said:

> The church is a precious gem of ancient Swedish Church architecture, little changed by time except for the subtle charm that only great age can bring. The walls are heavy gray stones, unrelieved by ornamentation inside and out. The church floor is heavy, red brick, while the oak high-back box pews lend the last sombre touch to the interior.
>
> Wandering out of the Churchyard the pilgrimage ends by the back of the Christina River, at the steamboat landing, where the old rock upon which the Swedish settlers landed on March 29, 1638, is preserved behind an iron railing. It stands near the old entrance of Fort Christina, about which the life of the early settlement was grouped. Here the Old Swedes' Church had its beginnings, in a log chapel standing nearby, which has long since disappeared, like the race of sturdy men who lived through those first bleak winters of gloomy fortitude.

In his "The Children of the Lord's Supper," Longfellow pictures the First Communion as celebrated by the Swedes, a beautiful reminiscence of early Swedish church days and customs in the New World.

GLORIA DEI (OLD SWEDES')
CHURCH
PHILADELPHIA

In spite of constant conflict between the Swedes and the Dutch, with the English eventually joining in, the Swedes slowly extended their settlements and influence, eventually erecting a settlement at Wicaco, now part of Philadelphia. There was no church near it, and in 1675 Governor Andros ordered that one should be built there. The site selected was what is now Christian and Swanson Streets, and the Rev. Jacobus Frabitius was assigned to its pulpit. It was Philadelphia's first House of Christian Worship and first clergyman to minister to the spiritual needs of its people.

This pioneer of churches in Penn's "towne" was as much a fort as a place of devotion. It was built on the order of a block house, from which, if occasion arose, the worshippers might protect themselves from savage Indians—a necessity, however, that seldom, if ever, arose.

In 1696, at the request of many of the Swedish settlers along the Delaware for clergymen, King Charles IX directed Dr. Olaus Suebilus, Archbishop of Upsal, to assign two, and equip them with supplies of Bibles, prayer books, hymnals, etc. The Archbishop thereupon sent the Revs. Eric Bjork and Andrew Rudman to assume charge of the churches at Christina and Wicaco, and the Rev. Jonas Auren to study and make a report on colonial conditions and needs. Mr. Rudman assumed the Wicaco pulpit; Mr. Bjork the Christina. Their letters home showed keen enthusiasm over their

GLORIA DEI (Old Swedes') CHURCH, PHILADELPHIA.

tasks and great admiration for the lovely land to which they had been sent.

About 1698 the block house church at Wicaco was burned, and while an effort was made by some members to have a new church erected elsewhere, it was eventually decided that the old site was best and the present edifice was built in 1700 and opened for worship July 2 of that year. The ground occupied by the church and burial ground was donated by the widow and daughters of Sven Svenson, from whom they had inherited it, and from whom the street was named.

This church was named Gloria Dei. It is of stone and brick. At first it had a low tower but no spire, and the porches were not built until 1703. The spire was added when the church acquired a bell already old. The present bell bears this inscription:

> Cast for the Swedish Church in Philadelphia
> Styled "Gloria Dei,"
> Partly from the old bell dated 1643
> I to the Church the living call
> And to the grave do summon all.

In June, 1719, the church bought twenty-five adjacent acres from Martha Cock for ninety pounds. Later it acquired ninety-six acres on the Schuylkill River banks. Had the church held possession of this property it would today be very rich and growing richer, although the lands have not acquired anything like the value of those held by Trinity Church, New York. But poor business management brought about their loss as the years rolled by.

In 1703, the Swedish King sent to the church a quantity of Bibles, prayer and hymn books and other religious equipment.

English settlers began to attend services in Gloria Dei, and Dr. Bjork came to summarize his sermons in their language. As early as 1710 the congregation lent their church to the English, who as a mark of appreciation sang their first hymn there in Swedish. In the course of time, as the English population grew and the Swedish waned, the English came more and more to use it, and in 1831, it became a regular church of the Protestant Episcopal denomination.

In the churchyard lie many of Philadelphia's earliest residents, and some of considerable distinction. Among the latter is that eminent ornithologist, Alexander Wilson, who expressed a desire that his body lie there "so that he would forever lie in a silent, secluded place where birds would always sing above his grave."

The birds sing above him, but his tomb is neither silent nor secluded, for a stone's throw away great steamships from distant lands now discharge or take on their cargoes and their myriads of travelers; the mighty river teems with traffic, and great trains virtually pass its doors to convey the discharged cargoes to their several railroad lines, thence to distribute them throughout the land.

Gloria Dei is its official title, but to Philadelphians it is ever affectionately known as Old Swedes', and is one of the most cherished possessions of that city of Penn that is so much richer than all its American sisters in historic treasures.

> There, as she mounted the stair to the corridor cooled
>   by the East Wind,
> Distant and soft on her ear fell the chimes from the
>   belfry of Christ Church,
> While intermingled with them across the meadows
>   were wafted

INTERIOR OF GLORIA DEI (Old Swedes') PHILADELPHIA. (*See page 242*)

Sounds of psalms that were sung by the Swedes in
their church at Wicaco.

—"*Evangeline,*" *Longfellow.*

SWAMP CHURCH

NEW HANOVER, PA.

This church, on or near the site of the original church
at Falkner's Swamp, bears the distinction of being the
House of Worship of the oldest German Lutheran congregation in the United States, according to the report
of the pastors of the United Congregation in Pennsylvania to the authorities in Halle. Previous to the erection of the first church, completed in 1703, the congregation had been gathered and services held with more
or less regularity, probably from 1694.

The primitive church remained in use until 1721,
when it was replaced by one more commodious, which
served until 1747. The fourth and present building
was erected in 1768. It was considered of such importance that the Synod met at New Hanover, November 6, 1747, to take part in the festivities of the dedication.

German immigrants had been arriving in America
singly and in groups for fifty years prior to 1700, and
after Penn's coming they began to arrive in larger numbers. But as early as 1638, fifty-four German families
settled chiefly at Olney and Falkner's Swamp, so named
for the Rev. Daniel Falkner, who led a large number of
them into the new land as the representative of the
Frankfort Land Company. These formed the nucleus
of the Swamp congregation, of which Falkner was the
pastor, the first of a German Lutheran congregation in
America.

MERION AND HAVERFORD MEETINGS

In the immediate vicinity of Philadelphia there are many Friends' Meeting Houses, and two of these bear the distinction of being the only buildings in the world in which William Penn himself preached.

The first of these, and probably the oldest in the world, is the Merion. This was built in 1695 by Welsh Quakers in Lower Merion Township, Montgomery County. It is at the corner of Montgomery Avenue and Meeting House lane, on the opposite side of the former from the borough of Narberth, and in it is still the wooden peg upon which the great Founder was accustomed to hang his hat. It is a tiny structure of stone.

The second is Haverford, which lies south of that suburb. It was built in 1700 and enlarged a century later. While larger than the Merion Meeting, it is still small, and if anything, plainer.

Still a third of these ancient Meetings is that of Radnor, at Ithan, built in 1718. It is larger than its neighbors in which the founder preached, and like them and all others erected by followers of George Fox, built to last apparently forever, of substantial lumber and enduring stone.

In connection with Friends' Meeting Houses, the following from Lippincott's "Early Philadelphia" is both informing and apropos:

Philadelphia owes its origin to religious persecution. It was undertaken as a "Holy Experiment." Penn went about the colonization of his province

FRIENDS' MEETING HOUSE, MERION, PA.
One of the only two buildings standing in the world in which
William Penn preached.

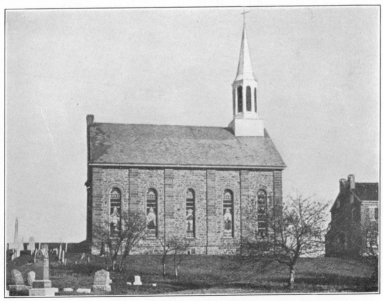

SWAMP CHURCH, NEW HANOVER, PA. *(See page 245)*
Oldest German Lutheran Congregation in the United States.

in a business-like way and with great advertising skill. He issued a series of immigration pamphlets in the interest of his project with a scrupulous regard for true statements and simple facts without exaggeration. He described the plentifulness of timber, game, and commodities, and granted all legislative power to the people and government. No law was to be made or money raised but by the people's consent.

It is plain to be seen what a sensible man Penn was and how earnestly he hoped for the success of his "Holy Experiment" without great material gain for himself. He described what to take on the journey, its cost, and what was first to be done on arrival. This was serious business, a journey in a little boat for two months on a great sea to an almost unknown wilderness, and they must not delude themselves with an expectation of "An ImmediateAmendment of their Conditions."

Indeed, he says, they must be willing to do without conveniences for two or three years. The passage money was six pounds a head for masters, five for servants and fifty shillings for children under seven years.

The earliest emigrants arrived before Philadelphia was surveyed. They stopped at Upland, now Chester, which was peopled by the Swedes and some English Quakers from Jersey. Philadelphia was located in 1683, "having a high and dry bank next to the water, with a shore ornamented with a fine view of pine trees growing upon it." In this bank they made caves to shelter their families and belongings and then went out into the wilderness with a warrant of survey to choose their land.

Upon his return to England in 1685 Penn wrote a further description of the province, telling of the divers collection of European nations represented there—French, Dutch, Germans, Swedes, Danes, Finns, Scotch, Irish, English, "and of the last equal to all the rest."

Much must be said about the Quakers. The province was theirs and they controlled, for nearly one hundred years, down to the summer of 1776, its policy and legislation. They were a solid lot, slow but sure, and in any account of the early city obviously became the most conspicuous of the diversified elements of the people. The other groups were for the first seventy years fewer in numbers. Many of the settlers, the German and Scotch-Irish particularly, went off into the wilderness of the frontier to live by themselves, leaving the Quakers in undisturbed control of politics.

Whittier, the "Quaker Poet" who quitted New England for some three years in the late 1830's to live in Philadelphia, and edit an anti-slavery paper, also wrote hymns, which have passed into general use, even among the Friends, who are not much given to hymn singing. Among his most popular hymns is:

> We may not climb the heavenly steeps,
> To bring the Lord Christ down,
> In vain we search the lowest deeps
> For Him no depths can drown.
> But warm, sweet, tender even yet
> A present help is He
> And faith has still its Olivet
> And love its Galilee.

While in Philadelphia, Whittier usually attended services at the Friends' Meeting House on Twelfth Street, near Market, which is still standing in the heart of a business section.

CHRIST CHURCH, PHILADELPHIA. *(See page 249)*
From an old etching

Where Washington with members of the First and Second Continental
Congresses of America worshipped and where Washington later attended
while President of the United States.

CHRIST CHURCH

PHILADELPHIA

In the days of William Penn the established church of England was not well represented in the colonies. Although English settlements were scattered all along the coast, there were few churches of that denomination and no resident clergymen at all. The chaplain at the fort in New York traveled about and did the best he could, but that, under the circumstances, was very little. In 1695, therefore, the Bishop of London sent the Rev. Thomas Clayton to Philadelphia to look over the field and do what was possible to establish the church.

Mr. Clayton found fifty adherents of the Church of England, which number rapidly swelled to seven hundred. The year of his arrival he and his parishioners built a modest little church on a lot near a duck pond, the site that is now at the northwest corner of Second and Church Streets, above Market, in the heart of the wholesale business district.

It wasn't business then, but a few residences were in its immediate vicinity and farms near by. This church had a seating capacity of five hundred. The founder and first rector did not live long to prosecute his labors, dying of yellow fever in Baltimore in 1699. The Bishop of London sent the Rev. Evan Evans to take his place, and under Mr. Evans the church grew and prospered. In 1702, it acquired a bell, and in 1708 built a belfry to hold it. Mr. Evans in that year visited England and brought back with him as a gift from Queen Anne, a full set of church plate. The flagon and chalice carry the inscription, "Anna Regina, in usum Ecclesiae Anglicanae apud Philadelphiam, A.D., 1708."

In 1711 the church building was enlarged and ninety pounds were realized from the sale of new pews.

The church suffered its second bereavement, this time in a highly dramatic manner, when the earnest and energetic rector, Mr. Evans, stricken with apoplexy in the midst of his sermon, fell dead in the pulpit. He was buried in the church and his body lies there yet.

When the church was enlarged in 1711, Governor Sir William Keith became a vestryman, and established a permanent "Governor's pew." Some of the city's most eminent citizens became members.

Until 1719, burials were in the yard adjoining the church, but this being small, a substantial burial plot was purchased at the corner of Fifth and Arch Streets, and it is in the corner of this that lie the bodies of Benjamin Franklin and Deborah, his wife, an iron fence there breaking the brick wall, that the passing people may see the grave.

When the Rev. Archibald Cummings assumed the rectorship in 1726, plans were laid to erect a new church building, and Dr. John Kearsley was not only the architect, but superintended the construction. The cornerstone was laid April 27, 1727, but it was not completed until 1744, and the tower and spire were not finished until ten years later, when the now famous chime of eight bells was installed. The bells were brought from England by Captain Budden, of the ship "Myrtilla," who charged no freight on them; hence whenever his ship arrived in port they rang a merry welcome to him. During the Revolution these

INTERIOR OF CHRIST CHURCH, PHILADELPHIA. (See page 249)

bells were carried to Allentown and hidden until after the British troops left Philadelphia.

The beautiful and dignified structure having been restored in 1882 (alterations having been made in 1836), is today virtually as it was when in 1754 the tower and steeple completed it. These, by the way, are at the rear of the building. The cost of building the spire and tower and installing the chimes was raised through a lottery, a form of gambling at that time, and until more than a century later, a legitimate form of business.

On July 20, 1775 the Continental Congress attended services in Christ Church in a body. George Washington attended whenever he was in the city, and regularly while there as President. On July 4, 1776, when the State House Bell (now affectionately known throughout the land as the Liberty Bell) started a joyous clanging to announce the adoption of the Declaration of Independence, the chimes of Christ Church quickly joined.

In the yard adjoining the church lie the bodies of several signers of the Declaration of Independence, including Robert Morris and James Wilson, the latter having been brought from the south about 1908 by his biographer, Burton Alvah Konkle, of Swarthmore.

ST. GEORGE'S METHODIST EPISCOPAL CHURCH

PHILADELPHIA

Philadelphia boasts the possession of the oldest Methodist Episcopal Church building in the world, in St. George's, Fourth Street below Vine.

The preaching of George Whitefield, who went through the colonies about 1738, winning tremendous success and many converts by his ministrations, planted the seeds of Methodism in this country, but as he died soon after his return to England, no effort was made to establish a church here for approximately thirty years. In 1768 came Captain Thomas Webb, a British Army officer, licensed by the Rev. John Wesley, founder of Methodism, to preach. He started with a class of seven, and services were held in the loft of a sailmaker's shop near the drawbridge that spanned Dock Creek at Front Street.

For a year the loft was occupied, and then came Messrs. Boardman and Pilmore, also sent by Wesley, to conduct services in New York and Philadelphia, Mr. Pilmore being assigned to the latter city. He began preaching from the State House steps, and later addressed large audiences in Centre Square, where City Hall now stands.

At that time the members of the German Reformed Church of St. George were building a church, the cornerstone of which had been laid in 1763, and had nearly completed it when in November, 1769, they were compelled for financial reasons to give up the enterprise. The building was purchased by Miles Penn-

St. George's Methodist Episcopal Church, Philadelphia.
Oldest Methodist Episcopal Church building in the world.

ington, a member of the new church, who promptly conveyed it to the Methodist Society for six hundred and fifty pounds, and it was immediately occupied. Since that time it has functioned regularly. For a while the congregation gave no name to their church, but as it had become known as St. George's, they at last decided to let the name stand.

In 1771 Bishop Francis Asbury, the first Bishop of the Methodist Church in America, arrived from England and preached his first sermon on American soil in St. George's. In July 1773 the first annual Methodist Conference in America was held in the church. It consisted of nine ministers, of whom only six took appointments, and circuits were organized covering Eastern Pennsylvania, New Jersey, Delaware, Maryland and New York City. The next two years the annual conferences were also held in St. George's, but owing to war conditions, that of 1776 was held in Baltimore.

The twentieth century was little more than a score of years old when construction of a bridge across the Delaware River, a project that had been talked of off and on for a century, was actually begun. This $39,-000,000 structure is nearly two miles long, and when the plans were revealed, to the horror of the then powerful Methodist Church, it was found that Old St. George's was partly on the line, and the entire church would have to go. But so great was the historical importance with which the building was regarded, the plans of the mighty engineering project were slightly altered, so that the building could be saved. Then it was announced that because the noise of passing traffic would interfere with services, the church would not be used for public worship, but would be preserved as a shrine of Methodism. *It is used*

FIRST PRESBYTERIAN CHURCH
ELIZABETH, N. J.

This oldest English-speaking church in the State, had its first building in 1666—a commodious and substantial edifice in good condition a century later. To its pastor, the Rev. James Caldwell, who served as chaplain to the New Jersey regiments, General Washington paid the rare compliment, "No man in New Jersey has contributed so much toward giving direction and energy to the thoughts and movements of her citizenry."

A new church, occupying the site of the first, succeeded it. This was set on fire in 1780 by a British emissary.

In the churchyard lies "Fighting Parson Caldwell" beside his wife, both shot from ambush while engaged in service for "both their country and their God."

On the walls of its recently added choir room may be read the inscriptions on two old tombstones embedded there, this means being taken to avoid disturbing the old graves.

THE FIRST REFORMED CHURCH

IN PHILADELPHIA, PA.

The First Reformed Church of Philadelphia may rightly be said to date its beginning to the arrival of the sloop, "William and Mary," which anchored in the Delaware River, at Philadelphia, on September 21, 1727. The list of passengers, as listed by the government officials, is headed by the name of George Michael Weiss, V.D.M.,—*i. e.*, Minister of the Word of God. Upon his arrival, he immediately set about the task of gathering the scattered members of the Reformed Church, whom, with those in his own party, he organized into a permanent congregation the same year. The charter, secured a few years later, which is still in possession of the congregation, is a large and detailed document, signed by John Penn.

In the year 1730, Mr. Weiss returned to Holland, and Rev. John Philip Boehm entered upon a pastorate which continued until 1746. The congregation at this time worshiped in an old frame house, near the Delaware River, alternating on Sundays with the Lutherans. But after the Lutherans built their own Church in 1744, the Reformed congregation rented a small Church-house, on Arch Street, from one William Allen for the extravagant sum of $20 a year. Here the Church continued to worship until December 6, 1747, when the Church which was erected on Sassafras (Race) Street, near Fourth Street, was dedicated and used for the first time. This building was very quaint in appearance. It was a brick structure, hexagonal in form, and with a hipped-roof which sloped from each of the

[255]

six sides to the cupola. It soon became apparent that the old hexagonal building was too small for the constantly increasing attendance, and, on May 1, 1774, a new Church upon the same site was opened and dedicated.

This Church building was ninety feet long and sixty-five feet wide. Concerning its size, Charles G. Finney, who held revival services in it during 1828, has this to say in his autobiography: "In Race Street there was a large German Church . . . Their house was then, I think, the largest house of worship in the city. It was always crowded, and it was said that it seated 3,000 people, when it was packed and the aisles were filled." That the location was a noisy one is evident from the fact that they were accustomed to stretch a chain across the street in front of the Church during the time of service in order to keep vehicles from passing; and in 1837 the building was moved farther back in the lot in order that the services might be more quietly conducted.

Race Street and its vicinity kept growing busier and noisier as a result of the influx of trade and the establishment of warehouses and, after another generation had passed, the congregation moved to Tenth and Wallace Streets in 1882. Here the congregation worshiped until 1915, when, following the tide of population, it moved to its new site at Fiftieth and Locust Streets, where in March, 1925, it dedicated a modern building at a cost of $200,000.

CONGREGATION MICHVEH ISRAEL

PHILADELPHIA

Benjamin Franklin in his autobiography alludes to
Samuel Keimer, a native of England, by whom he was
employed in 1723,—a printer and the publisher of the
Pennsylvania Gazette, who "wore the long beard and
kept the Jewish Sabbath with greatest strictness." Official documents of 1725 refer to Arnold Bamberger, a
Philadelphia Hebrew who "held lands and trade."

Further early records relate that as early as 1747, a
number of Hebrews who had joined together for the
purpose of divine worship, met for services in a small
house in Sterling Alley. At this spot they seem to have
remained until the outbreak of the Revolution, when
their membership was increased by some who were
forced to quit New York City after the occupation by
the British soldiers. The house in Sterling Alley was
no longer of sufficient size to accommodate the growing
numbers, and so the congregation moved to a house in
Cherry Street, where a room of the second story was
fitted up for Hebrew worship. This house became in-
adequate, and a meeting was convened on March 24,
1782, by Isaac Moses, to consider means for the purchase of ground on which a suitable synagogue might
be erected. The Synagogue in Cherry Street, the cornerstone of which was laid Tamuz 6, 5542 (June 19,
1782), and which had a seating capacity of about two
hundred, was completed at a cost of 1815 pounds sterling.

The following curious description of this church appears in Dr. Mease's "Picture of Philadelphia," August, 1830:

"A Synagogue, situated on the North Side of Cherry Street, above Third Street, is forty feet in front by seventy feet in depth, being two stories in height, built in Egyptian style of stone from the Falls of Schuylkill. The principal entrance is through an elevated doorway, formed with inclined jambs, supporting a large covered cornice, in which are scultpured the globe and wings. The interior embraces two semi-circular blocks of seats, displaying to the North and South the Ark and the Altar. The dome is supported with Egyptian columns copied from the temple at Tentyra. . . . In the center of the dome is a lantern which gives light to the Altar.

"The Ark is situated immediately opposite the Altar and is neatly decorated with pilasters, supporting a covered cornice, enriched with the globe and wings, together with a marble tablet, containing the Ten Commandments in Hebrew. It is approached by a flight of three steps between symmetrical blocks, which support two handsome tripods crowned with lamps. The galleries are semi-circular, supported by columns, which extend to the dome."

Congregation Michveh Israel included in its numbers then, as it has ever since, men who rose high in the community, and in serving the State and nation, men of true patriotism, whose acts tested their devotion to the cause of the young Republic and its institutions.

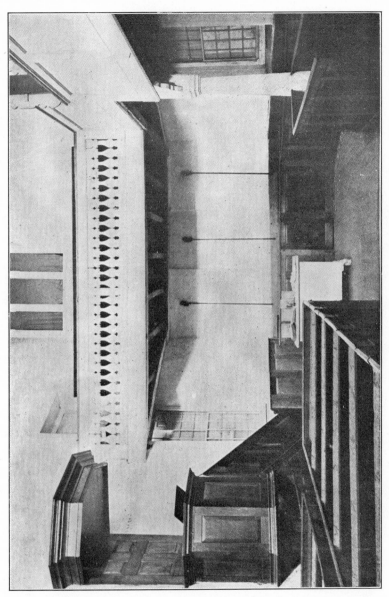

AUGUSTUS LUTHERAN CHURCH, TRAPPE, PA. (*See page 259*). Oldest Lutheran Church in America.

AUGUSTUS LUTHERAN CHURCH
TRAPPE, PA.

The Stone Church (Augustus Church) at Trappe, Pa., is celebrated as the oldest Lutheran Church in America.

The first traces of congregational life are found in a baptismal record of March 8, 1730, in the handwriting of John Casper Stoever, Jr. Henry Melchior Muhlenberg, the first regular pastor, preached his initial sermon in a barn December 12, 1742. On January 5, 1743, the congregation decided to erect a church building, at which time a log schoolhouse had already been erected, which Muhlenberg himself, as the first teacher, opened January 10, 1743. Plans for the church building were sent to Germany for confirmation. It was to be constructed of stone, fifty-four "shoes" long by thirty-nine wide, and to cost two hundred pounds sterling.

On May 2, 1743, when the cornerstone was laid, Muhlenberg preached in German and made an address in English. The service opened with the old German hymn, "Commend thy Ways and all that grieves thy heart to God." The congregation worshipped within the bare walls of the new church for the first time on September 12, and two years later, when it was completely paid for, it was dedicated October 6, 1745, at which time the dedicatory stone was placed over the south entrance, where it still remains. The original floor consisted of native stones, laid on the ground. It was covered with straw in winter, and there were no stoves. In 1814, a wooden floor was laid.

The gallery on the east side was erected in 1751, to receive the pipe organ, purchased in Europe. Henry Melchior Muhlenberg married Anna Maria Weiser, daughter of Conrad Weiser, Government interpreter and Indian agent.

On September 19, 1777, Washington's army passed the church, one regiment encamping in front of Muhlenberg's house nearby. On September 26, General Armstrong took up his headquarters in the church and the schoolhouse.

After the Battle of Germantown, October 4, 1777, the church was used as a hospital, and the next day Washington visited the wounded soldiers. The old church still stands in its original condition, a Mecca for historians and churchmen alike.

It was Dr. Muhlenberg's son, the Rev. John Peter Muhlenberg, who, exactly one hundred and fifty years ago, preached a most stirring sermon in his church at Woodstock, Va. He closed his discourse at that time by saying—"There is a time to pray and a time to fight; and this is the time to fight." Throwing back his vestments, he stood forth clad in the uniform of a Colonel of the Continental Army and called for volunteers. That day witnessed the recruiting of between 700 and 800 men, the nucleus of the Virginia State militia. Later he became a Major-General.

General Muhlenberg while in winter camp at Valley Forge several times preached in the old Stone Church at Trappe. After the Revolution, he served as a member of the First and Third Congresses; Vice President of Pennsylvania under the Supreme Executive Council, 1787-1788; United States Senator from Pennsylvania; Supervisor of Internal Revenue and Collector of the Port of Philadelphia.

BAPTIST TEMPLE
PHILADELPHIA

One of the largest and most notable churches in Philadelphia was built on a capital of fifty-seven cents.

Moreover there has grown out of this church several other churches, three hospitals and a great University. It is not an old church at that; but what it lacks in age it makes up in achievement, and the mighty things it has done have been due to the genius, devotion and indomitable energy of the superman at its head.

In 1871, a number of Baptists living in a growing neighborhood with no church of their denomination near, organized the Grace Baptist Church. They procured a lot on the northeast corner of Mervine and Berks Streets, and for months held services there in a tent. Presently they began to build a church of stone, but funds ran low when the walls were up, so a temporary wooden roof was placed upon it, and for some years this served until the money was obtained to put a real roof on and thus complete the building.

For ten years the church thrived under three pastors in succession. The congregation, its pulpit vacated by death, sought some one to fill it, and selected a hustling young man of thirty-eight years who was preaching in a small Massachusetts town. His name was Russell H. Conwell.

This young man was a native of Massachusetts. At nineteen he donned his country's uniform and for three years fought through the Civil War, winning his way to the rank of Lieutenant-Colonel. Then he studied law and was admitted to the bar, beginning to practice in his native State. He had been a newspaper correspondent, traveler and writer, and had toured the world with Bayard Taylor.

One day Russell Conwell was called upon to go to a little country town and sell a tiny church because the members could not pay $300 that was due upon it. He went. The people stood about in tears, helpless to save their cherished house of worship. The great heart of the lawyer was touched. He announced that services would be held every Sunday, and paid the $300 out of his own pocket.

Conwell, the lawyer, went into the pulpit himself and conducted services until an ordained minister could be found to take it. He studied for the ministry, and was ordained at Lexington, Mass., in 1879.

This was the man that Grace Baptist Church induced to come to Philadelphia. From the first Sunday, when he electrified the congregation with his masterly preaching, his fame grew. In a few Sundays it became necessary to issue tickets of admission to limit the size of the congregation to the capacity of the church. The Sunday school grew, too, and soon overflowed. The name of Conwell was soon as well known in Philadelphia as that of the Mayor.

One Sunday afternoon he came to a little girl who was fruitlessly seeking a seat in the crowded Sunday school. He lifted her to the window sill, saying: "Never mind, little one, some day we will have a Sunday school big enough for all children who want to come. Just as soon as we can raise the money."

The child pondered. She began to save her pennies. In a few months she was stricken with fatal illness, and asked to see Mr. Conwell. He went to her bedside and she asked for her little bank, which she handed to the pastor, saying that she had saved this money to build a Sunday school, and asked him to take it. He did so, and the little one died happy in the promise that her savings would be so used. The bank, when opened yielded fifty-seven cents.

There was a vacant lot on the southeast corner of Broad and Berks Streets that Mr. Conwell had long coveted as the site for the church of his dreams. He had an inspiration. Putting the child's money in his pocket he sought the owner and asked the price, stating his object. The owner held it at $25,000. The clergyman said he would buy it if the owner would take part payment and let the rest stand on mortgage.

"How much do you plan to pay?" asked the owner.

"I have only fifty-seven cents," replied the pastor, simply.

Long and loud laughed the other at such a preposterous idea. Mr. Conwell waited until he quieted down, and then, simply, quietly, he told the story of the fifty-seven cents. As he talked the owner sobered. When he finished there was a moisture in the owner's eyes.

"Mr. Conwell," he said, "you shall have that lot, not for $25,000, but for $20,000. I will take the fifty-seven cents as first payment and take a mortgage for the rest."

The papers were drawn up, a receipt given for the money and a mortgage drawn for $19,999.43. Then the man who had owned the land handed back the fifty-seven cents, saying, "Mr. Conwell, if I were you I would never part with that money." And that same fifty-seven cents remains to this day locked in the church safe, a possession it holds sacred.

The church was built of white stone, fireproof, with heating plant outside. Instead of pews, it is equipped with cushioned opera chairs, for this unusual minister expressed the opinion that people would be more likely to be religious if they were comfortable. The church cost $250,000.

"Where," cried the congregation, aghast, "are we going to find the money to pay for it?"

"I will lecture," replied Conwell, "and thus raise the money myself."

"But suppose you should die?"

"Insure my life for enough to cover it."

And this was done. The church grew in membership to thousands. The indefatigable pastor lectured on many subjects. The favorite was "Acres of Diamonds," which he has delivered throughout the world a total of 6,150 times. He wrote books which brought substantial revenues. Money rolled in to him, and yet he never had any. No appeal for help was ever made to him in vain. His hand was always in his pocket. It is related that his wife on several occasions went to the trustees to get some of his salary in advance to do the family marketing. To assure him of a home free from landlords, the congregation bought and presented him with a house, 2020 North Broad Street.

One day two young men went to him and stated their desire to study for the ministry, and asked how they could get the preliminary education necessary. "Make up a class of ten and come to me Friday night," he told them, "and I will teach you myself." They came, but instead of ten there were forty. He put them off for a week to study the situation. The incident convinced him that there were many poor young men who desired a college education, but could not obtain it for financial reasons. He rented a room, engaged a teacher and the Temple School started. The room became a house; the house became two houses; the two houses became a large building adjoining the church and Temple School became Temple College. It grew to cover the whole square and became Temple University. And still other buildings in other parts of the city were needed to house its Medical, Dental and Music departments.

The Baptist Temple functioned, but not as a church. It would not be a church until it was dedicated, and it would not be dedicated until it was fully paid for. It was occupied March 1, 1891, and at last, free of all debt, it was formally dedicated December 1, 1907.

Dr. Conwell, once the needs of the temple and the university were provided for, devoted all his remaining income to paying for the tuition of poor boys through the college, and hundreds have him to thank for the education they have acquired. Yet so quietly has the benefaction been made that few of them know to whom they are indebted.

Three splendid hospitals, the Samaritan, the Garrettson, and the Great Heart were founded by him because they were needed in their neighborhoods. He has financed struggling young churches until they were able to travel alone. In 1924, he received the Edward Bok award of $10,000 for the Philadelphian who had done the most for the city in that year.

Had he kept what he earned, or even half of it, he would be today a millionaire several times over, but he has nothing but his salary and retains only enough of that for his simple wants.

So this great church, university and associated enterprises thrive and grow in importance and power which are always exerted for the good of mankind. And it was all done on a capital of fifty-seven cents.

And the church still has the fifty-seven cents.

The Rev. Dr. Russell H. Conwell died Sunday, December 6, 1925, at his home on North Broad Street, Philadelphia, at the age of 82 years.

QUAKER MEETING HOUSE
FLUSHING, L. I.

One of the quaintest landmarks of Long Island is a Friend's Meeting House, the original of which was erected in 1694 with funds obtained two years earlier, when the Friends were the only organized religious denomination on the island. It had no floor and no heat.

The present edifice was erected in 1719 and has had few alterations. In this plain meeting house in 1719 was held the first public meeting for the abolition of slavery. At the annual meeting of 1718, William Burling is said to have delivered an address considered the first anti-slavery address published in this country.

As early as 1672, we are told, George Fox traveled in Long Island, which adds weight to the tradition that Flushing had a Meeting House, even as early as 1670. The first actual protest against slavery, however, was made by the Germans who settled Germantown, Philadelphia, in 1683. The protest was framed at a meeting in the home of Thomas Kunders (still standing), and addressed to the Friends' Meeting of Philadelphia.

Moravian Church, Bethlehem, Pa. *(See page 267)*

MORAVIAN CHURCH
BETHLEHEM, PA.

For a motto they took the words "In commune oramus, in commune laboramus, in commune patimur, in commune gaudeamus," (together we pray, labor, suffer and rejoice).
—*"History of Moravian Church," Hutton.*

This church was born of the intense missionary zeal of the Moravians, organized in 1722, under the patronage of Count Zinzendorf (1700-1760). Their headquarters were in the Moravian city, Herrnhut ("Lord's Watch") where, driven by persecution, they had settled in 1722. As early as 1740, the American Province of the Unitas Fratrum (not to be confused with the "United Brethren") purchased a large tract of land in eastern Pennsylvania, naming it Bethlehem and intending it to be the central point for missions among the Mohican and Delaware Indians. Previous to this they had formed settlements in Georgia and along the Savannah River under the direction of Governor Oglethorpe.

In 1742, Count Zinzendorf himself visited the new mission center, dedicating the small Chapel House, erected the year before, and completing the organization. This is now recognized as the Mother Congregation of the Moravian Church in America. The Chapel House, the Bishop's House, and the residence of the Moravian Sisterhood were on the original tract of land purchased in 1740. Numerous Indian Missions sprang up. The first convert buried in the flat-stoned graveyard was an Indian. Today it is said that fifty-eight Indians lie buried there, representing the several tribes, which Moravian ministrations served.

The chapel dedicated in 1742, to which a large room was annexed in 1751, served for many years. In 1805 the present church was dedicated.

The hospital under the care of the Moravian Sisterhood is credited with having had General Lafayette as one of its patients during the Revolution. Count Pulaski, assigned at that time to protect it against the British and Indians, carried away with him the banner celebrated by Longfellow in his "Hymn of the Moravian Nuns."

This banner was of silk, embroidered by the Sisters, and Pulaski carried it streaming from an upright lance at the head of his legions, until he fell at Savannah, Georgia, in October, 1779. It was preserved by his comrades and carried in the procession that welcomed Lafayette upon his visit to this country in 1824. In 1844, it was presented to the Maryland Historical Society, in whose posession it still remains.

"Zinzendorf's Hymn," "Jesu geh voran, auf der Lebenshahn," said to be the first hymn taught children in every German household, well expresses his strong faith and that of his humble followers:

> Jesus, still lead on
> Till our rest be won,
> And although the way be cheerless,
> We will follow calm and fearless,
>   Guide us by Thy hand,
>   To our Fatherland.

At Winston-Salem, North Carolina, is the Home-Moravian Church, one of North Carolina's three Eighteenth Century Churches yet in existence. It was erected in 1788.

SHEARETH ISRAEL (REMNANT OF ISRAEL)

NEW YORK CITY

About 1650, Spanish and Portuguese Hebrews probably made their first settlement in New Amsterdam. There are records of a settlement of London Hebrews at Savannah, Ga., in 1733, and of Hebrew Congregations at Charleston, S. C., in 1750 and Montreal in 1768. A building consecrated in 1763 by the Yeshnath Israel Congregation of Newport, R. I., is in one of the country's historic spots and is celebrated by one of Longfellow's most touching poems. This latter congregation apparently resulted from a removal of part of the New Amsterdam settlement, about 1654 to Newport, for greater freedom of religious worship. Embury says that the Jewish Synagogue of 1775 at Newport is the oldest Jewish place of worship existing in the country.

Sheareth Israel, formed in 1680 by the descendants of the earlier settlement in New Amsterdam, was probably the oldest regular Hebrew congregation in the United States. The first records of this congregation, written in Spanish and in English, dated 1729, refer to records of 1706, at which time services were held in a small frame synagogue on Mill Street. In 1729 a neat stone building was erected on the site, in which the congregation worshipped for nearly a century. In 1838 it moved to "a spacious and elegant synagogue" in Crosby Street. The Rev. G. Sexias, who was active in the organization of Mickveh Israel, Philadelphia, served as the second Rabbi from 1787 to 1815, and was also a trustee of Columbia College (now University).

Temple Emanu-El, Forty-third Street and Fifth Avenue, a modern building, erected at a cost of $700,000, has a seating capacity of 2,000, and its lecture room will accommodate 1200. It has eight large school rooms in the basement, and boasts a male membership of more than four hundred of the most prominent Hebrews in New York City.

FIRST DUTCH REFORMED CHURCH
FLATBUSH, L. I.

The Long Island settlers, in attendance at the Dutch "Church-in-the-Fort" in early New York City, were dependent upon the crudest methods for crossing the East River, their ferry consisting merely of a small flat boat rowed by some farmer, who was summoned by a horn which hung conveniently on a neighboring tree for the purpose. The length of the passage depended upon the weather and tide, and the ancient Long Islanders decided it was time they should make their church-going less hazardous. In 1654 was organized, accordingly, the First Dutch Reformed Church of Flatbush, Long Island. The cost of the building was $1,800, to which fund Governor Peter Stuyvesant, the last Dutch Director General of the New Netherlands, contributed liberally.

First Huguenot Church, New York City. (*See page 271*)

FIRST HUGUENOT CHURCH
NEW YORK CITY

The Huguenots were among our country's earliest settlers. As early as 1564 they landed near Seloy, an Indian village on or near the site of St. Augustine, later moving on to the St. John's River. Early in the seventeenth century the West India Company sent out its first body of emigrants, as has been noted, to colonize Manhattan. Many of them were French Huguenot immigrants. By 1628 they had laid the foundations of a church under the leadership of the Rev. Jonas Michaelis, who conducted services in their own language, the Huguenot services being very similar to the Dutch Reformed.

In 1687-1688 a fourth of the population of New York were Huguenots, due to the immigration of French driven out by Louis XIV through his Revocation of the Edict of Nantes in 1685. Accordingly the First Huguenot Church of New York was organized, called Eglise des Refugees Français a la Nouvelle York. It was built in 1688 in the street then known as Petty Coat Lane. Until 1704, this church was the chief Huguenot center of worship, not only for the French in the city, but from distances as far out as what is now Long Island and New Rochelle. Many devoted worshippers set out on Saturday evening and traveled all night to be at church in time.

In 1704 a second and larger church was erected, the Huguenots by that time being recognized as a strong and wealthy congregation, second only to the Dutch Reformed.

In 1804 the French Church conformed to the Episcopal régime of worship, becoming the French Chapel of Saint Esprit, an interesting relic of the union at that time being the adaptation of the English Book of Common Prayer to the use of the Huguenot worshippers. The French Church was generously assisted by Trinity in its early organization and development.

ST. MICHAEL EVANGELICAL LUTHERAN

PHILADELPHIA

The mother church of all Lutheran churches in Philadelphia was founded April 5, 1743, by the Rev. Henry Melchior Muhlenberg, of Trappe, assisted by the Swedish pastor of Gloria Dei.

Zion Church was fostered by St. Michael and served by its pastors. In 1806, the English section of St. Michael's built St. John's.

St. Michael Evangelical Lutheran Church. Philadelphia.

FIRST PRESBYTERIAN CHURCH

NEWARK, N. J.

"They lived in the shadow of a fort-like structure
which was at once the Hall of Justice and Records and
the original House of God on the Soil."—*Bacon.*

A church much venerated by New Jerseyites is the
First Presbyterian at Newark, born of the necessity for
the Presbyterian training of the youth of the pioneer
settlers in the vicinity of Newark. For many years it
was ministered to by the Rev. Abraham Pierson, a
Scotch Presbyterian Minister, whom they had brought
with them for this purpose.

The original church was a crude building, planned
September 10, 1663, and ready for occupancy eighteen
months later. Two additions built on each corner,
called "flankers" served as a palisade to conceal and
protect the guards who patrolled during the service and
warned of Indian attack. During King Philip's War
the church was used as a fort.

This Presbyterian Meeting House, used also as the
town house, was the scene of all the important religious, civil and military transactions of some half century. In 1716 a plain and substantial stone church
was dedicated, which in 1753 was chartered by King
George III. This was desecrated by the British during the Revolution, just after it had been repaired, but
after the war it was restored with little change.

In front of the pulpit was the seat for the precentor.
To its right the pew for the minister's family and to
its left one for representatives of the royal family of
England. The congregation sat on the customary

plain benches. From the belfry the bell rope hung down into the middle aisle.

In 1787 the present church was erected, preserving in the main the old arrangement and calling the congregation to worship with the original bell, purchased twenty-five years after the erection of the building of 1716. The old church takes pride in a large Venetian window in the rear wall which is the admiration of all who see it.

On the banks of the Passaic, just outside of Newark, stands the old Dutch Reformed Church of Belleville, another of Jersey's landmarks. In its possession until recently was a Dutch Bible printed in Holland in 1768, which is now among the relics of the Belleville Free Library.

DUTCH REFORMED CHURCH
HERKIMER, NEW YORK

In her intense zeal to Christianize the Indians in the new land, Queen Anne caused the erection of several churches in the Mohawk country. Of these there are now only three remaining, and only one of these is still used for divine worship—the one that is a proud possession of Herkimer.

It is of stone. The curious drum-shaped pulpit, quaintly carved, is perched on a pedestal and reached by a steep, winding staircase. It is at an unusual height, and from it the preacher looks down upon his congregation, who are compelled to sit with heads bent back to see him. This pulpit, says Wallington, is one of the greatest curiosities to be found in ecclesiastical architecture in America.

[274]

FRIENDS' MEETING HOUSE, PHILADELPHIA. (*See page 275*)

FRIENDS' MEETING HOUSE
PHILADELPHIA

The first Friends' meeting was held in 1681 at Shackamaxon (now the Kensington district of Philadelphia) in a house opposite Penn's famous Treaty Elm. The meetings were first held in private houses. After these meetings men turned out to help new neighbors erect their small houses. Heavy work, such as wood cutting, was divided among many hands and a jovial rustic meal sweetened the toil.

In 1693, a site was chosen for the Center Square Meeting House, the present location of City Hall. This was succeeded in 1695 by a larger house at Second and High (now Market) Streets, erected on ground given to George Fox, the founder of the Society of Friends. There the Government of Pennsylvania and Council met until the building was destroyed in 1755 and replaced by a third which served until 1804, when the present brick house at Fourth and Arch Streets was erected on a site that had been donated by William Penn for that purpose. This historic Meeting House is the largest of all the Friends' Houses of worship in Philadelphia, and is said to be the largest in the world. It is 180 feet long. It is not only the largest, but also the oldest of these Houses now standing within the corporate limits of Philadelphia.

Like all Friends' Meeting Houses, it is severely plain, yet restful in its atmosphere of peace. There are the wooden benches for the worshippers and pegs upon which hats may be hung; and to it on the days of Meeting go throngs who are still of the faith of Fox and Penn, many to this day appearing in garments plain of cut and drab of color.

———— ◆ ————

PENNYPACK CHURCH
PENNYPACK, PA.

The Pennypack Baptist Church, founded in 1688 by twelve men and women settlers from Ireland and Wales, is the oldest church of this denomination in Pennsylvania and the third oldest in the country. Its pastor for a time served the Presbyterian congregation of "Old Barbados" previous to 1698. In 1707 a small place of worship was erected near the site of the present edifice. Two additional buildings were erected in 1770 and 1805, the latter being the one which stands today. This historic church was in its early days the center of denominational activity not only in Pennsylvania but throughout New York and New Jersey, Delaware and even as far south as Maryland.

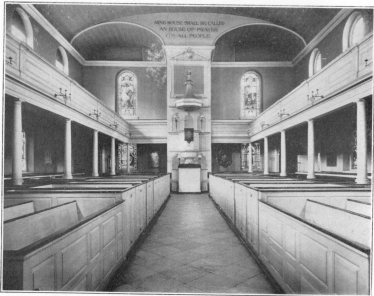

ST. PETER'S CHURCH, PHILADELPHIA. *(See page 277)*
Exterior and Interior Views.

ST. PETER'S
PHILADELPHIA

St. Peter's, Philadelphia, the second Protestant Episcopal Church in the city and one of the few, the interior of which has not been modernized, was erected on ground given by Thomas and Richard Penn, the proprietaries of Pennsylvania and loyal churchmen, for a chapel for Christ Church parishioners living in the southern part of the city. The first stone was laid by the assistant minister of Christ Church, the Rev. William Sturgeon, in September, 1758. It was to be "upon equal footing with Christ Church and under the same government withal," and "the first and best pew was to be set apart for the accommodation of the Honorable Proprietary's family and their governors for the time being." Benjamin Franklin, it is said, went with other worshippers from the mother church.

In 1842, the present tower and spire were added, also the large gilt cross which, it is said, was at that time the only cross on an American Episcopal Church. The church building stands today as one of the very few colonial churches of our country that have undergone no changes. It has lost none of the stern simplicity of its old colonial lines, within or without.

It was in this church that the Rev. William White, chaplain of the Second Continental Congress, and the first Bishop of English consecration in the United States, preached his first sermon in his new position.

One winter during the Revolution, whenever he was in the city, Washington attended St. Peter's. In the churchyard lie buried many of the city's prominent early residents, among them the Rev. Jacob Duché, Rector of both Christ Church and St. Peter's, whose prayer opened the First Continental Congress; Commodore Stephen Decatur, who proposed that inspiring American toast, "Our Country; may she always be right, but right or wrong, Our Country." A monument rises above him, and somewhere in the yard lies the body of Lewis Hallam, the younger, whose father founded the drama in America, and who, as his successor, established it firmly.

FIRST PRESBYTERIAN CHURCH
PHILADELPHIA

The First Presbyterian Church of Philadelphia owes its origin to the visit of the Rev. Francis Makemie to the city in 1692, a pastor sent to America in 1684 by the United Brethren of Presbyterians and Congregationalists of London. Previous to this visit to Philadelphia, he had been organizing churches in Maryland and Virginia, having organized the church at Rehobeth, Md., in 1683. His first congregation assembled in Barbados store, a small building belonging to a trading company, chartered by William Penn and called "Society of Free Traders" or "Barbados Company." The congregation was composed of Protestant "dissenters," including English, Welsh, Calvinists and French Huguenots. For a time (around 1695) a group of Baptists worshipped with them, the Rev. John Watts, a Baptist minister from Pennypack, serving them every other Sunday.

In 1698, the congregation formally organized and called its first pastor, Jedediah Andrews, from Boston. He was an Independent or Congregationalist, who had been ministering to a congregation largely composed of immigrants from Scotland and Ireland. So harmoniously and effectively did these two pastors work for the upbuilding of their churches, that they have been called the "Fathers of Presbyterianism in America."

In 1704, the congregation erected its own building on Market Street, above Second, affectionately called "Old Buttonwood," which was enlarged in 1729 and rebuilt in 1794 in "more spacious and elegant style, and served as their house of worship until 1822, when the congregation moved to its present edifice" at Seventh and Locust Streets.

Among the noted worshippers and pewholders of the old Presbyterian Church was Benjamin Franklin, also "an attendant and vestryman of Christ Church for five years."

———————

THE SECOND PRESBYTERIAN CHURCH
PHILADELPHIA

The Second Presbyterian Church, of Philadelphia, organized in 1743, had as its first pastor the Rev. Gilbert Tennent, eldest son of the famous Rev. William Tennent of New Jersey. Its organization is attributed to the preaching of the Rev. George Whitefield in Philadelphia with its attendent spiritual awakening.

In the Presbyterian Church in Germantown, which obtained its site in 1732, Count Zinzendorf is said to have preached his first and last sermons in America.

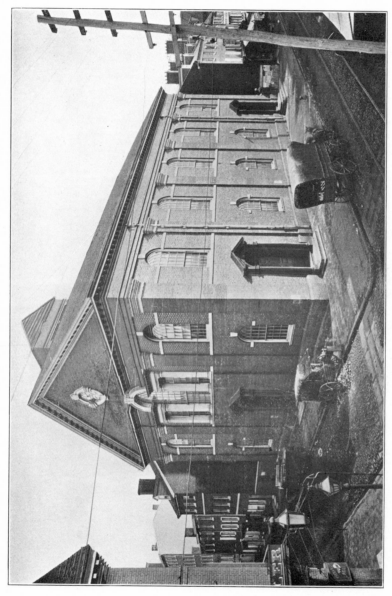

ZION EVANGELICAL LUTHERAN CHURCH, PHILADELPHIA. (See page 281)

ZION EVANGELICAL LUTHERAN

When built, and for many years afterward, Zion Lutheran was the largest church building in America, the outgrowth of St. Michael's, the first Lutheran Church in Philadelphia. The cornerstone had been laid by the Rev. H. M. Muhlenberg some quarter of a century before. Zion Evangelical Lutheran Church was dedicated on June 25, 1769, with fitting ceremony. In 1770, the Rev. George Whitefield preached in the church.

On November 27, 1777, pews were torn out and the church was used as a British hospital, with nothing but bare walls remaining. It was well called "Desolate Zion." On October 10, 1790, the great organ, built by a self-taught Moravian artisan, was used for the first time. It was the largest and grandest organ in America, having over two thousand pipes and three banks of keys, and costing $10,000.

On March 1, 1791, among distinguished guests gathered there in a commemorative service to Benjamin Franklin, were President and Lady Washington, Vice President and Mrs. Adams, and members of the Senate and House of Representatives.

This church, destroyed by fire in 1794, was replaced by a new church dedicated on November 27, 1796.

At the funeral services for General Washington (December 26, 1799) held in this church, Major General Henry Lee, the orator of the day and father of General Robert E. Lee, referred to Washington as "First in

War, First in Peace, and First in the Hearts of his Countrymen." On October 31, 1817, the third centennial of the Reformation was celebrated in Old Zion, participated in by all the clergy of the city.

Final services were held in Old Zion November 1, 1868, and a new church dedicated September 1, 1870.

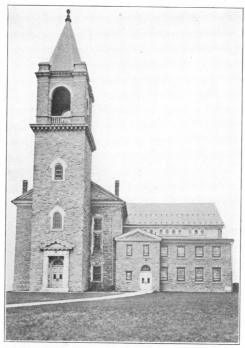

First (Tabor) Reformed Church of
Lebanon, Pa. *(See page 284)*

Donegal Reformed Church, Milton Grove, Lancaster County, Pa.
(See page 284)

ZION REFORMED CHURCH

ALLENTOWN, PA.

Zion Reformed Church at Allentown, Pa., remains a monument to the faith of the early settlers of that vicinity, who were, in the main immigrants from Switzerland and the Palatinate, and loyal supporters of the Reformed faith. In 1762, the year of the founding of the town, a log Meeting House was erected, one of the first buildings, which served also as a schoolhouse for many years. In 1770, by permission of Governor Penn, plans for a new church were made and in 1772, the cornerstone of a new stone church to cost some $1,500, was laid near the site of the old log church. This second church was succeeded in 1838 by the present building, completed in 1840.

Zion Reformed Church holds a place of peculiar historic interest, because of its protection of the Liberty Bell amidst the misfortunes of Revolutionary War times. Fearing that the bell would be taken from Independence Hall by the British, then occupying Philadelphia, to be made into cannon, some of the patriots loaded it on a wagon and started with it to the mountainous districts. When they reached Bethlehem, where the State Hospital for the Continental Army was located, the wagon broke down. With difficulty the bell was conveyed to Allentown, where it remained hidden under the floor of the church until it could be safely returned to Independence Hall.

[283]

Tabor Church (First Reformed), Lebanon, Pa., built in 1792, though remodeled and added to, still retains its original walls.

Donegal Reformed Church, Milton Grove, Lancaster Co., Pa., was built in 1744.

St. David's Church. Radnor, Pa. Interior. *(See page 285)*
In the graveyard adjoining lies buried General "Mad" Anthony Wayne.

ST. DAVID'S
RADNOR, PA.

What an image of peace and rest
Is this little Church among its graves!
— *"Old St. David's at Radnor," Longfellow.*

St. David's Church, some sixteen miles out from Philadelphia, stands a historic monument to Welsh Episcopalians of 1700. Parish records in possession of the church refer to an original building, on the site of the present church, built of logs and used also as a garrison against the Indians.

On May 9, 1715, the cornerstone of the present St. David's was laid. It stood, according to plan, "East and West with main door south and a sharp pitch to the roof to shed water, snow and summer rain." An unusual feature of its construction was the choir loft, reached only by a stairway from the outside of the church.

The interior was severely plain, having no heat nor seats and for forty years only the ground for a floor. In 1765, scanty equipment and floor covering were added. A few years later pews were put in and rented, to increase the church income. Though scantily furnished, St. David's had a few cherished possessions, thus referred to in its records of a robbery of the church in 1740: "One large folio Bible; one quarto Bible; one black gown made of Spanish cloth; one chalice; two plates, and one basin, being stamped Radnor Church," —a gift to the parish from Queen Anne.

At the outbreak of the Revolution, St. David's sturdy and patriotic congregation resorted to physical force to prevent the rector, who was a staunch loyalist, from using the liturgical references to the King and the Royal family. His resignation judiciously followed. The church became a rendezvous for Continental soldiers. The lead of the windows was contributed for bullets. British soldiers lie buried in the graveyard.

In 1809, the remains of General "Mad" Anthony Wayne, whose family was closely connected with the church, were buried with appropriate ceremony at St. David's. His monument reads: "Born in neighborhood, worshipped in church, was member of vestry, body brought from Presque Isle to rest here!"

At that time the church was remodeled and has remained since then much as it is now.

BRUTON PARISH CHURCH, WILLIAMSBURG, VA. *(See page 287)*

ST. DAVID'S CHURCH. RADNOR, PA.

BRUTON PARISH CHURCH

WILLIAMSBURG, VA.

Bruton Parish Church at Williamsburg, Va., was dedicated in 1684, nine years before the chartering of William and Mary College, the oldest institution of learning in our country, next to Harvard. The church was named in honor of the Ludwells, who were born in Bruton, in the County of Somerset, England, as one reads on the tomb of Sir Thomas Ludwell (died 1678) at the entrance of the north transept door.

The Rev. James Blair, who represented the Bishop of England as head of the church in the colony, served as its pastor thirty-two years. He also served William and Mary College as President about fifty years. To the students of the college, sons of Virginia planters, Indian youths and young ministers, the gallery was assigned.

Though authentic records are destroyed, it is probable that there was an earlier church at Middle Plantation, probably dating back to 1665. It was referred to as "already old" in 1674, when it was ordered that a new church be built of brick.

With the removal of the seat of State Government from Jamestown to Williamsburg, some seven miles distant, in 1669, Bruton Parish Church became the Court Church of Colonial Virginia, counting among its worshippers, the Governor and his staff, members of the House of Burgesses, and celebrated State visitors. The Council of State and members of the House of Burgesses, had officially assigned pews. With the enlarged congregation, a new edifice was deemed necessary and was erected accordingly in 1710-1715. Since then services have been regularly held in it. Among Old Bruton's cherished furnishings are the baptismal font and silver communion service of the old Jamestown Church.

Old Bruton Church was restored in 1905 at a cost of $25,000 and appears today much as it was in Colonial times, with pews arranged in colonial style and the Governor's pew covered with its canopy. It has been called the most interesting and historical Episcopal Church in the United States.

Blanford Church, Blanford, Va., now only the ruins of a brick church finished in 1736, was named in honor of Theodoric Bland, an Englishman, who went to Virginia in 1654 as a merchant from Spain. It was constructed by order of the church wardens of Bristol Parish and around it the town of Blanford was built. The Blanford family enjoyed distinction and influence in England and America for some six hundred years. John Randolph, of Roanoke, was one of its illustrious members.

INDEPENDENT PRESBYTERIAN CHURCH
SAVANNAH, GA.

This church of white marble, replacing in exact facsimile of design an older wooden church of 1800, is one of the most famous and beautiful of southern churches.

CHRIST CHURCH, ALEXANDRIA, VA.   *(See page 289)*
To whose erection, George Washington gave generous assistance.

CHRIST CHURCH

ALEXANDRIA, VA.

One of America's most historic landmarks is Christ Church at Alexandria, to whose erection and growth George Washington gave generous assistance. The family pew, for which he paid the highest price ($100) on the day of the completion of the church, February 27, 1773, still stands marked with his name. At that time he also presented a handsome brass chandelier with crystal pendants, which likewise still may be seen in the church sacred to his memory.

Church records say that as early as 1765, the parish of Fairfax was created and that for five years the Father of His Country served as an active vestryman. Among his other duties while in this office was the supervision of the collection of the tax of 31,000 pounds of choice Oronoko tobacco, sold to provide funds for the building of the church. The contract, for $3,000, for the erection of the church was signed in 1767.

Its style is simple Colonial and the appearance handsome. Its architect was from the family of Sir Christopher Wren.

Records tell of some interesting methods of Church financing: The poor were cared for by fines imposed for killing deer out of season, or hunting on the Sabbath. The clergyman's salary was paid in tobacco. His rectory was luxurious beyond all Colonial church customs, with glebe of some five hundred acres and "a dairy, meat-house, barn, stable and corn-house."

There is also the account of the baptism and confirmation of Robert E. Lee in Christ Church. When the Federal Troops occupied Alexandria, the church was held by military authorities. In a large mound in the churchyard lie buried thirty-four Confederate soldiers who died in Alexandria hospitals.

ST. LUKE'S
SMITHFIELD, VA.

At Smithfield, about ten miles from Fortress Monroe, is St. Luke's, one of the oldest churches of the South. Erected in 1632, it was used for some two hundred years with little change. Restored in 1887, through the generosity of not only native Virginians, but patriotic parishioners from twenty-one other States, St. Luke's stands today preeminent among examples of early southern Colonial church architecture.

Distinctive features of this interesting church are its twelve memorial windows, among which are those in memory of George Washington, General Robert E. Lee, Sir Walter Raleigh, Captain John Smith, John Rolfe and the Rev. Dr. Blair, founder of William and Mary College, the Alma Mater of President Jefferson and President Monroe. In the building are incorporated bricks taken from the ruined walls of the church at Jamestown.

St. John's, Hampton, Va., used as a barracks in 1812, has "survived three wars, twice in ruins, twice it has risen again."

The Hebron Lutheran Church in Madison County, Virginia, was built in 1740.

St. Luke's, Smithfield, Va.

ST. MICHAEL'S
CHARLESTON, S. C.

St. Michael's Protestant Episcopal Church at Charleston, S. C., distinguished among church buildings as a notable specimen of early British church architecture, was opened for worship February 1, 1761. The interior is rich and imposing with its lofty carved pulpit, high colonial pews and gallery supported by twelve Ionic pillars. The graceful, imposing tower, about one hundred sixty-eight feet high, with spire of ornamental chambers, its most beautiful feature, is one of the city's ornaments. It is said that during the Revolutionary War, when the tower was used as a beacon light, it was painted black by General Hood to prevent the enemy from using it as a guide to the harbor. In the Civil War the steeple was used as a lookout station. Its chimes of eight bells were imported from England and cost five hundred eighty-one pounds, fourteen shillings, four pence. They were taken from the city when it was captured by the British in the Revolution and sent to London, where they were bought by a merchant of that city and restored to St. Michael's.

Later in the War between the States, at the suggestion of General Beauregard, the bells were sent to Columbia to be cast into cannon, but were pronounced unfit. They were injured by fire when Charleston was besieged, and were recast in 1866. These "charmed" bells, after their various vicissitudes, still serve in this historic church.

Until 1882, the chimes gave warning of all fires. No American church, it is claimed, ever possessed a better set of chimes than St. Michael's, which also prides itself on its many highly prized pieces of eucharistic silver and rare church plate, zealously and successfully concealed by the vestrymen during the country's three great wars.

Though suffering great damage in 1863 from bombs from United States batteries at Fort Morris; again in 1885 by cyclone, and in 1886 by earthquake, all mutilating the beautiful spire, St. Michael's, restored, still stands an exceptionally beautiful Colonial church.

Previous to the erection of St. Michael's, its site was occupied by St. Philip's Church, built about 1681, the site having been designated for it on the first plot of the town. It was in this church—the State Church until St. Michael's was built—that the citizens worshipped until 1723, until then the only English church in the city.

VERMONT AVENUE CHRISTIAN CHURCH
WASHINGTON, D. C.

In this church, President Garfield worshipped. He was a member of the Christian Church, whose members are also known as "Disciples of Christ" or "Campbellites," the denomination having been founded by Thomas Campbell and Alexander Campbell, his son, in the latter half of the eighteenth century. Its strongest centers are in the Middle West. At Springfield, Mass., is "The Little Church at the Cross," an influential New England Christian church.

[292]

St. Paul's Church, Norfolk, Va. *(See page 293)*

St. Michael's Church, Charleston, S. C. *(See page 291)*

ST. PAUL'S

NORFOLK, VA.

St. Paul's Church of Norfolk, Va., cruciform, with walls of glazed brick, dates from 1739. But "Norfolk Towne" had chapels and churches even earlier. The records of 1637 show that one "John Wilson was minister of Elizabeth Reves Parish." Long before the town was incorporated in 1705 (laid out 1682) its parish had been organized.

On New Year's Day, 1776, when the town was bombarded under Lord Dunmore and was laid in ashes, only one home and the walls of St. Paul's were left. In the south wall of the church, restored in 1785, may be seen a twenty-four pound cannon-ball fired from the "Liverpool." The churchyard shelters the remains of many patriots of both wars and original Huguenot settlers of Virginia and is considered one of the most beautiful cemeteries of the South.

Pohick Church, in Truro Parish, organized by the Assembly in 1732, for which site was chosen in 1769, still stands, not far from Alexandria. George Washington served on its building committee and later worshipped in its pews.

ST. PETER'S

To St. Peter's, erected in 1703 by English settlers, belongs the coveted distinction of having been held in such high social and spiritual repute as to have been the church in which the marriage of George Washington to Mrs. Martha Custis was solemnized in 1759.

In architectural style it is similar to the old English parish churches,—the pulpit is high and above it the sounding board and beside it the inevitable hourglass. The communicants occupied family pews. After service the Virginians, always a social people, collected in groups and passed the time in friendly converse, while the negro servants brought the riding horses and the coaches to the door.

BRICK REFORMED CHURCH, GUILFORD COUNTY, N. C. *(See page 295)*

BRICK REFORMED CHURCH
GUILFORD COUNTY, N. C.

Founded by George V and Ludwig Klapp (1748), this historic church, near the Alamance battleground of the Regulators and Tryon, was known for many years as the "Klapp Church," later taking its name from the present brick structure.

Here in 1831 was organized the Classis of North Carolina of the Reformed Church in the United States. In 1844, the pioneer prohibition sentiment of the State, centered about this church, led by its pastor, the Rev. G. W. Welker.

Many soldiers of the Revolution who fought at Alamance and at Guilford Court House, lie buried in the adjoining cemetery, and also William Montgomery, member of the twenty-eighth United States Congress.

THE WORLD'S SMALLEST CHURCH.
Near Latonia, Kentucky. Built of granite; has stained glass windows and
seats only three worshippers. Built about sixty years ago by Monks.

MODERN CATHEDRALS, CHAPELS AND CHURCHES

ST. LOUIS CATHEDRAL
NEW ORLEANS, LA.

As royal patents provided for the erection of churches wherever settlements were made, it follows that in the plans of New Orleans specifications for Place d'Armes included a site for the Cathedral.

Other churches had preceded it. The first regular services were held in 1699 at the Fort, by the chaplain accompanying D'Iberville. An early Parish Church, said to have been known as St. Ignatius, built probably between 1718-1722, was destroyed by the hurricane of 1722. The new church, erected in its place, was burned to the ground in 1788. On the same site another edifice was constructed which was replaced by the present Cathedral, erected in 1850.

St. Louis Cathedral, of irregular architecture exteriorly, presents a rich, artistic and majestic interior. The beautifully frescoed ceiling bears, as its central picture, "The Transfiguration." A semi-historic presentation of St. Louis and the First Crusaders appears behind and above the main altar.

It was in this church that General, later President, Andrew Jackson, hero of New Orleans, worshipped after his great victory at Chalmette in 1815, and in his honor the Place d'Armes at that time became known as Jackson Square. The picturesque setting of this old Cathedral is suggested by the following appreciation:

A still, sultry, dreamy atmosphere pervades the romantic quarter of streets surrounding the Cathedral of St. Louis, which forms the hub of the city. Once in a while a cassocked priest steps from his transept door to a simple house opposite, reserved for the

[299]

clergy, whose frugal living room stands open to the street, disclosing to passersby its devotional pictures and anchorite furnishings.

"The Hispanic Southwest," Pexiotto.

CATHEDRAL OF ST. NICHOLAS
NEW YORK CITY

In this Russian Orthodox Church the first solemn mass celebrated in English was offered on the anniversary of Lincoln's Birthday, February 12, 1924. This service was arranged as a tribute to Lincoln and to show the desire of the Russian ecclesiasts here to Americanize their church.

The many visitors, who included a number of Episcopal clergymen, sat, but those of Russian birth and descent stood, as is the custom in the churches of the Old World. The textbook used was the translation of the Slavonic ritual, which was first brought out in 1906 by the Holy Russian Orthodox Synod and Czar Nicholas II.

"This," said a writer, "is the first step toward the Americanization of the Orthodox Church in the United States, where about two million communicants are living, who until now have been using in their churches the languages used in their former mother countries."

The Russian choir sang in English. The clergy wore brilliant cloth-of-gold vestments, and the Archbishop in addition wore a gold crown sparkling with stones. The Cathedral was redolent with incense.

[300]

MORMON TEMPLE, SALT LAKE CITY, UTAH. (*See page 301*)

ST. LOUIS CATHEDRAL, NEW ORLEANS, LA. (*See page 299*)

MORMON TEMPLE

SALT LAKE CITY, UTAH

In Temple Square, a ten acre tract near the center of Salt Lake City, stands the Mormon Temple, a massive, granite edifice sacred to the rites and ceremonies of the Latter Day Saints, and open to none but the members of that faith, and only to those in good standing. It was begun in 1853, two years after the organization of the city, and completed in 1893, at a cost of $4,000,-000. The granite was hauled by oxen from the Wasatch Mountains, twenty miles distant, and the timber from Cottonwood Canyon, also twenty miles away. At first the huge blocks of stone were carried on specially constructed carts, drawn by four yoke of oxen, but travel was so slow that it often required four days to transport one block. In 1873, a railway was built to the quarry, thus greatly expediting the work. The foundation walls of the Temple were laid less than six years after the pioneers arrived.

In the Tabernacle, an adjacent one-story elliptical building (two hundred fifty feet long, one hundred fifty feet wide and eighty feet high) having a great arched dome unsupported except by the walls, is the famous pipe organ, the largest in the world. It was manufactured in 1867 by a home architect where it stands, under the supervision of an Englishman, Joseph H. Ridges. All the wood, metal and other materials used were brought from forests and mines in Utah. The case is polished pine of elegant simple design. The wood for the pipes was taken from Pine Valley, three hundred miles south of Salt Lake City, after experimenting with specimens of wood from all over the State. The organ is known to the musical world as one of the largest and most perfect in existence and the Tabernacle is famed for its organ recitals and chorus concerts, and acoustical perfection.

The present Tabernacle occupies the site of an older Tabernacle built in 1851-1852, replacing "The Bowery"—a primitive structure of timbers and tree boughs, used for a temporary place of worship.

———◆———

JUDSON MEMORIAL
NEW YORK CITY

The Judson Memorial Baptist Church, believed to be the successor of the Berean Baptist Church (possibly incorporated 1835) was given its name in commemoration of the services of Adoniram Judson, pioneer missionary to Berma, and his son Edward, both ministers of that denomination, and the latter the pastor of the earlier church in 1881. Stanford White (slain in 1906) at that time (1892) considered among the greatest American artists of church architecture, was the architect. The tower, surmounted by a cross, illuminated at night, typified the ideals of the church for the surrounding neighborhood, as suggested by its motto, "The Church with the Lighted Cross."

ST. PATRICK'S CATHEDRAL, NEW YORK CITY. *(See page 303)*

ST. PATRICK'S CATHEDRAL

NEW YORK CITY

Old St. Patrick's, the cornerstone of which was laid
in 1809, under the supervision of old St. Peter's, on
Barclay Street (established 1784), has a quaint reference in its records to a "college, in a center spot, not of
Long Island but of the Island of New York, the most
delightful and healthy spot of the whole island, at a
distance of but four small miles from the city and one
half mile from the East and North rivers, both of which
are seen from the house, set between two roads (which
are very much frequented), opposite the Botanic Gardens, which belong to the State. It has adjacent to it
beautiful lawns and a garden and orchard."

The romantic spot so pictured is now occupied by
St. Patrick's Cathedral, on Fifth Avenue at Fiftieth
Street.

This spacious Cathedral of the New World, begun
in 1858 and completed, except the spires, in 1879, is in
the decorated Gothic style, prevailing in Europe from
1275 to 1400. It simulates the Old World Cathedrals (Rheims, Amiens and Cologne, Exeter, York
Minster and Westminster), with which it compares
favorably in beauty of material and design, purity of
style, harmony of proportions, and finish of workmanship. The exterior building material is, in the main,
of white marble from the quarries of Westchester
County, N. Y., and Lee, Mass. Its façade, richly decorated, carries twin towers with octagonal spires in two
stories, rising to a height of three hundred thirty feet.

The beautiful Lady Chapel is the gem of the new

Cathedral, the stained glass windows, for size, number, richness of coloring, variety and artistic beauty unsurpassed in America, were made in France near the Cathedral of Chartres, where it is universally admitted the most beautiful specimens of the thirteenth century painted glass is preserved.

James Renwick (1819-1895), an American, was the architect of St. Patrick's.

First Church of Christ, Scientist, Boston. *(See page 305)*

FIRST CHURCH OF CHRIST, SCIENTIST

BOSTON

"Erected Anno Domini, 1894" one reads on the pink granite tablet built into the circular wall of the tower of the "Mother Church" of Christian Science, in Boston, organized in 1879, and erected under the direction of Mary Baker Eddy (1821-1910). In June, 1906, the temple extension of white granite and Bedford stone was dedicated.

The architectural style of the Mother Church is Romanesque, the building material of New Hampshire granite. The interior, the decoration of which is in exquisite harmony with this church's symbolical interpretation of religion, is renowned for its beautiful windows, with color tones determining the color scheme of other interior decorations. Floor mosaics, fresco designs, marbles, and hangings carry out to the last detail the rich tones of the windows. Conspicuous for its rare beauty is the Rose Window memorializing "The Raising of Jairus' Daughter," the lower sections of palms and lamps signifying light, intelligence and victory. Another Rose Window of marked beauty and significance is "The New Jerusalem." Other windows which win much admiration are, "The Resurrection of Lazarus" (a double window); "Isaiah," "St. John on the Island of Patmos," and the "God-crowned Woman."

A distinct feature of the church is the Mother's Room, at the entrance of which one reads, inlaid in colored stones in the landing before the door, "Mother's

Room, The Children's Offering." Above the door in letters of gold on a white marble tablet is the word, "Love." Testimonial windows of exquisite beauty in this room, sacred to childhood and mother love, are "Christ and Christmas," "The Star of Bethlehem," and "Suffer Little Children to Come Unto Me." An onyx beehive contains the twenty-eight hundred names of "Busy Bees," the band of children to whom the church owes the Mother's Room.

A large oil painting pictures the little black haircloth rocking chair in which the Founder sat while writing her celebrated works. A bookmark given to the "Mother's Room" by two little girls bears the sentiment to which the room is dedicated:

> And so I find it well to come
> For deeper rest to this small room;
> For here the habit of the soul
> Feels less the outer world's control;
> And from the Silence, multiplied
> By these still forms on every side,
> The world, that Time and Sense have known,
> Falls off, and leaves us God alone.
>
> —*Whittier.*

ST. JOHN THE DIVINE
NEW YORK CITY

Among the great Cathedrals of New York is that of St. John the Divine representing, in its present unfinished condition, an outlay of several millions of dollars and fifty years of preparation and planning, the charter having been granted in 1873.

The prevailing style is French-Gothic. The plans propose two towers 265 feet high and a central tower 500 feet high. When completed, it is estimated that it will cost $20,000,000, taking its place among the great cathedrals of the world in vastness of dimensions and beauty of design.

Notable works of art in the Cathedral are the Potter Memorial Pulpit of Knoxville marble, and the Eagle lectern of bronze, on the north side of the choir. This lectern is said to be a replica of an ancient one found in a lake near St. Alban's Cathedral where it had been cast at the time of the destruction of that Cathedral during the Saxon invasion.

The choir stalls, rising four tiers on either side of the chancel, are of carved American oak. The canopies are copied from those in one of the chapels in Westminster Abbey. The finals of the stalls are figures of great musicians and composers of church music. The high altar is white Vermont marble, containing statues of Our Lord, seven feet high, of Moses and of St. John the Baptist. The great rectangular panel in the lower part of the reredos is filled with rare Spanish embroidery of Arabesque design two hundred years old.

[307]

The eight great columns of light gray Maine marble in a semi-circle around the sanctuary are among the marvels of the Cathedral, and are approached in size only by those of St. Isaac's, in Leningrad. The organ contains 7,000 pipes and chimes. Among the Cathedral's treasures are twelve Barbaric tapestries, woven in the first half of the seventeenth century on the Papal looms, and purchased for $45,000.

THE NATIONAL CATHEDRAL

When Washington drafted the plans of the federal city, a large plot of land, centrally situated, was reserved for a national church "in due recognition of that God of Our Fathers, under whose fostering care the Republic was founded and has grown to its present commanding position among the sovereign States of the world."

The present completed apse, a fragment of the proposed Washington Cathedral, whose erection was begun in 1915, does not occupy this site, but one considered more advantageous. It comprises some sixty acres of beautifully wooded land, lying picturesquely on the summit of Mt. St. Alban and overlooking the Potomac.

When completed, the proposed Cathedral, in pure Gothic style, measuring some five hundred feet from the western front to the apse at the eastern end, will equal in length any English church except York Minster. The crowning glory will be the great central tower rising two hundred sixty-two feet and rivaling in height and beauty the lovely Angel Tower at Canterbury, which it will exceed by thirty-three feet. In the perfection of its proportions and the purity of its style, it is believed the Washington Cathedral will stand without a peer.

Bethlehem Chapel, of the National Cathedral of St. Peter and Paul, is built over the foundation stone of the Cathedral brought from the fields of Bethlehem, and bearing the inscription, "The Word was made flesh and dwelt amongst us." Inlaid in a piece of American granite, it was set in place in 1907 in the presence of President Roosevelt and 20,000 people. The beautiful stained-glass windows of the chapel, representing scenes in the life of Christ, came from England.

In the crypt of this chapel lies the body of Woodrow Wilson, the "World War" President of the United States. When the Cathedral is finished, his body will be placed in a permanent sarcophagus that will be provided for it therein.

In the temporary Baptistry is the Jordan font of white Carrara marble, carved with Biblical scenes and lined with stones from the Damascus ford of the River Jordan, where tradition holds, Christ was baptized.

How the ground was chosen for this Cathedral makes an interesting story. Joseph Nourse, first Registrar of the Treasury, was the owner of a tract of land on part of which the Cathedral is being built. He was a friend of Washington and a Church-of-England man. He lived in a mansion on Mount St. Alban. Looking down from the heights of his home, he felt that it was the ideal home for a National Cathedral. It was his prayer that some day the country would build a shrine there.

After his death his home was made a church school for boys. An upper room was used as a chapel. There on Sundays, the students and many of the people in the outlying districts, would gather for services.

Phoebe Nourse, granddaughter of Joseph Nourse, attended regularly until her health failed. While confined to her room, she spent her time doing fancy work, which she sold. Nobody knew why she did it, or what she did with the proceeds of the handiwork. It was thought to be the whim of a suffering lady, and therefore humored.

In 1848, Phoebe Nourse died. Among her effects was found a small box, which upon being opened laid bare forty gold dollars. A note accompanying the money read, "For a Free Church on Alban Hill." The sincerity of this offering touched many of her friends, and, with the forty dollars as a nucleus, enough was collected to build a small, free church on Alban Hill. That little church still stands, the mother church of the Cathedral.

WEST POINT AND ANNAPOLIS

Although not yet old enough to become famous or classed as historic, the United States furnishes for its future Generals and Admirals church buildings that are richly significant as well as architecturally dignified and beautiful, and well worthy to be included among the important church edifices of the world.

On the hills overlooking the Hudson river which its guns command, upon ground held sacred for its Revolutionary associations, stand the group of buildings where future officers of the Army are trained and developed, known as the United States Military Academy, or popularly, West Point. Few, if any, institutions of the kind in the world equal it, and none surpass it; and one of the most important and beautiful of the buildings is the Cadet Chapel.

The architects, Cram, Goodhue and Ferguson, designed a structure modern Gothic in style and military in appearance. Construction was begun August 25, 1908 and completed April 30, 1910. It was consecrated June 12 of the latter year. Its exact cost, including furnishings and the Chaplain's quarters was $487,-392.12. From the entrance to the Altar, it is 210 feet long; the nave is 60 feet wide and the transept 87 feet. It is 56 feet high inside. The seating capacity, including the choir is 1,500.

With the exception of the two large windows at either end of the Chapel all windows are memorials of the various classes that have gone before. The large stained-glass sanctuary window, a memorial to departed graduates and the gift of the Alumni Association, represents the Genius and Spirit of West Point, symbolized by the heroes of the Bible, every one of the many sections having its individual significance in harmony with the central thought the whole typifies.

The large window over the entrance was installed in January, 1923, as a memorial to members of the Alumni who died in the World War. This window, as a whole, is based on St. John's Revelation, vouchsafed him on the Isle of Patmos for the comfort of the early Christians in the midst of persecution and war. The central theme is the victory of Christ over sin and death. "As the vision of St. John revealed to the Apostle many mysteries of the millennium in all its radiant glory," says an anonymous writer, "so this Apocalypse in glass impresses one at first as a jewel of glory and light." Close study of the window reveals the many subordinate visions that make up the entire revelation.

One of the features of the West Point Chapel is its organ, installed in 1911. While paid for as it stood originally by funds appropriated by Congress, donations and memorials have trebled its size. It now contains 102 separate ranks of pipes, totaling 6,874, with 174 stops. There are really seven different organs, each having its part to play. The mechanical equipment includes five electric motors aggregating 21 h. p. The pipes range from those smaller than a lead pencil to one thirty-two feet long and eighteen by twenty-one inches in diameter weighing half a ton. The organ is as large as a three-story house. The console, one of the largest in the world, has four manuals of sixty-one keys each, with 287 stop keys, 135 manual accessories, 32 pedal keys and 49 pedal accessories.

The choir composed of 155 cadets, is the largest male choir in the country. The chimes in the tower were presented in 1919 by Mrs. James M. Lawton as a memorial to her father, General Robert Anderson, who commanded at Fort Sumter, the attack upon which marked the opening of the Civil War.

Under the chapel is the crypt, the door to which is of hammered copper into which has been wrought a shattered hour glass and a broken sword. Along the walls are twelve recesses for the illustrious dead.

The banners in the chapel are regimental standards figuring in all our wars since and including that with Mexico.

Over the entrance is a great two-handed sword buried in a cross. As that of King Arthur, "Excalibur," could be drawn from the stone into which it had been plunged only by one destined to be a king, so this symbolizes that it may be drawn only in the defence of the things the cross represents, the ideal qualifications for a King.

As it is with the school for soldiers at West Point, so it is with the Naval Academy at Annapolis, Maryland. This institution, too, has been rebuilt and modernized and made of world-challenging beauty and effectiveness. More showy, yet richly dignified is the golden-domed marble chapel, with its ornate bronze doors, through which the Middies march to worship. Guns captured by the Navy in the Mexican war guard its entrance, and inside are three stained glass windows, memorials to Admirals Farragut and Porter, of Civil War fame, and Sampson, who commanded the American fleet off Santiago during the War with Spain.

But chief interest in the chapel lies in the fact that it is the tomb of our first Admiral, John Paul Jones. The great sea fighter died in Paris and was buried there, but both place and cemetery were forgotten until a century had passed, when through the efforts of the American Ambassador, General Horace Porter, the body was found, identified, and removed to the United States. When this chapel was built an imposing mausoleum was provided in the crypt for the body, and there it was placed, it is hoped, for all time, a symbol of victory accomplished, an inspiration to the sturdy American lads who are following in the profession he so splendidly graced.

BIBLIOGRAPHY

American Churches . . . . *The American Architect*
Famous Buildings . . . . *Barstow*
Historic Churches (private editions) . . . . . . *Phila. Free Library*
Quaint Corners in Philadelphia . . . . *Jackson*
Book of Philadelphia . . . . *Shackleton*
Early Philadelphia, Its People, Life and Progress . . . *Lippincott*
Penn's Green Country Towne . . . . *Hotchkin*
Old Meeting Houses . . . . *Hayes*
History of Moravian Church . . . . *Hutton*
The Presbyterian Church in Philadelphia ⎫ *Historic Library*
The Reformed Church in Philadelphia ⎪ *Witherspoon Bldg.,*
Historic Manual of the Reformed Church ⎰   *Philadelphia*
   in the United States ⎭
The Jews of Philadelphia . . . . *Morais*
Wesley and His Preachers . . . . *Pike*
History of New York City Churches . . . . *Greenleaf*
Earliest Churches of New York . . . . *Disosway*
History of St. Patrick's Cathedral . . . . *Farley*
Early American Churches . . . . *Embury*
Old New England Churches . . . . *Bacon*
Old Time Meeting Houses of the Connecticut Valley . . . *Wight*
Historic Buildings of America . . . . *Singleton*
Historic Churches of America . . . . *Wallington*
Francis Asbury in the Making of American Methodism . *Carroll*
Missionary Explorers Among the American
   Indians . . . . *Humphreys*
Sabbath in Puritan New England . . . . *Earle*
Historic Shrines in America . . . . *Faris*
California Padres and Their Missions . . . . . *Chase and Sanders*
Romantic California . . . . *Pexiotto*
Hispanic Southwest . . . . *Pexiotto*
Texas the Marvellous . . . . *Winter*
Old Franciscan Missions of California . . . . *James*
Campa and Camino in Lower California . . . . *North*
Missions of California and the Old Southwest . . . . . . *Hildrup*
California and Its Missions . . . . *Church*
Stories of the Old Missions of California . . . . *Carter*

[317]

Utah the Land of Blossoming Valleys ....*James*
Modern Mexico .... *McHugh*
Mythology of Ancient Mexico and Peru........... *Spenge*
Monks and Monasteries .... *Wishart*
In the Land of Mosque and Minarets .... *Miltoun*
The Spell of Switzerland .... *Dale*
The New Jerusalem .... *Chesterton*
Out of Doors in the Holy Land .... *Van Dyke*
Land of the Prophets .... *Heussar*
Egypt and Its Monuments .... *Hichens*
Lectures .... *Stoddard*
China the Long Lined Empire .... *Scidmore*
Great Cathedrals of the World .... *Meagher*
Great Cathedrals of the World .... *Allen*
English Cathedrals .... *Van Renssalaer*
An English Cathedral Journey .... *Kimball*
Cathedral Churches of England .... *Pratt*
Cathedrals of England .... *Farrar*
English and Welsh Cathedrals .... *Atkinson*
Roll Call of Westminster Abbey .... *Smith*
Cathedrals of England and Wales .... *Bumpus*
French Cathedrals .... *Pennell*
Churches and Castles of Medieval France .... *Larned*
How to Visit English Cathedrals .... *Singleton*
Turrets, Towers and Temples .... *Singleton*
Famous Cathedrals as Described by Great Writers ... *Singleton*
Stories of Paris Churches .... *Wolff*
What Pictures to See in Europe in One Summer ...... *Bryant*
Life of Luther .... *Kostlin*
Homes and Haunts of Luther .... *Stoughton*
Famous Hymns of the World .... *Sutherland*
Hymns That Have Helped .... *Stead*
Everyman's History of the Prayer Book .... *Dearmeer*
Early European History .... *Webster*
How to Study Architecture .... *Caffin*
Cathedrals of the Old and New World (National Geographic Magazine, July, 1922) ...... *J. Bernard Walker*
Cathedral Overlooking Washington (New York Times Magazine, March 23, 1924) ....
Canterbury Tales .... *Chaucer*
Thomas à Becket and Other Dramas .... *Tennyson*
Sketch Book .... *Irving*

With Byron in Italy .... *McMahon*
Joan of Arc .... *De Quincey*
Lorna Doone .... *Blackmore*
The Cathedral .... *Lowell*
Evangeline and Other Poems .... *Longfellow*
Ramona .... *Jackson*
Notre Dame de Paris .... *Hugo*
Stones of Venice .... *Ruskin*
Rob Roy .... *Scott*
Lay of the Last Minstrel .... *Scott*
The Cathedral .... *Walpole*
The Shadow of the Cathedral .... *Ibanez*
Corinne .... *De Stael*

INDEX

Abbey Church, Mont St. Michael, France, 65
Aix-la-Chapelle, France, 72
Alamo, The, Texas, 166
Amiens Cathedral, France, 109
Apostles, Church of the, Cologne, Germany, 84
Art Treasures in Notre Dame, Antwerp, 145
Augustus Lutheran Church, Trappe, Pa., 259

Baptist Temple, Philadelphia, 261
Beauvais Cathedral, France, 106
Belen Church, Havana, 164
Bells: Ancient Bell, St. Pierre, Geneva, 100
    Angel Tower, Canterbury Cathedral, 56
    Belfry of Bruges, 146
    Campanile, Florence, Italy, 64
    Campanile, Santa Maria del Fiore, Florence, 64
    Christ church, Oxford, England, 94
    Christ Church, Philadelphia, 250
    Dunstan Bell, Canterbury Cathedral, 56
    First Baptist Church, Providence, R. I., 206
    Golden Pagoda, Rangoon, 9, 10
    Great Paul, Westminster Abbey, London, 67
    Great Peter, Exeter Cathedral, England, 127
    Great Peter, York Minster, England, 126
    Great Tom, Lincoln Cathedral, England, 94
    Kaiser-Glocke, Cologne, 84
    Liberty Bell, Philadelphia, 251
    Malines, Belgium, 146
    Metropolitan Church, Toronto, Canada, 146
    Oldest Belfry and Bell in Colonies, 199
    Santa Fe, New Mexico, Cast 1350, 173
    Santa Maria del Fiore, Bell Tower, 64
    Santa Maria Guadalupe, Mexico City, 160
    St. Joseph's, St. Augustine, 181
    St. Michael's, Charleston, S. C., 291
    St. Nicholas Collegiate Church, New York City, 218
    St. Patrick's, Dublin, 136
    St. Peter's Church, Morristown, N. J., 146
    St. Stephen's, Vienna, 149
Bethlehem Chapel, National Cathedral, Washington, D. C., 309
Bibliography, 317
Bishops of Canterbury, 57
Black Stone, The, Mecca, 37
Blanford Church, Blanford, Va., 288
Bones of Ste. Anne, The, Quebec, 176
Brick Church, Boston, 193
Brick Reformed Church, Guilford County, N. C., 295
Bruton Parish Church, Williamsburg, Va., 287
Burgos Cathedral, Spain, 143

Cathedrals: Amiens, France, 109
    Antwerp, Belgium, 145
    Ascension de Maria Sanctissima, Mexico City, 159
    Ascension, Moscow, 126

Assumption, Moscow, 142
Beauvais, France, 106
Burgos, Spain, 143
Canterbury, England, 54
Chartres, France, 105
Cologne, Germany, 83
Columbus Cathedral, Havana, Cuba, 162
Como, Rome, 82
Durham, England, 95
Ely, England, 118
Exeter, England, 127
Glasgow, Scotland, 133
Gloucester, England, 89
Grenada, Spain, 91
Holy Trinity, Quebec, Canada, 164
Lichfield, England, 150
Lincoln, England, 92
Malines, Belgium, 146
Milan, Italy, 97
Monreale, Sicily, 29
Murano, Italy, 119
Naples, Italy, 53
National Cathedral, Washington, D. C., 309
Our Lady of Guadalupe, Mexico, 179
Oxford, England, 113
Peterborough, England, 120
Pisa, Italy, 101
Ratisbon, Germany, 85
Rheims, France, 107
Rouen, France, 141
St. Etheldreda and St. Peter, Ely, England, 118
San Fernando, San Antonio, Texas, 167
St. John the Divine, New York City, 307
St. Joseph, St. Augustine, Fla., 181
St. Michael the Archangel, Moscow, 126
St. Louis Cathedral, New Orleans, La., 299
St. Nicholas, New York City, 300
St. Patrick's, New York City, 303
St. Peter, St. Paul and St. Andrew, Peterborough, England, 120
St. Peter's, Rome, 30
St. Rombold, Malines, Belgium, 146
St. Stephen's, Vienna, 148
Salisbury, England, 69
Seville, Spain, 77
Siena, Italy, 62
Strassburg, Germany, 111
Toledo, Spain, 103
Tours, France, 68
Trondhjem, Norway, 137
Vasali, Moscow, 85
Venice, Italy, 52
Verona, Italy, 123
Wells, England, 152
Winchester, Hampshire, England, 116
Worms, Germany, 84
Chapel of Edward the Confessor, Westminster Abbey, 59

INDEX

Chapel of Henry VII, Westminster Abbey, 59
Chapel at U. S. Military Academy, West Point, N. Y., 312
Chapel at U. S. Naval Academy, Annapolis, Md., 314
Chapel of St. Helena, The, Jerusalem, 28
Chapels of St. Peter and St. Paul, Tower of London, 147
Charlemagne's Royal Tomb Church, Aix-la-Chapelle, 31, 72
Chartres Cathedral, France, 105
Chester Church, New Haven, Conn., 212
Christ Church, Alexandria, Va., 289
Christ Church, Bennington, Vt., 215
Christ Church Cathedral, Dublin, 136
Christ Church Cathedral, Oxford, England, 113
Christ Church, Philadelphia, 249
Christ Church, Philadelphia, Burial Ground, 250
Christ Church, Shrewsbury, N. J., 232
"Church in the Fort," New York City, 216
Church in which Washington married, 294
Church of the Brethren, Germantown, Pa., 228
Church of the Holy Sepulchre, Jerusalem, 27
Church of the Nativity, Bethlehem, 25
Church of the Pilgrimage, Plymouth, 189
"Church of the Town Meetings," The, Boston, 195
Clock, Antwerp Cathedral, 145
Clock, Exeter Cathedral, England, 127
Clock, Strassburg Cathedral, 112
Collegiate Church (Dutch Reformed), New York City, 216
Collegiate Church of St. Nicholas, New York City, 218
Collegiate Church of St. Peter, London, 58
Cologne Cathedral, Germany, 83
Colonial Churches, 185
Como Cathedral, Rome, 82
Concepcion la Purisima de Acuma, San Antonio, Texas, 165
Concord's Old Meeting House, Mass., 215
Congregation Michveh Israel, Philadelphia, 257
Constantine's Church, Jerusalem, 27
Conwell, Rev. Russell H., D.D., 261
Coronation Chair, Westminster Abbey, 59
Court Church of Colonial Virginia, 287

Early Christian or Basilican Churches, 21
Eddy, Mrs. Mary Baker, 305
Edict of Theodosius, 17
Ely Cathedral, England, 118
Emerald Buddha, Bangkok, 10
Escorial Church, The, Madrid, Spain, 76
Exeter Cathedral, England, 127

Famous Wat Phra Kao, or Royal Temple for the Emerald Buddha, 10
First Acceptance of Unitarian Faith in United States, 203
First Baptist Church, Providence, R. I., 205
First Church, Boston, 192, 200
First Church, Hartford, Conn., 204
First Church of Christ, Scientist, Boston, 305
First Congregational Church, Salem, Mass., 214
First Dutch Reformed Church, Fishkill, N. Y., 219

First Dutch Reformed Church, Flatbush, L. I., 270
First Huguenot Church, New York City, 271
First Mennonite Church in America, Germantown, Pa., 228
First Methodist Preaching House in America, 231
First Protestant Church in America, Jamestown, Va., 187
First Protestant Episcopal Church in New England, 202
First Presbyterian Church, Elizabeth, N. J., 254
First Presbyterian Church, Newark, N. J., 273
First Presbyterian Church, New York City, 229
First Presbyterian Church, Philadelphia, 279
First Reformed Church, Philadelphia, 255
First Reformed Church, Tarrytown, N. Y., 237
First sermon preached in America, 189
First Thanksgiving in New England, 191
Foreword, v
Franciscan Church of Santa Croce, Florence, 57
Franklin's Grave, Philadelphia, 250
Friends' Meeting House, Haverford, Pa., 246
Friends' Meeting House, Merion, Pa., 246
Friends' Meeting House, Philadelphia, 275

Glasgow Cathedral, Scotland, 133
Gloria Dei (Old Swedes) Church, Philadelphia, 242
Glastonbury Clock, 123
Gloucester Cathedral, England, 89
Golden Pagoda, Rangoon, 9
Golgotha Chapel, Jerusalem, 28
Grace Baptist Church, Philadelphia, 261
Grace Church, New York City, 225
Grave of Benjamin Franklin, Philadelphia, 250
Great Mosque, The, Mecca, 37
Greek Temple of Diana, 16
Grenada Cathedral, Spain, 91
"Grotto of the Nativity," Bethlehem, 25

Havana, Cuba, Columbus Cathedral, 162
Haverford, Pa., Friends' Meeting House, 246
Hebron Lutheran Church, Madison Co., Va., 290
Herod's Temple, 8
Holy Apostles Church, Constantinople, 51
Holyrood Chapel, Edinburgh, 102
Holy Sepulchre, Jerusalem, 27
Holy Trinity Church, Wilmington, Del., 239
Home Moravian Church, Winston-Salem, N. C., 268

Images of Buddha, 9
Independent Presbyterian Church, Savannah, Ga., 288

Jerusalem Church, Bruges, 100
Jesuits, Church of the, Cologne, Germany, 84
"Jewel Box of Constantinople," The, 46
John Eliot's Bible, Indian Language, 201
John Street Methodist Church, New York City, 231
Judson Memorial Baptist Church, New York City, 302

INDEX

Justinian's Church, Constantinople, 45

Kaaba, The, Mecca, 37
King's Chapel, Boston, 202
Koran, The, 41

La Merced "Our Lady of Mercy," Havana, 163
Lateran Palace, The, Rome, 29
Largest Church in the world, St. Peter's Rome, 80
Leaning Tower of Pisa, 101
Lichfield Cathedral, England, 150
Lincoln Cathedral, England, 92
"Little Church Around the Corner," The, New York City, 226
"Little Church at the Cross," The, Springfield, Mass., 292
"Little Church of England," The, 199
Little Dover Meeting House, Dover, N. H., 214
Llandaff Cathedral, Wales, 152
Lorna Doone's Church, Devonshire, England, 121

Madeleine, Church of the Paris, 153
Malines Cathedral, Belgium, 146
Marble Collegiate Church, New York City, 217
Mother Church in America, Dunkards, Germantown, Pa., 228
Marseillaise Hymn of the Republic, 87
Martin Luther's Church (Schloss-Kirche) Wittenberg, Germany, 86
Mayflower Pilgrims, The, 189
Medieval Cathedrals, 49
Meeting House of First Presbyterian Society, 1756, Newburyport, Mass., 211
Meeting House-on-the-Green, Lexington, Mass., 209
Melrose Abbey, Scotland, 131
Merion, Pa., Friends' Meeting House, 246
Mexico City Cathedral, 159
Milan Cathedral, Milan, Italy, 97
Mission of the Concepcion, San Antonio, Texas, 165
Mission Dolores, San Francisco, Calif., 183
Mission of San Xavier Del Bac, Arizona, 182
Monastery of Mar Saba, near Jerusalem, 34
Monreale Cathedral, near Palermo, Sicily, 29, 94
Moravian Church, Bethlehem, Pa., 267
Mormon Temple, Salt Lake City, Utah, 301
Moscow Cathedrals:
  St. Michael the Archangel, 126
  Ascention, 126
  Assumption, 142
Mosques, Temples of Mahomet, 35
  Amru, Cairo, 44
  Cordova, Spain, 41
  Damascus, 44
  Ispahan, Persia, 44
  Kait-Bey, Egypt, 44
  Machpelah, Hebron, 44
  Omar, The, Jerusalem, 39
  Sultan Hassan, Cairo, 42
  Sultan Mahomet II, 51

"Mother Church" of Christian Sceince, 305
"Mother Church of England," 54
Mother Congregation of Moravian Church in America, 267
Murano Cathedral, Italy, 119

Naples Cathedral, 53
Nativity, Church of the, Bethlehem, 25
National Cathedral, Washington, 309
Naval Academy Chapel, Annapolis, Md., 314
New England Sabbath Day, 191
New South Church, Boston, 197
Notre Dame, Antwerp, 145
Notre Dame, Paris, 73
Nuestra Senora de Guadalupe, Church of, Mexico, 179

Old Dutch Sleepy Hollow Church, Tarrytown, N. Y., 236
Old Dutch Reformed Church, Bellville, N. J., 274
Old Franciscan Missions of California, 168
"Old Jerusalem," Portland, Me., 213
Old Meeting House, Concord, Mass., 215
Old Mission Church, Mackinac Island, Michigan, 180
Old Mission Grapevine, California, 170
Old North Church, Boston, 192
Old North Church, Portsmouth, N. H., 208
Old St. Patrick's, New York City, 303
Old St. Peter's, Rome, 30
Old St. Peter's, Philadelphia, 277
Old Sarum, Diocese of, London, 69
"Old Ship" Church, Hingham, Mass., 198
Old South Church, Boston, 195
Old South Church, Newburyport, Mass., 211
"Old Swedes" Church, Philadelphia, 242
"Old Swedes" Church, Wilmington, Del., 238
Old Tennent Church, Monmouth Battlefield, N. J., 233
Oldest Baptist Church in Pennsylvania, 276
Oldest Church in the United States, 173
Oldest English-speaking Church in New Jersey, 254
Oldest German Lutheran Congregation in United States, 245
Oldest Lutheran Church in America, 259
Oldest Meeting House in United States, 199
Oldest Methodist Church in the World, Philadelphia, 252
Oldest Regular Hebrew Congregation in United States, 269
Our Lady of Guadalupe Cathedral, Mexico, 179
Oxford Cathedral, Oxford, England, 113

Pantheon, The, Paris, 117
Pantheon, The, Rome, 18
Parthenon, The, Athens, 14
Paul Revere, Boston, 194
Peking, Ancient Tartar City, 11
Penn's "Holy Experiment," 247
Pennypack Church, Pennypack, Pa., 276
Peterborough Cathedral, England, 120
Philadelphia's First House of Christian Worship, 242
Pigeons of St. Mark's, Venice, 53

Pisa Cathedral, Baptistry and Leaning Tower, 101

Plymouth Pilgrim Meeting House, Site of, 190

Pohick Church, near Alexandria, Va., 293

Pre-Christian Temples and Shrines, 3

Quakers in Pennsylvania, 247

Quaker Meeting House, Flushing, L. I., 266

Quebec Cathedral, Canada, 164

"Queen of French Cathedrals," 73

Queen's Chapel, Portsmouth, N. H., 207

Quincy Church, Quincy, Mass., 213

Ratisbon Cathedral, Germany, 85

Rheims Cathedral, France, 107

Roman Basilica, 21

Roger Williams Settlement at Providence, 205

Rosario Chapel, Santa Fe, N. M., 164

Rouen Cathedral, France, 141

Russian Orthodox Church, New York City, 300

Russian Orthodox Church, Sitka, Alaska, 177

Sabbath Day in New England, 191

Sacred Tablet of Confucius, 11

St. Alban's, England, 114

St. Andrew's, Richmond, Staten Island, N. Y., 230

St. Anne de Beaupre, Quebec, 175

St. Apollinare Nuova, Ravenna, 32

St. Basil, Church of, Moscow, 126

St. Chapelle, Paris, 144

St. Charles, Vienna, 79

St. Clements, Rome, 31

St. David's Cathedral, Wales, 151

St. David's, Radnor, Pa., 285

St. Genevieve, Paris, 117

St. George's Methodist Church, Philadelphia, 252

St. Gervais, Geneva, Switzerland, 99

St. Gudule's, Brussels, 115

St. Helena, The Chapel of, Bethlehem, 28

St. Isaac's, Leningrad, Russia, 140

St. Jacques' Chapel, Antwerp, 145

St. John the Divine, Cathedral of, New York City, 307

St. John's, Hampton, Va., 290

St. John Lateran, Rome, 29

St. John's, Portsmouth, N. H., 207

St. Joseph's, St. Augustine, Fla., 181

St. Louis Cathedral, New Orleans, La., 299

St. Luke's, Smithfield, Va., 290

St. Maria dei Cappuccini, Rome, 82

St. Mark's-in-the-Bowery, New York City, 255

St. Mark's, Venice, 51

St. Martin's at Canterbury, 55

St. Martin's Hill, Church of, England, 54

St. Mary and St. Donato, Murano, Italy, 119

St. Michael's, Charleston, S. C., 291

St. Michael Evangelical Church, Philadelphia, 272

St. Michael's, Marblehead, Mass., 197

St. Oven, Rouen, France, 141

St. Patrick's, Dublin, 135

St. Patrick's Cathedral, New York City, 303

St. Paul's, London, 66

St. Paul's, New York City, 223

St. Paul's, Norfolk, Va., 293

St. Paul-Without-the-Walls, Rome, 33

St Peter's, Albany, N. Y., 224

St. Peter Collegiate Church of London, 58

St. Peter, St. Paul and St. Andrew, Cathedral of, Peterborough, Eng., 120

St. Peter's, Philadelphia, 277

St. Peter's, Rome, 29, 30, 80

St. Peter's, White House, Va., 294

St. Philip's, Charleston, S. C., 292

St. Pierre, Geneva, Switzerland, 99

St. Roch's, Paris, 104

St. Simeon Stylites, Kelat-Seman, 28

St. Sophia, Constantinople, 45

St. Sophia, Green Jasper Columns, 17

St. Stefano Rotondo, Rome, 30

St. Stephen's Cathedral, Vienna, 148

St. Thomas, Salisbury, England, 71

St. Ursula, Cologne, Germany, 84

St. Vitale, Ravenna, 31

San Ambrogio, Milan, 149

San Augustin, Oldest Church in Havana, Cuba, 163

San Carlos Borremo, Monterey, Calif., 169

San Francisco de Assis Solano, Mission, 183

San Gabriel Mission, Calif., 170

San Jose de Aguayo, near San Antonio, Texas, 166

San Juan Capistrano Mission, 172

San Luis Rey de Francia Mission, Calif., 171

San Marco Chapel, Venice, 51

San Miguel, Santa Fe, N. M., 173

San Miniato, Florence, Italy, 108

San Xavier del Bac, Arizona, 182

Santa Barbara Mission, Calif., 171

Santa Clara Mission, Calif., 172

Santa Croce, Florence, 139

Santa Inez Mission, Calif., 172

Santa Maria de Belen, Havana, 164

Santa Maria della Pace, Rome, 82

Santa Maria della Salute, Venice, 88

Santa Maria del Fiore, Florence, Italy, 63

Santa Maria Formosa, Venice, 130

Santa Maria Maggiore, Rome, 26

Santa Maria Novella, Florence, 57

Santo Domingo, Havana, 163

Salisbury Cathedral, England, 69

Sanctuary of Shinto, Japan, 13

Saviour, Church of the, Moscow, 85

Schloss-Kirche, Wittenberg, Germany, 86

Second Presbyterian Church, Philadelphia, 280

Seville Cathedral, Spain, 77

Sheareth Israel (Remnant of Israel), New York City, 269

Siena Cathedral, Italy, 62

Site of Tomb of Abraham, Isaac and Jacob, traditional, 44

"Sleepy Hollow Church," Tarrytown, N. Y., 236

Solomon's Temple, Jerusalem, 7

Stadt-Kircke, Wittenberg, Germany, 86

Stone of Scone, Westminster Abbey, 59

Stone of Unction, The, Jerusalem, 28

Strassburg Cathedral, 111

Swamp Church, New Hanover, Pa., 245

Tabernacle, The, Salt Lake City, Utah, 301

INDEX

Tabor Church (First Reformed), Lebanon, Pa., 284
Tell's Chapel, Lake Lucerne, Switzerland, 128
Teocalli, The, Guatusco, Costa Rica, 167
Temple of Athena at Athens, 14
Temple of Diana, Ephesus, 16
Temple Emanu-El, New York City, 270
Temple of Edfu, Egypt, 5
Temple of Heaven, The, Peking, 11
Temple of Jupiter, Erected by Agrippa, 18
Temples of Nikko, Japan, 13
Temple University, Philadelphia, 264
Toledo Cathedral, Spain, 103
Tombs and Monuments in Westminster Abbey, 60
Tombs of: Admiral John Paul Jones, Chapel, Naval Academy, Annapolis, Md., 314
Christopher Columbus, Seville, Spain, 78
Gen. "Mad" Anthony Wayne, 286
Michael Angelo and Galileo, 139
Raphael, the Painter, 19
Rubens, in Antwerp, 145
Sts. Ambrogio, Gervasio and Protasio, 149
St. Mark, Patron Saint of Venice, 51
St. Olaf, Norway's Patron Saint, 137
Former President Woodrow Wilson, 310
Tombs in: Durham Cathedral, England, 96
Old St. Peter's, Philadelphia, 277
Peterborough Cathedral, England, 121
St. George's Chapel, Windsor Castle, England, 130
St. Peter's Chapel, Tower of London, 147
St. Patrick's, Dublin, 135
St. Paul's, London, 67
Winchester Cathedral, England, 116
Tours Cathedral, France, 68

Tower of London, Chapels, 147
Translation of Bible into Indian Language, 200
Trinity Church, Boston, 210
Trinity Church, Fishkill, N. Y., 219
Trinity Church, New York City, 220
Trondhjem Cathedral, Norway, 137

United Church, New Haven, Conn., 201

Vasali Cathedral, Moscow, 85
Venice Cathedral, Italy, 52
Verona Cathedral, Italy, 123
Vermont Avenue Christian Church, Washington, D. C., 292
"Vinegar Bibles, The," 207
Votive Church, The, Vienna, 79

Wall Street Church, New York City, 230
Washington in St. Paul's, New York City, on his first Inauguration Day, 223
Wells Cathedral, England, 122
Westminster Abbey, London, 58
West Point Chapel, West Point, N. Y., 312
Where Andrew Jackson Worshipped, 299
Whittier, Quaker Poet, 248
William Penn, where he preached, 246
Winchester Cathedral, Hampshire, England, 116
Worms Cathedral, Germany, 84

York Minster, England, 124

Zerubbabel's Temple, 8
Zion Evangelical Lutheran Church, Philadelphia, 281
Zion Reformed Church, Allentown, Pa., 283

[325]